FIRE on the WATER

or

THE ONE

By

Andrew Therriault

Printed in the United States of America

First Printing, 2020

ISBN 978-1-7338944-4-9

www.AndrewTherriaultBooks.com

To
My Mother, Father, and Nas

Fire on the Water
or
The One

Chapter 1

I stood in a bright room on black tiles. There was a door and one window and the light that flooded through glared like snow in the sun and to see I had to squint. From floor to ceiling the room was illuminated gold and silver, and my eyes strained but from where I stood it appeared to be my foyer. The glossy black tiles, the bifold doors, everything blurred. And then I heard a faint knock at the door and the door pushed open. Outside it was bright like the blaze of a diamond and the source of light came from far beyond. I threw both hands in front of my face to dull the luster of the tiles, and then peering through widely splayed fingers what appeared bright was quite divine, the room, the space, everything outside. And then as if he had hailed from the ether a man appeared in the doorway and stood and faced the expanse of pale light.

"Hello," I said.

The man turned around in a swift movement. I dropped my hands and immediately recognized him. It was my friend's father, Mister P. "Hey buddy!" He stepped inside and like an aura the light from outside glowed around his slender body. He walked over and we greeted each other with a handshake. "How are you?"

It was unbearably bright and hard on the eyes, and even Mister P gleamed in the light and there was not a shaded nook or niche in the room to look at.

"I'm all right." I squinted and then looked around this lustrous space and the space behind Mister P. "Where's George?"

"Oh, he's skiing in the Alps."

"The Alps?"

"Yes! Mont Blanc in France. I thought you might have known. He'll be there for two weeks."

"No, I didn't. But that reminds me. I should be in Colorado—skiing Beaver Creek."

Mister P laughed dubiously. "Well I'm not so sure that would be a good idea right now. But buddy, I'm so glad that you're doing well. We were all praying and rooting for you—everyone!"

With that, I could sense a pretense. Maybe they were praying, but was it for the right reason?

Mister P continued, "Then just a couple days ago I was asked to come into town for work. Right across the street actually! It really is a small world, don't you think? Well anyway buddy, I made it my top priority to check in on you. And just by looking at you now I think you'll be more than fine…"

"Thank you," I said, and at that moment a wave of euphoria spread through my body like the onset of morphine. All around the room a brilliantly bright light flashed in a wavelike sequence. That's all there was, a flash of light that lingered and with each surge its silent intensity slowly escalated. This caused my eyes to line with tears and my vision to blur.

"Hello?" I heard Mister P ask. "Buddy? You there?"

I tried to speak but not a sound came out and the light now beamed like an aging sun. I blinked twice and rubbed my knuckles on my eyes and after the last blink the man was gone and the door slammed shut. My vision faded and the room gradually dimmed to a black nothingness. Every sense was gone, and I found myself not in my foyer but somewhere else. Someplace vastly spacious while standing weightless and surrounded by darkness as a comfortable numbness slowly crept in. And then…

My eyes opened and I blinked once, twice, thrice, adjusting to the first light of a new life. I lay stiff in a strange bed and it must have been some time in the morning. The light streaming into the room was grey and dull like clouds on a foggy day. My bed was small, and it felt arid and worn and older than what was normal. Everything seemed unfamiliar, the sheets, pillows, noises, smells, setting; and even the fibrous tiles that lined the ceiling seemed new to me.

I rubbed my eyes and the crisp rheum crumbled away. My head ached and a humming buzz faded apace and then returned. In my ear it swelled as if a horsefly thrummed about, and with my fingers I plugged my ears and this rousing ring stopped. But a throbbing pain then suddenly arose from the back of my head and I reached behind to probe around and what I felt was a scabbing wound. Then gently brushing the crusted flesh my feeble fingertips traced the shape of an X. And it stung terribly to touch.

"Where the hell am I?" I said under my breath, gazing shell-shocked directly at the ceiling. And then the closet door to the side of the room slammed shut and my heart skipped. I turned my head to the right and walking across the room was a woman with curly hair, pushing a cart with a laptop on top and drawers underneath. She looked almost identical to my aunt Barbara, I thought, and she appeared to be about the same age. But I wondered if this discreet woman was some sort of apparition, because she walked silently to the door and then simply left without speaking a word.

"Barbara?" I called out as she disappeared around the corner. She did not respond, and there I lay on this unusually cramped bed wondering where I was and what was going on. Everything was bizarre, and then I began to enjoy the strangeness of the situation. From face to feet my entire body felt numb and weightless save for the back of my head which rested on a pillow. Or at the very least it was a lightly plumped up so-called pillow, not much softer than a slab of Styrofoam and I hardly seemed to care. For a moment it was pleasant, peaceful and I even felt at ease.

And then there was a knock on the door to my room and I slowly rose in bed and the pain was strong and shocked my mind out of its trance. Back to reality I went, just in time to hear the doorknob turn and a man routinely enter the room. He wore a white lab coat and in his right hand held a clipboard. *Thin black hair, muscular build, tall wide frame—this man is strictly business*, I thought.

And that's when it all hit me like some sort of epiphany: for some reason I was dazed and in pain in a hospital; and the man that I was looking at was a doctor with Eastern European features; and the woman that had left the room and looked like my aunt Barbara was a nurse; and I was lying on what seemed like a shabby hospital bed but I had no idea why…

"Andrew!" the doctor said as he walked to the foot of my bed. "You look good today."

"Thanks," I said. "But who are you?"

"My name is William, and I'm here to help."

Feeling intruded and confused I didn't say anything.

"I worked alongside Doctor Trey during your operation, and I'll say it right now. It certainly wasn't easy, but it was successful."

I furrowed my eyebrow. "What."

"The operation was successful."

"What do you mean 'operation'?"

"Well. I mean that we performed a six-hour operation on your pelvis last Tuesday."

I laughed. "What are you, an apparition? A dream?"

"No, I'm not."

"Well then look, I woke up not even five minutes ago. In this godawful bed. What is this place and where am I?"

"Yes, yes. That can happen with a severe brain injury."

"William, I'm not so sure if I follow you."

"You're not so sure?"

"Brain injury, pelvic operation—don't ask me, answer me."

"Well. You didn't *just* wake up. Maybe from a nap, yes. Today is Saturday but you have more or less been awake since Thursday. Hardly responsive—but awake. Before that you were in a coma, first naturally and then medically induced. You sustained several severe injuries, Andrew. I see a lot of patients, a lot of outcomes that can easily be determined on the spot. We weren't certain about you. We did our best as we always do. But this—I'll say this. You're very lucky to be alive."

"Aren't we all," I replied. "Well I guess I'm not really sure what else to say. Yeah I have more questions. I have a lot of questions but it's pretty hard to think right now. You never answered where we are. Where am I?"

William pulled back his white sleeve and looked at his watch.

"And what time is it?" I said.

"This is Massachusetts General Hospital. The time is quarter to four."

"We're at a hospital—that seems about right. But I'll be honest with you, and this is probably why what you told me doesn't make a lot of sense, I feel great."

William laughed. "I'm glad that you feel good. And let me put it this way. I've never felt what you're probably feeling right now."

"Oh yeah?"

"Well. I've never been on any more pain medication than what I was given after my wisdom teeth were pulled. Right now, you're on a lot—I mean a whole array of pain medication. It's good to know that they're doing what they're supposed to do. But even with their help you should still feel some pain and discomfort."

"I do actually—right around my lower back and bottom."

"Yup, that's exactly where you should feel it. Your pelvis was critically injured, fractured in three locations, all of them were very serious. That's what we operated on, and even though we repaired those fractures you may never be able to walk the same again—or at all even. It just depends how *everything* heals."

There was not a single word at the moment that I could think of to say. Shock, surprise, stupor, call it whatever you'd like. The room then settled and chilled as my heart thumped like a pump and William continued.

"If you ever want to walk again," he said. "You have to be very cautious of your movements. Along with pelvic fractures you have several spinal fractures, mostly to your lumbar spine and sacrum, all of which are generally in the same vicinity, and that's why you feel pain in your lower back and bottom—there's a lot of damage all in the same area. Not to mention the other parts of your body. You have a fracture to your cervical spine—that's your neck—and with that and everything else in mind it's imperative that you stay mindful of every move you make. The fractures to your spine are just millimeters from your spinal cord. You cannot twist or bend your back or else those could easily expand. We don't want that to happen. You're young, and you're very lucky as it is to be talking right now—very lucid if I must say so. I've seen it happen before, and trust me, you do not want to become paralyzed."

After his last comment my vision blurred and tunneled and through this dazedness I managed to say, "You're right, I don't."

"Here," said William. "I'll show you the X-rays from imaging."

He opened the manila folder and inside was an array of black and white images. They were all taken from different angles and focused on isolated areas of white bone that were likely all a place of fracture. It was incredibly hard to focus on anything in particular with my mind everywhere else but the present moment. All that I remember seeing were three large and bright white screws sticking through the right hip bone and beyond the lower spine a line of ten or twelve bolts connected. I thought that it looked kind of like a bullet belt, and this I didn't mention until much later to friends and family.

William pulled out and showed me an image of my abdomen. "See those cracks?" he said, circling around my lumbar spine with his pen.

"Yeah." There were what appeared to be a few splintered black cracks along the lowest vertebra.

"That's why you have to be mindful of your movements, and please don't move around in bed or anywhere else recklessly. For now at least. Those cracks could easily expand to your spinal cord, and like I mentioned before, we do not want that to happen…"

"That's right," I said, and what else could I say? In fact, neither of us said anything as if everything was understood. The room was quiet and through the walls a frantic bustle begun, and during this wave of commotion it finally occurred to me to ask how long I had been in the hospital.

William pondered for a moment and then looked inside of his manila folder. "Six days," he said.

"Six days."

"Yes."

"So I arrived here last Sunday and was in the coma for four or five days."

And again, he looked inside of the folder. "*Wow.* You're right."

"Yeah?"

"How did you know that?"

"Well I remembered when you told me that today is Saturday and that I first woke from the coma on Thursday. I did the math. It's simple mathematics that's based on memory."

"You know," said William. "You're very sharp. I heard that you were smart but have you always been like this?"

"It's hard to say," I said. "I can't remember anything…"

"But I thought you just said—"

"No. My memory's very clear after I woke from my nap today. That's what you called it but to me it seems more like that's when I woke up *woke up*. Before that there's no memory."

"Nothing?"

I shook my head. "Nothing."

"So your memory has yet to come back."

"It's the weirdest thing. My mind is like a void."

William nodded his head. "Well yes, experiencing amnesia is very common among those who suffer a brain injury."

"I've heard of amnesia but I've never really thought about it."

"I've never experienced it."

"It's… I guess you could say it's peculiar."

"I have another minute," said William. "You can tell me about it if you'd like."

"Well there's nothing to tell, because there's nothing there! And besides, my mind feels spent. I can hardly think anymore."

"Your brain's in a fragile state," said William. "And right now, I told you, you're on a lot of narcotics."

"Well that must be it," I said. "I'm getting pretty dizzy. If you don't mind I'd like to continue my afternoon nap."

"That's a good idea. Do you need anything before I leave?"

"No."

"Well if you ever do, or if you ever start to experience any pain, just call out and a nurse will get you pain medication. Or anything else that you might need. Enjoy your nap."

William turned around and left the room and I rubbed my eyes and stared at the ceiling. The white fibrous tiles blurred and moved like musical chairs. In this tiny room, and even after everything that I had just learned, it still felt like a dream, and like a dream when you don't say or do the things that you want to say or do, I quickly realized that I forgot to ask what had happened—maybe the most important question that at the moment was best unanswered. Did I really want to know what had happened, why I was in a coma and why I was so lucky to be alive? The truth is, it was hardly much of a concern at the moment and seemed like something to put off for tomorrow, or the next day, or the next day, or the day after that. I closed my eyes and hoped to wake up in my own bed.

Chapter 2

I woke the next morning in a cold sweat and from head to toe my body hurt. I felt pain everywhere and a stale smell pervaded the still air, a smell like spoiled milk in the hot sun on a summer afternoon. Where it came from I didn't know. But the smell and the feeling of damp bedsheets and blankets, and knowing that they were fully soaked in sweat, made my belly churn and growl at the foulness. I closed my eyes to escape this place for a brief moment, but when they opened I was still in the same room and in the same bed that I had learned was on the fourth floor of the intensive care unit at Mass General. There was no way out and I was forced to stay in bed all day, unallowed to eat solid foods and stoned on a plethora of prescription narcotics. The narcotics helped with the pain and lying in bed I hardly felt it. Yet somehow the scab on the back of my head itched and stung against the pillow, and this caused some problems. One was undoubtedly the worst—I absolutely could not sit upright to relieve the sting and itch without my lower back and bottom flaring up in pain. In that case, I was uncomfortably stuck in bed with nowhere to go—yet.

My mind was slow and it was hard to think. But I was able to remember some basic information: my name and how it's spelled and that I was a teenager from Maine and that I went to school at the University of New Hampshire.

I also remembered that I had been arrested for a naive prank. It was at the mall and I was charged with burglary, trespassing, and theft when I had lost a bet and tried to stay in the mall overnight. It sounds senseless, I know, but because of my taciturnity after the event, which stemmed mostly from shock and regret, that was how I remembered it, and frankly I'm unbothered and could care less. It's doubtful that things escalated and being charged with a felony seemed excessive. They said that it looked like I had intent and without further ado I was arrested. Now when I locked my hands together in bed my wrists felt cuffed and the rigid steel and the flashing lights and shameful talk ran through my mind whenever it darkened however unoften.

This only happened the day before when the lights went out and my wrists were dry and the thought of the cuffs and their hold on life all at once came to mind. All of this probably felt similar to a phantom sensation.

In any case, I knew my mother's name is Martina and that she was short and Italian but I forgot what her face looked like. It was on the tip of my memory but like many memories it struggled to surface. Little details and large hadn't come back. But before you get on my case for forgetting the appearance of my own mother's face you should know that it wasn't only hers—I forgot what my face looked like too! Strangely there was not a mirror in the room that I could look at. And it was the same case with my father Leon and his appearance too.

Under the current circumstance the room began to feel slightly homely, probably because the situation was accepted for what it was and there was not a lot that I could change about it. For one, I could barely move, but I managed to lean up in bed and just then I saw Nurse Barbara walk by in the hall. Around my torso the pain was drastic; throughout my back and on the back of my head and inside of my head and behind my eyes and the X-shaped scar it was very sore. *Perfect timing*, I thought. *Just what I need.*

"Nurse," I yelled. "Barbara."

She appeared in the doorway. "Yes? What is it?"

"I need you to help me with the pain."

"Hold on. I'll get you a round of medicine."

Barbara walked out of the room and then came back, pushing a cart with a laptop on top and drawers underneath. The nurses were always pushing those carts. Barbara went through the sorted drawers and the next thing I knew there was a small paper cup the size of a shot glass filled with pills that sat in my hand.

"You know," I decided to mention. "Yesterday I thought that you were my aunt Barbara when I first woke up. Are you?"

"Oh, that's cute," she laughed. "But no, I'm not."

"Well I thought I had a dream about you and me last night. But since you're not my aunt I don't know who it was."

"I hope it was a good dream," said Nurse Barbara.

"It was all right," I said. "She just took me to McDonald's."

"*Oh!* Well that sounds pretty interesting."

I shrugged, didn't say anything.

"Can I get you anything else?" she asked.

"No, I'm fine."

"Okay!"

Nurse Barbara left the room and I swallowed the pills and on the pillow recalled my one and only dream from the night before.

It was nighttime and Barbara and I were driving and then went to McDonald's and parked out front and went inside. I sat at a booth, Barbara went to the counter, three girls sat at a table to the right and ogled in my direction. That's when I realized that it must be a dream—the dream was in control. Barbara set a tray full of questionable food on the table and sat at the booth.

"Thanks," I said. "Now where to begin…"

"You can't."

"Yeah, okay."

I reached for a greasy burger and brought it up to my mouth and before I sunk my teeth and savagely chewed the savory food that smelled of ambrosia mixed with obesity Barbara grabbed my wrist. I tried to pull away; she would not budge.

"I said that you can't," she said.

"What the hell are you talking about?"

"No food, remember?"

"No, I don't remember, Barbara."

"I'm only here to enforce the rules."

"You're a tease," I said and then tried for the Sprite. Her hand seized my wrist.

"You can't—you can't have any of this!"

"Fabulous," I said. "Then what can I have?"

Barbara glanced down at a small paper cup in the corner of the tray.

"And that is?"

"Ice."

"What?"

"Those are ice cubes," said Barbara. "They're all that you can eat right now."

I laughed. "I'm good. You're right, I don't want this *food...*"

"Well what do you want?"

"We're at McDonald's. How should I—you know, maybe it'll just come my way."

Barbara got up and left the joint, and I looked to my right and toward the booth the three girls gently tiptoed. They each sat down opposite me and I abruptly fell back to reality from the click of the door to my room. It was William, and he walked inside and asked about me.

"I'm pretty hungry," I said. "But I'm all right."

"Great. Well I'm just going to ask you some basic questions to evaluate your brain injury."

"Sounds good."

"But first," he added. "How do you pronounce your last name: Therriault?"

"Terrio," I said.

"Okay." William looked as if he wanted to write a note on his clipboard. "Well," he said. "Let's get started."

"All right, shoot."

"Where were you born?"

"Portland, Maine."

"What is the day of the week?"

"I don't know."

"It's Friday."

"Right."

"What's the date today?"

"I have no idea."

"Do you know what year it is?"

I drew a perfect circle on the linen sheet with my index finger. Deep inside of my shattered mind the years appeared to be out of order and scattered about like stars in the sky. There was no time to overthink. "2017," I said.

"That's right," said William. "The date is January 29, 2017. Do you know when your birthday is?"

"February 24, 1997."

"Tell me something about yourself."

I tilted my head. "What?"

"It can be anything."

"That's pretty broad," I said.

"Give me one sentence about yourself—anything."

"One sentence. Well. I'm a Pisces and I usually get along with anyone."

"That's fascinating," said William.

"If you think so."

"For one sentence—that's pretty good."

"It's the narcotics."

"They were wrong about you."

"We done?"

"Almost. Just a few more questions and exercises." He raised his sleeve and looked at his watch. "How old are you?"

"Nineteen."

"And do you know who the president is?"

This I was quite certain of. "Obama," I said.

"No." William wrote a note on his clipboard. "He used to be but now our president is Donald Trump."

At that, I laughed immensely. "That's right," I said.

"Are you a Trump supporter?"

"I'm nineteen. I can't remember ever voting in my life."

William put his pen into his breast pocket and held out one hand with four fingers raised and his thumb folded into his palm. "How many fingers am I holding up?"

The pills had just taken effect and I was feeling funny. "Eight," I said.

William put his hand down and seemed discouraged.

"I was joking. There were four fingers…"

"Correct. Now I want you to follow my pen with your eyes. Try and keep your head still this time."

I didn't know what he was talking about. As far as I knew this was the first time. He said nothing more and neither did I, and then he grabbed the pen out of his breast pocket and held it out in front of his face. I glued my eyes to the tip of the pen as he moved it back and forth from left to right and all around in narrow circles, and my eyes followed the pen like they would follow a pendulum, up close and careful, but like I said, the pills had kicked in and it was very hard to focus. Under a painfully eloquent gravity I was laughing in a woeful ecstasy.

"All right," said William. "That's all for now. Good job. Good work." Then he placed his pen back into his breast pocket and left the room. I stayed in bed, laid back and sprawled out. My body felt numb and flat, warm and tingly. The narcotics were survival, a true necessity, and best of all were fun to use. But not everything would stay as is. The status quo would soon change and whether it would change for better or change for worse was up in the air but stoned on all sorts of narcotics it hardly seemed to matter. The question of how I actually ended up here at Mass General was becoming less and less relevant, as it all seemed more and more like a cyclical repetition of lying idle, waiting for the next encounter, a conversation with a nurse, eating ice cubes from a cup, the pain leaving and then returning, and when it returned another dose of narcotics, and after that a few hours of sleep. Circumstances were bleak but not everything was as bad as it seemed. For now at least. And I closed my eyes on a positive note and dozed off into a deep sleep.

Chapter 3

My parents came to visit me one day and that one day could have been any day. It was very hard to gauge the time without a routine or even a sleep schedule. I took a round of narcotics when the pain was unbearable and usually an hour later I would pass out, but at what time and for how long varied from day-to-day. Every day either William or a nurse would remind me of the time and date while assessing my brain injury, and if it was a nurse that meant that it was time for a round of narcotics. Those silent killers were purely pleasure, relief from the perpetual pain, and conversations that I had amid their false elation were superbly bizarre! Much to the doctors' surprise my brain was healing good and proper, but for some reason for the life of me I could not remember the date. I was told that my memory would get better in time but the sound of their voice had a tone of uncertainty. It was really only the trivial things that were hard to remember, and in this case, the date was always changing and the clock constantly ticking—why remember the date, the sequence of numbers organized between two lines or dashes of what will soon become what will never again be? I will say that it's better to recall what yesterday was made of rather than what yesterday officially was. But even with this logic I had a hard time remembering, mostly because I stayed in the same spot each day, doing the same thing, fighting the same pain, and quenching the same thirst. No solid food or liquid for the first few days was absolutely brutal! Being at the hospital seemed very redundant, and at this point it was time to go! If my existence was restricted solely to lying in a bed and all cooped up for several hours on end I often wondered why I couldn't heal in the comfort of my own home! But precautionary measures had to be taken—if I fell out of bed or moved in a way that re-shattered a bone or tore a tissue, I would have then received immediate care that was unavailable at home. So Mass General it was, and man was it rough. Pain rose and eased like the ocean's tide and days and nights all blended together. Time stood nearly still. Yet it was constantly ticking and that's probably what confused me. My mind wandered, and slowly but surely my energy restored and my mind recharged and self resurfaced. Yet I could not remember the date or day of the week or even spot a clock on the wall, and with that being said, I'm not exactly sure when my parents came to visit, but whenever it was, the timing was bad.

I had been told and urged on several occasions to use the toilet. But the toilet was located right inside of my room and there was all but nothing for privacy. Wisely I held off. I relieved myself in bed through a catheter, and together all of the narcotics made it very hard to go number two. But I'll be honest, I never actually tried to go until right now after Nurse Barbara had convinced me. In other words, why the timing was bad, my parents walked in on me taking a shit.

"Oh my." My mother laughed. "We'll wait outside…"

I wiped the beads of sweat off of my forehead. "No, don't. It's not happening."

"Are you sure?"

"Yes, it hurts too much to sit down."

I stood up on my left leg and using a walker I hopped to my bed and lay down. Besides the chronic pain, that was probably the main reason why I hardly got out of bed—I was unallowed to use my right leg by any means. The doctors said that even the slightest stress to my right leg would have a bad outcome for my pelvis. *Say no more*, I thought. That was enough to confine me to bed. Both of my parents walked over and they each had a smile on their face and their eyes were likely wider than mine. They were noticeably tired but seemingly happy to see their son alive.

My mother hugged me. "Oh, Andrew! It's so nice to see you!"

"You too," I said as she sat down in the chair next to my bed. "Actually, I hardly recognized you at first."

"What!"

"Well. I forgot what you looked like."

"Oh, no. Your father and I were afraid of something like that happening." And my father walked toward the window and looked out.

"That's a nice view you have," he said sarcastically.

With that, I gently flipped over in bed and moved the blind to the side on the window behind me. Outside there wasn't much of a view. A brick wall stood about twenty feet away and between us was a courtyard and a small walkway with grass on either side. Thick grey clouds filled the sky completely.

"Marvelous," I said. "That's what this place is."

"Are you hungry?" my father asked. "We just ate down in the cafeteria and the food here is actually pretty good."

"You didn't know? I'm not allowed to eat food…"

"Oh, that's okay. I'll go get you something."

"No, Leon. If he's not allowed to eat he shouldn't eat."

"I'm starving," I said.

And there was one of those minor parental disagreements but of course my mother had her way.

My father said, "Well I guess we should probably listen to your mother."

I shook my head. "I'll just starve and keep eating ice cubes."

"Ice cubes?"

"Yeah. That's what I eat and if I'm thirsty. I let them melt inside of my mouth."

"That sounds awful." My father laughed.

"I don't really notice. The narcotics tie me over pretty well but sometimes they give me serious cravings like the munchies. And think, I know that I can't eat anything."

My parents looked at each other.

"A little food would be nice!" I said. "Look, the other day I had a dream. Aunt Barbara took me to McDonald's and she wouldn't let me eat. What does that tell you?"

"That's funny," said my mother. "The last time that we were here you kept calling one of the nurses Aunt Barbara. I mean she *did* kind of look like Barbara."

17

I thought about it for a moment, but nothing came to mind. "When were you here?"

"Oh geez. Almost every day for a week straight."

"Was I in the coma and then mostly unresponsive?"

"Yes! How did you know that?"

"One of the doctors told me."

"Well yes, you were in a coma for the first three or four days and after—well after that you were in critical condition. We didn't know if you were going to make it."

"Maybe someday I will."

"What?"

"Nothing. I'm here, I'm all ears."

"Okay, so we stayed overnight in Boston," she said. "And then we got a call in the morning that you—and I don't know how—but you fell out of bed and now you're suddenly awake. We rushed over and you *were* awake, but you were so out of it. You could barely talk, Andrew." She laughed. "Now that you're okay I have to say that it was kind of funny. Then later in the day you kept calling that nurse Aunt Barbara."

"I didn't see a resemblance." My father's two cents.

"When was that?" I asked.

"About—no actually, exactly a week ago."

"That means that it's my eleventh day here, and it's a Thursday. What's the date?"

My mother looked at her phone. "February second."

"Thanks," I said.

My parents looked at each other. "Well I have to say, you look and sound so much better now than when we saw you last."

"I'm glad that you've noticed improvement."

"Have you been able to do anything?"

"Not a lot, but I explored the hospital for a while with Alfonso yesterday."

My father laughed. "Oh, we remember Alfonso. You asked him over and over to push you around on the wheelchair. He was very nice about it."

"He was!" my mother agreed.

"Well hey," said my father. "I have to use the bathroom. Do you know where it is?"

"Bathroom? I don't even know if there's a clock or mirror."

"I'll find it," my father said as he walked toward the door and then left.

"How are you doing in bed?" my mother asked.

"Fine."

"Are you comfortable?"

"Not really," I said. "But it could be worse."

She frowned. "I wish there was something that we could do. I should've brought your pillows and some blankets."

"You should've brought my weed," I joked.

"No, you'd get arrested again if you had it in here!"

"No, not happening."

"You know, I spoke to Robert and he said the case should go smoothly. He said don't worry, but any more trouble and there could be some serious obstacles."

"You're right, I won't worry. I really can't. Right now my mind is chock-full of nothing."

"Andrew."

"What."

"Did that arrest have something to do with what happened to you?"

"Not that I know of."

"What do you mean?"

"I mean I don't see how it would have anything to do with what happened to me. I don't even know what happened."

"Well what happened was just a week after you called us from jail…"

"I know. I can remember that. I debated calling you guys in the first place. It was pretty late."

"It was at three in the morning," my mother said. "And then a week later we got a call that you were in a coma in the hospital and that you might not make it."

"I know," I said.

"Did you owe someone money?"

"No. Right now I don't owe anyone anything. You know that it was a very poor choice."

"I know that you said it was a prank but what am I supposed to think?"

"It's up to you. In this context you control your own thoughts. It's hard to remember what actually happened but it was a prank, I know that. What I don't know, and what I'd like to know and what no one seems to know around here is what happened to me."

"Well we don't know what happened either," said my mother.

"Okay."

"Do you remember anything from that night?"

"I have basically no memory."

"Well they said that it appeared like you were a victim of foul play."

"Yeah, it does feel like that."

"And they said that your phone and wallet were missing, and you had cuts and wounds all over your hands—those nice hands."

I looked at my hands. It's true, my knuckles were scabbing and scarred on both. "My eye's all tender," I said. "It's hard to see out of this eye. What's wrong with it?"

"Your eye, it's swollen and bruised. It's a black eye, Andrew."

"Great. Well what in the fuck happened?"

"We don't know," she said and then rubbed her eyes with her sleeve. "They said that an anonymous caller tipped them off early in the morning—and this was two Sundays ago—and it was about a body lying on the ice beneath a railroad trestle in Dover. Well it was you, and *oh my God* I was horrified. I was like—"

"Hold on a second," I said. "*What?*"

"That's what I was like! Oh, it's so bizarre. I almost fainted after the first phone call that we got."

"Why?" I asked, knowing why but that word naturally coming out.

"Well. You were first taken to Colonel Cole hospital in Dover and that's when they called us at home. I was still in bed! Just past eight in the morning—on a Sunday! I told you that. They asked if you were my son and I said yes. Then their next words—and I'll never forget these words—were all flat. 'He's in cardiac arrest. He's flatlining.' That was it, what they said. I forgot what happened after that but those words are that all a mother can bear to hear. I begged it to stop, that somehow it can't be real. I asked why, why, why—I got only uncertain updates."

My mother collected and bottled her emotions. She took her phone out of her pocket and opened a picture. "Have you ever seen this railroad trestle?"

I studied the picture. Stretched over and across a frozen river was a rusted trestle and above the sky was grey and the ice below a color without color. If right there my soul had departed my body and moved on—there was no light.

"No," I said.

"It's in a shady part of Dover."

"I believe it, but that's miles away. How did I get there?"

"We don't know. It's about five miles from campus, and the night before you were at Blake Carrington's apartment and I guess Chuck and Smiley drove down that night and were there with you. They said that they spent the night and that you left at about three in the morning. Do you have any memory of this?"

"No. This makes no sense."

"Something happened on your walk home. The police are still investigating but they don't have any leads to follow."

"Of course not."

"How are you holding up?"

"Well I'll say this. I had a round of narcotics long enough ago to think clearly but enough at once to dull the shock."

"Wow. Is that good?"

"Given the circumstance," I said. "But this is all really messed up."

"You know," said my mother. "I've never really liked college campuses at night."

"Good point," I said and then covered my face with my hands and rubbed my eyes with my fingers. There in the darkness sparse dots of light whirled about and shone like stars. For the first time in my life I was horrified. And it was hardly the situation that was shocking, or even the pain or the dry hunger or my mother's sullen expression. What surprised me most was my lack of concern. The turn that my life had taken was a blind one and I was thrilled to see where it would go from here. But the circumstance itself had yet to sink in. For now it was entirely superficial, the pain, hurt, thirst, hunger, pleasure. Everything was external, nothing was internal. I didn't feel much of anything on the inside and that part was the most shocking.

Outside of the window light snow fell from the sky and whirled in the wind and a few spots on the ground in the courtyard were dusted white. I had carefully maneuvered to the side of the bed to get a better view, but it was hardly a view to admire. I looked down at my damaged knuckles, which as it were, made me a damaged white boy. I turned back around.

"It's just horrible," said my mother.

And I completely agreed, and then she got up and grabbed a tissue by the sink and blew her nose. My breathing slowed down and I rubbed my eyes repeatedly, mostly because it felt satisfying, like the feeling a cat gets when his head is scratched and groomed. In his head he sees his mother, and in my head stars and bright colors of exotic shapes and patterns danced behind my eyelids. My mother sat down. She had cleared her mind and her mood was much lighter.

"I feel much better now that I know you're okay."

"Well in my eyes I've always been okay. I woke up 'okay.'"

"We didn't know. I mean you fell fifty feet onto ice and being dropped off—who knows?"

"That's disgusting," I said.

"It's inhuman. You must have angels looking over you."

"I'm sure I do."

"Did you see the light? Some people that have had near-death experiences say that they saw the light."

"It was something. Maybe they saw their own light dimming. Maybe I'll tell you someday or maybe I'll write about it."

"Yes, please! Alfonso said that you wanted to. He said that you kept going on and on saying that you're going to write about your time here. He said that you spoke with determination."

"I don't remember that. But yeah, I'll write about this place."

"I guess it was pretty funny. He said that you're a funny dude."

"Well I don't feel funny. Actually, I feel abnormal, and I'd like to rest and process all of the information."

"Yes, please rest. It's good for your brain injury." My mother got up from the chair and walked to the door. "I'm going to find your father. Do you need anything before I leave?"

"No."

She left the room and with her gone the air was filled with the sweetness of solitude. I propped up the pillow and thought, *Now what's missing?*

The room was quiet. A clock ticked but there was not a clock in sight. Rosa walked by in the hall. *Oh, I know what it is…*

Rosa was the best nurse. She was very caring and she had an ethereal voice that when she sang rose from her soul effortlessly. Her accent was thick and where it originated from was anyone's guess. Occasionally when she talked—which seemed to happen at the worst times, whether it was the pain that was bothersome, or the confinement or noise or some other untold frustration—I'd close my eyes and let my mind drift to some place spectacular.

"Rosa," I groaned. She came around the corner.

"Yes?"

"I need some medicine."

"More?" She laughed. "No way, boy. I gave you a dose three hours ago."

"Please…"

"Oh, well I can give you a partial dose. Okay?"

"Okay."

"You don't want to overdo it."

"No.

Rosa dropped three small pills into the center of my palm and I said thanks. They were bitter enough for your face to pucker and this time the numbness commenced immediately. I closed my eyes and to my surprise from a nook nearby I heard music and waves and sensed the salt on the tip of my tongue and felt the sun and all around the light blue sky and beneath my feet the pink sand beach and the soft sweet breeze and it was a very good and very warm spectacular place until a pushcart wobbled and the cloudy reality once again set in.

Chapter 4

Time at Mass General went nowhere yet elapsed like everywhere else. With little to do in my dainty room I began to think about what might have happened that night about twelve days ago, and why right now amnesia felt so right, but like any vulnerable person would do amid unusual unpleasantness, you soon find a crutch to slowly stop the ugly thoughts. There were not many options in my condition, and it came down to two things: relying on narcotics and spending time with Alfonso. My miniature world inside of Mass General seemed much better after a heavy dose of narcotics. The room felt bigger, the atmosphere brighter, fulfillment came easily. It occurred to me once that I might be addicted, but I brushed the thought aside and replaced it with a crutch—both actually! First came the pills and then the sudden urge to explore the hospital with Alfonso. He always offered to push me in the wheelchair, and I have to say that he might have been the kindest person that I had ever met. He was from Dorchester, but he grew up on a piece of land outside of the United States. Under the influence of several opioids his accent to me seemed purely Dominican, and many times in the chair while highly intoxicated I thought that he was David Ortiz, and on the comedown, that he was his brother. Much of this conception of course had to do with the brain injury. Alfonso hardly looked like David Ortiz at all! He was close to my height and had dark skin and a wavy buzz cut. Besides entertaining myself by strictly using my own mind, the wheelchair rides were the first and really only line of entertainment. Often while sitting stoned in the wheelchair I'd imagine what the hospital might be like if instead I was stoned on cannabis—much better! But it was not allowed, and I had no control over federal laws, so narcotics it was. Nonetheless, they made our travels around the hospital both tolerable and amusing.

Rosa and Alfonso were buddies at work. They both seemed to like me and this was likely because while being in such a deliriously jocular and damaged state I was unlike any other patient that they had come across. On the afternoon of my thirteenth day I believe, through the unremitting noise of an intensive care unit—patients screaming, doctors and nurses aiding, wheels squeaking, timers and machines beeping, a continual buzzing—I heard footsteps from down the hall enter my room.

"My boy," said Rosa. "How are you feeling?"

With my hand I formed a ringlike gesture. I asked, "Is Alfonso around?"

"Yes! We were on the same T coming into work."

"Do you live in Dorchester too?"

"No, Quincy."

"*Quinzy*—my roommate Gonzo is from Quinzy."

Rosa laughed. "It sounds like it. Quinzy boys don't play."

"Can I have a round of medicine?" I asked.

"Already? When was your last dose?"

"A long time ago."

Rosa logged onto her laptop and quickly checked the system. Hospitals record everything.

"Hold on," she said. "I'll be back with your dose in a minute."

"If he's not busy," I said. "Come back with Alfonso too."

Rosa said that she would try and she left the room and down the hall I heard her voice and Alfonso's voice and then they both walked into the room.

"What's up, my man!" We bumped fists. "You hanging?"

"Just gliding," I said.

"You hear that Rosa? I told you he's ahead. My man's already thinking about the wheelchair."

"Is that true?" asked Rosa.

"Yeah," I said. "It's time to get out of bed."

"Are you ready to go now?"

"Hold on. I need a round of medicine first."

Rosa handed me a cup that was filled with exactly a dozen and one pills. This I know—I counted them. The extra pill that they had added was a purgative, and even though it was extra strength up until now it had been totally ineffective. I tipped the cup back and swallowed the pills dry.

"Now I'm ready," I said as I maneuvered into the wheelchair.

Alfonso said, "Let's go!" and then pushed from behind and we made a left turn and lying on a bed in the room next door was a man with burns and bandages. My heart ached for the sufferer.

"I want to tell you a story about my kid," said Alfonso.

"And I want to hear it," I said. "I'm all ears for any story."

"So after work yesterday," he said. "I go home. I kiss my wife. I hug my kids. My youngest, that little devil is always up to no good. I love him the most. He's not around and I ask my wife where he is. She says in his bedroom. I hear laughter inside and I wonder, *what's he doing now?* I go in and I laugh. He's covered in peanut butter. The walls, carpet, everything. He's playing with an empty jar of peanut butter. I ask him, 'What are you up to, my little man?' and he just laughs an innocent laugh." Meanwhile, Alfonso was laughing his one of a kind laugh. "I go to pick him up—to clean him off you know—and he bites my hand. Look at this. See?" Laughing hysterically a hoarse laugh that in my condition sounded like a seal Alfonso held out his right hand. There was a bandage covering the flesh beneath his thumb. "He sank his teeth right in."

We were both still laughing when we made it down the hall and to an intersection. To the left lay a woman on a stretcher by herself and ahead walked a janitor down the hall who then stopped. We turned right and carried onward.

"You heard of Spaulding Rehabilitation Hospital?" I asked.

"Oh yeah, my man."

"Well I was told that they're transferring me to Spaulding."

"Really? Who told you?"

"My mom. She claimed that they're good with brain and spinal injuries. I guess my voice was heard."

"Your voice?"

"Yeah, I complained very well about my room here. One day back when I was very touchy. I called their home phone—that's the only number that I remember! It was late at night, because you know how my sleep schedule is very out of whack, and I gave them a piece of my mind about the struggles here."

"Ahh," laughed Alfonso. "Well Spaulding, it's a good hospital. I know that. Full of smart doctors and therapists."

"Alfonso, are you upset?"

"When do you leave, my man?"

"When there's an open room. I'm next on the list."

We turned the corner down a crowded hallway and ably wove through many people and much ruckus.

Alfonso leaned in closer to my ear. "That will be a sad day! A sad day, my man!"

"Come to Spaulding!"

"I will try!"

We made a right turn down another hall to escape the madness and in an open room at the end stood a man throwing patient pants and shirts into a washing machine. "Ay, there's my man Avi. Hey Avi!"

Avi turned to us and waved. He and I had played a game of chess on my ninth day and it was the last game of chess that I had played at Mass General. The pain was too great to focus on any strategy or move; we had to stop the game short.

"Ey yo!" called Avi. "When's our next game?"

"Come to Spaulding with Alfonso!" I said, and then we rolled by and wheeled back into the ICU and into my room. I got out of the chair and hopped into bed. "You know what else my mom had to say on the phone?"

"What's that?" Alfonso asked.

"Weed might have saved my life."

"What!" Alfonso laughed his hoarsely laugh that sounded like a seal. "Weed—the ganja? You're always talking about it! I know you like the ganja!"

"Yeah. I have some waiting for me when I get home. I can't wait!"

"You're funny, my man."

I sniffed my nose and in the air smelled the scent of laboratory lilacs or quality detergent. The smell of freshly cleaned sheets. Rosa was washing her hands in the sink and then as if she was waiting to ask she shut off the water and turned around. "Do you like rap, Andy?"

"Good rap," I said and then thought, *What a random question.*

"Good rap, huh."

"And good rappers."

"Yes. Who's your favorite rapper?"

I smiled sagely. "Nas."

"Oh, I like Nas!"

"He's brilliant."

"Yes! Very talented."

"Can you get me a pillowcase?"

"Did I not—oops." Rosa got a pillowcase out of the closet and slid it over my pillow. "There you go."

"What time is it?" I asked, and Rosa looked at her watch.

"Four-thirty."

"In the afternoon?"

"Yes…"

"All right. I'm taking a nap."

"You like afternoon naps, don't you?"

"Here I do—love them."

"Write to Nas when you wake up."

"When I finally do, I will."

There was a loud knock at the door and I opened and rubbed my eyes. Alfonso rushed in and rolled a wheelchair beside my bed. "I was just in the cafeteria," he said. "I heard Rosa in the lobby. She's singing."

"Mmmm. I was sleeping," I said.

"Afternoon nap?"

"Yes…"

"Come on, my man. It's nighttime now and she sounded good. Let's go check it out."

"You know that many countries in Europe and throughout the world shut down in the afternoon for daytime rest."

"No, how do you know."

I shrugged and said, "They know how to live life."

"Let's go, my man."

"All right, one second."

I reached for a partial does of medicine on the table beside my bed and brought the cup to my mouth and swallowed the pills dry. I got out of bed and sat in the wheelchair and we left the room. The hospital was quiet and perfectly peaceful at night, an entirely different world. The hall that we were in had white walls and the fluorescent lights on the ceiling made our exploration feel almost unreal. We were on our way to room 101.

But we were not! There were other rooms and other patients inside of each room, most of which flashed with light from the TV, and in one man's room his bedsheets appeared to be bobbing. I made no judgement. Then everything changed as soon as Alfonso spoke. Being half-stoned and sleepy I thought that he was David Ortiz and in my mind an image arose and he smiled and talked and we strolled around the diamond at Fenway Park. The memories came back, memories at baseball games, the doleful games, in the flesh, somewhere else.

"You hear that?" Alfonso asked.

"Uh—"

"You hear her voice?"

"Yeah," I said. "Sounds exceptional."

We weren't very close but we used her voice as a guide through the maze of hallways, and her voice grew steadily and we stopped in a hallway beside a small lobby. Inside the voice of Rosa echoed.

"Melodious," I said.

"I think she's in this lobby," said Alfonso.

"I don't know…"

We rolled inside and the lobby was dim and in the air the mood was mellow. Rosa stood on top of a chair toward the back of the lobby where the ceilings were high and round. Her arms were spread and her eyes were closed and she did not seem to notice us. Nothing else occupied her conscience.

We listened by the entrance and her voice rose from her soul and swelled through the lobby. I felt connected and enjoyed this free show much more than flirting with my own thoughts in bed. In a sense her happiness was my happiness and her pain was my pain. And for a brief moment the whole world seemed welcome, everything inside was right in this very room, all news and talk and worry and hurt and presidents and problems and debts and taxes all fougasse. I began to hum my own melody. And then Alfonso slowly clapped his hands, the jokester that he was, and the whole room fell silent. Rosa had immediately stopped singing and she stood looking our way arms akimbo. "What are *you* doing here?" she said.

"We wanted to hear you sing," said Alfonso.

"Of course you did."

"You sing with emotion," I said.

"So what do you think?"

"It was great."

"Lovely, Rosa. It was lovely."

"Oh, stop that."

"We want to hear more," Alfonso said.

"Well. Okay."

Rosa promptly began singing and we stayed until I could handle the pain no longer. The pain while sitting down even on a dose of pain medication was more than could possibly be endured. We said goodbye to Rosa and then quickly turned around and rode through the halls in a hurry and this brought to mind a dream that I had in the coma. A shockingly realistic dream inside of a vintage train and I fell through the clouds and through its roof and onto a tiny bed with frayed sheets and squeaky wheels. Whenever we went around a turn the bed rolled across the floor and noised a screech that split my ears and people passed by ordinarily and then at last all of those people were doctors and nurses and we rode along and no one cared to help. Not even I, being strapped to a small cot on wheels, could help myself. Oh, what a nightmare! Outside there was fire everywhere and if we were on earth it was Hell on Earth. The front lines, the saga began. I threw a near frenzy whenever one of those automatonic doctors walked up to me helpless on that miserable cot. In that condition it was my only means of self-defense and this dream was not nearly powerful nor lucid enough to break free. To make sure that I went nowhere this automaton stabbed my chest with a full syringe filled to the brim with a bronze liquid thick like syrup and then immediately the lights went out and I'd soon wake up and fall from the sky and land in the same bed in the same dream in the same nightmare in the same manner as before.

Back inside of my dainty room I told Alfonso that it was time for me to sleep. I hopped out of the chair and into bed as fast as possible. There was very little pain while lying down in bed and what little there was was easily tolerable. Under the covers I lay on my side and thought, *You know, this bed isn't very different from that awful cot on wheels… Spaulding can't come soon enough.* I very much liked the healthcare workers at Mass General, but I was dead fed up with the hospital and ready to come back to life. There's no denying the struggles of living inside of an ICU, in that wretched environment with eternal noise and light. A convalescent needs eternal peace.

Chapter 5

I was transferred to Spaulding Rehabilitation Hospital on February 7 and what an exciting day. I had been at Mass General for sixteen days and technically conscious for ten. Looking back at it, those days breezed by like any other day, but come to think of it, when you're clearly suffering and all that you can do with yourself is toy with fantasy or desire or put up a fight with the pain time elapsed is as slow as molasses. And though I was heavily sedated, for most of this time I yearned to go home, and if that was not an option, then someplace else. I got what I wanted, but in life there are two simple tragedies: the first is not getting what you want, and the second occurs eventually after you get it. Everything else is meant to be. Sadly home was not an option but a room at Spaulding had recently been vacated and it was now my turn to occupy it. As soon as they informed me of an open room I was placed on a stretcher and transferred in an instant. Spaulding seemed to be an amazing hospital, fully living up to the hype, other than inside of the elevator in which I was now riding up. It smelled almost like an outhouse and stank like eggs and sweaty crotch. I looked up at the ambulance driver who had driven me about one mile from Mass General to Spaulding. He had a guilty grin on his face.

"Stuart, did you just..." the medic began and then stopped.

The medic's name was Ralph, and he had told me this while he and I rode in the back of the ambulance. I had learned very little about Ralph. By day he was a medic, by night an alcoholic. He told me that he lived in South Boston, and like many Bostonians and people from New England he was a passionate Patriots fan. He talked continuously about the Patriots and praised the Super Bowl and this year it was a number, an anniversary so to speak, that I did not even register. It's fair to say that the ambulance ride was even entertaining. I was strapped to the stretcher then, and still strapped to the stretcher now.

Stuart rolled his eyes back and forth and said nothing, grinning widely, unacknowledging Ralph and his attempted question.

"Oh, hell. Stew!"

Silence in the elevator and mixed with it a smell of sulfur. Stuart rubbed his eyes and laughed. "All right, you caught me," he said. "Stew me!"

At that I also laughed for a painful second.

Jim shook his head. "Not in front of the man! At least wait until we get out of the elevator." Ralph looked at me "Hey, man. Don't laugh at him. You're egging him on! Get it? Egging—it smells like rotten eggs in here! This guy has so much gas he does that all day. Whenever he wants to. Just to piss me off!"

All right, Ralph, I thought, and to be frank about it, I couldn't laugh anymore even if I tried to. It was absolutely brutal. Without narcotics that is. On the face of it nothing seemed very funny, and my tragedy had only just begun.

The bell rang and the elevator stopped and from the middle the steel doors spread apart. Before my eyes sat a squeaky-clean green lobby. Stuart walked out. Ralph pushed the stretcher from behind. I glanced at the panel on the elevator wall. Button number eight was lit up.

We moved through the lobby and went under an archway and into the central area on the eighth floor. We made a left turn and I rolled in front of a group of nurses. I was all eyes, and one of the nurses noticed and smiled.

Ralph pushed me toward a room and hanging on the wall to the left of the door like a nametag stuck to a person's chest was a small plaque that read 832. I rolled into the room and could not have been more thrilled! It exceeded my expectations, but I'm not sure what my expectations even were at this point. I was going where I was going.

"Here we are," said Ralph.

"Nice place."

"He'll like it. You like it?"

"Yeah," I said.

"Oh, hold on. Let me get those."

Stuart and Ralph unfastened the straps and freed me from the stretcher. It was rough sitting upright but better than being locked down.

"You need anything?"

I nodded to the corner of the room. "That walker. Thanks."

"Is that it?"

"Yeah."

"Well listen. It was great to meet you. You'll be all right. I just know, I have a feeling."

"Oh no," said Ralph. "Whenever Stew has a feeling—that's his gut feeling. It's going to be a long day…"

The two medics walked toward the door. "Take care, man."

"You too," I said as I sat on the edge of the bed.

Ralph was a football fanatic, one of those men who had never played the sport but knows just about all there is to know about it. At the spectator level, he knew offence, defense, players, teams, and he never mentioned it, but most of his knowledge probably came from fantasy football. I played the sport, didn't care to watch it. In the ambulance Ralph mentioned that the Patriots had won the Super Bowl.

"So I heard," I said.

"Today's their Super Bowl parade!"

"The weather's perfect for it."

It was really the most dreary winter day that to my knowledge I had ever seen. Overnight a blustery snowstorm had swept through New England and by morning it had changed to a wintry mix of snow, rain and sleet.

"How about that ending!" said Ralph.

"That's pretty much what I've heard everyone say."

"You didn't watch it?"

"Only the first quarter. That's it."

"Oh, but it was a great game!"

"I couldn't focus. Honestly I've never really been interested in watching games. I was planning to since I had nothing better to do, but before I knew it, it was the start of the second quarter and I had already passed out."

"I don't blame you! That was the sad part of the game."

"Yeah, well. My attention was elsewhere."

"What do you mean?"

"Well. A nurse gave me a round of narcotics."

"There you go! That makes the game fun to watch."

"I was hardly watching the game to begin with—"

"I don't blame you," Ralph said.

"Yeah… It was a new nurse. Hadn't seen her before. Maybe an intern. She had given me the pills and then came back and asked if I wanted a foot rub. I couldn't remember the last time that I had gotten one of those—my memory's not very good right now you know. Of course I said yes. Her hands—so soft. She was talented too! It wasn't long after being overwhelmed with euphoria when I passed out."

"Yes! Do you think that she stopped once you did?"

"That," I said. "Is hard to say."

Ralph laughed. "Well I don't know what I'd rather like—foot rub or watching the game. Probably watching the game!"

"Makes sense!"

"It was the best Super Bowl game that I've ever seen, man!"

"Tell me about it—the highlights."

"Well the Patriots were down by—"

"Woah!"

"Pickle nips!" yelled Ralph. "What the hell was that!"

It felt like the ambulance had flown over a speed bump but based on the time of year and the weather outside there's a good chance that it was a pothole. Ralph was slightly whiplashed, and luckily I was strapped to the stretcher.

"Sorry…" we heard from up front.

"You watch," said Ralph. "He'll get all shy after this."

"That's funny."

"You wanna hear the highlights?"

"In a minute. Let me think for a minute."

And I thought for a minute about those hands and Ralph told me about the game and it was clear that I did the right thing and now at Spaulding from down the hall a timer beeped and the pain came back. Well that'll wake you out of a daydream! I rose out of bed and stood on my left leg and grabbed the walker and hopped away. My room had its very own private bathroom and from the room that I was used to at Mass General this was like upgrading from a Motel 6 to the Bellagio. Yet it was simple, and I like simple. I stood before the sink and blankly looked at the mirror. The thing in the reflection had a slovenly thick beard that grew out beneath the cervical collar on its neck. He looked nothing like me but he didn't look bad, and the collar had always been there for support but because of the narcotics I had hardly noticed it. The more that I studied the reflection the more that I recognized myself; really only the beard had confused me slightly at first. I took off my shirt. Even in the mirror I was noticeably thin. Eating only ice cubes for two weeks will surely do it! I liked this. Now I didn't mind so much the forced famishment. Everything else seemed to be in order except for two scabbing scars on the side of my chest and above my ribcage. The room was quiet. I had been looking in the mirror for far too long and there was nothing more to see. Now with no catheter attached and ample privacy I could piss at my pleasure into the toilet. I set the walker to the right and then pivoted around and closed the door. *Click*.

Chapter 6

My new room had many remarkable features and what stole my attention right away was the window and the view outside in every direction. Sitting on the edge of the bed and facing directly south was the best view in the whole city. I sat there for a short while and studied the cityscape, unintentionally meditating, knowing that for every day that I'm here this will be my view but as soon as I leave it will become a memory. Memories will fade and they can vanish—you remember as much as you can, and I absorbed as much of the view as I could.

Toward the bottom of the frame sat dozens of yachts floating on the water that were covered for winter and tied to a pier, and to their rear was a wharf with modern condos that jutted out from the peninsula and into the pallidly blue harbor, and towering above these exclusive homes amid an overcast sky and foggy air stood the stark skyline of Boston. Lustrous steel structures stretched high off the ground and above the horizon into the clouds and the harbor below swelled with whitecaps at the mouth of the Charles River. Those lost souls of the sea. A massive red and black cargo barge entered the channel off to the left and its deck was full of assorted intermodal containers. It furiously honked its horn. Like a child crying it screamed, "*WAAANG!*"

Suddenly, to my brief disappointment, there was a knock on the door and I turned around and lay in the bed. In the doorway stood a young nurse with a welcoming smile and her tone of skin a light olive color. What a fine complexion! She had dirty blonde hair and looked like a nice girl. "Hey Andy," she said. "I'm Jess. Can I come in?"

"Yes," I said.

"How are you feeling?"

"Right now, much better."

"Good!" Jess flipped through the pages in her manila folder to signal something. "I was just looking at your file and saw all of the injuries. That's horrible!"

"I know. It felt surreal at first."

"Wow. I didn't know what to expect when I first came in. But when I saw you I couldn't believe it—that the injuries in the file actually happened to you."

"Yeah…"

"You look great."

"So do you, Jess."

She smiled. "There must be something else out there."

"Oh, there's something else."

"Do you believe in God?"

"The gods—uh. Well absolutely. Now I do. You?"

"I had never thought about it before but now I do too."

And as she said that I lost focus and recalled that the most tested beings are the most holy beings, and though I was not even slightly religious the word of it had a promising ring and resonated with me after all of this time. Why the gods had spared me I had no idea. Maybe there was more to life that I was destined to live. Right now I was smack in the middle of an intersection.

"Andy…" said Jess.

"Yeah?"

"Are you okay?"

"Yeah."

"You were just staring at my—hands. You didn't respond."

I smiled. "Oh."

"Are you in any pain?"

"I'm fine. There's always some pain, sí."

"See what?"

"I mean yes."

Jess brushed the end of her hair with her hand and laughed. "I *see*," she said. "Is it one of those things that lingers?"

"No, it's more intense. The right word might be chronic."

"*Oh!* Well just let me know if I can help."

"I will."

"See that intercom on the side of your bed?"

"This, yes."

"Sí. Now if you ever need anything just press that red button. I'll answer your call." Jess laughed. "And then you speak into it."

I pressed the red button.

"Well don't press it now," she said.

"Hello?" a voice spoke through the intercom.

We were both silent.

"Hello?" it said again.

Jess laughed warmly. "Andrew, I have to go to a meeting…" She turned and walked away. "Call me if you need anything."

I was surprised to hear her say it and glad to be on a first-name basis, and then I propped up the pillow at the head of the bed and leaned back against it. The mattress was surprisingly comfortable, much firmer than those at Mass General, and advanced too. On the intercom were buttons that could raise and lower the bed and incline or recline the frame, and on each side there were plastic guardrails to prevent a patient from falling to the floor. Those would have been valuable features to have on beds in the ICU, and it would have saved me from falling out at least once, but then would I have ever awakened from the coma? It's true that some people never wake up from a coma. The guardrails were there to prevent the unfortunate, but sometimes I like to dangle my arms or legs over the side of the bed. But in this case I was restricted and confined within the bedframe. Compared to Mass General, you'd make the sacrifice. I inclined the bed and looked out through the window. I tried to meditate by counting the windows on a building instead of my breath to ease my mind and relax my thoughts, and it worked. The pain, the cervical collar, my beard beneath the collar, my escalated heart rate, everything was hardly noticeable, and after I counted the windows on one building I moved on to the next one. And this was very meditative, and about all that I could stand to do in the moment.

Deep amid my self-given solace the doorknob turned and the door opened. A doctor with black hair and delicate eyes walked in.

"Andy?"

"Yes."

"My name's Chris."

"Call me Andrew."

Chris held out his hand and we greeted each other.

"It's nice to meet you."

"You too."

"I'm a specialist in traumatic brain injuries here at Spaulding. I was informed just about a week ago about your coming here. Well. A severe TBI. How are you?"

"I'm good."

"You have a lot of other injuries too."

"Yes."

"How does everything feel?"

"Well. It hurts."

"On a scale of one to ten what is your level of pain?"

I rubbed my chin. "That's different for everyone. On average a five and when I'm sitting upright a solid eight or nine."

Chris made a note on his clipboard. "I ask because I wanted to talk to you about pain management. I've noticed that your intake of pain medication was… Well it was astronomical!"

"Woah—" I jerked back.

"We think that it would be best if you stopped altogether. They can be bad for your health, and we do not want to see you become dependent on them."

"That's funny. I was actually just about to ask for a dose."

"Hmm. You can have one five milligram Oxycodone, but after that I'd like you to stop."

"That's okay. I was going to ask, but now I'm fine."

"I'm glad to hear that. You've passed the test!"

"Well I've had a feeling that I might already be addicted."

"Oh. There's always Tylenol…"

I looked outside and watched one airplane approach another as Chris wrote a note on his clipboard.

"Logan airport is just across the river," he said.

"Behind some trees and East Boston."

"Have you ever been?"

"I believe so."

"How's your memory?"

"No bueno."

"Can you remember anything from the incident?"

"No. I've tried to. That's what I spent doing for hours at Mass General. But it's like this. The harder I try the further it goes."

"Interesting. I suppose that if it wants to come back it will."

"Well I'm not sure if I want it."

"I understand. It may never happen, and we may never know what happened. Amnesia is not your typical field of study. That's, well that's what this entire floor is—the eighth floor, brain injury floor. Amnesia and brain injuries are different for each person, just as each person and place is different from one another We have a community meeting tomorrow in the conference room. We'll have a few guest speakers. It should be a fun event. You should go. We'll welcome you."

"Oh, I don't know."

"There will be plenty of good food."

"Count me in," I said.

"It's in the afternoon. Looking at your schedule you should be finished with therapy by then."

"Perfect."

Chris glanced at the clock on the wall. "Well. I'll leave you be. See you tomorrow."

"Thanks," I said. "See you."

Chris left the room and on his way out he softly closed the door. Sitting through an entire meeting in a wheelchair, I could clearly see all of it now even with a lacking imagination. My body sank into the firm mattress and the dread set in and the thought, *Oh, the things that I do for good food!*

That night was a terrible night and for all of it I tossed and turned and never found the right position. As the night went on a gentle fasciculation arose and by morning if my eyes were closed they quivered. There had been only one other time at college that bore any sort of similarity. It was after a long week of abusing ourselves and getting very little sleep, and when I finally tried to get a full six hours it didn't work, as if my body repelled any attempted rest, any means of revival, any kind of cooperation, and it twitched its eyelids to show that it had complete control. The human body is complex and very smart, and if it's not treated right it will raise you hell but if it's taken care of it will show you love. Only after it is wholly destroyed and then properly nourished can it fully flourish and that will happen over time. This eye twitch at Spaulding had other contributing factors. There was a restlessness in each involuntary movement either as a revolt or out of resentment. It was my body's way of expressing its displeasure with me and I could not blame it, but I also couldn't do anything about it and there I found myself in yet another bind. The back pain was tolerable and inconstant. It came and went but rarely lingered like the tide on a planet in hyper-rotation. But what did it for me was the cervical collar, wrapped tightly around my neck and fastened by Velcro which scratched at my skin. It was not to be loosened according to the doctor. William had given fair warning against loosening the collar—"For obvious reasons," as he put it—because the cervical fracture could easily expand if the collar was even slightly fiddled with. That was a good enough reason for me! My beard was thick and beneath the collar it itched like ivy, and even though I've never had poison ivy I can imagine that it was similar to this. My beard squished against my skin under the compression of the collar, and for breathing room it had only a few air vents on each side, and I myself had a very hard time breathing as it was. And to complete the misfortune, every twenty minutes a high-pitched *BEEP!* chirped from the hall outside of my room like the sound of a fire alarm low on batteries. And I'd think, *What are the chances!* Very clearly I remembered that a fire alarm at my apartment beeped almost exactly the same way, and then I made sense of it in the best way that I could. Technology is like a puppy. For the most part it's very good and a great pleasure to have, but it can also bite you in the ass when you least expect it. By three in the morning a visceral rage had built up within and I looked at the intercom and pressed the red button.

"Hullo," the voice said.

"Hey, Jess?"

There was hard laughter on the other end of the speaker. "Jess went home about ten hours ago. This is Carol."

"Oh. Well hello, Carol."

"Hullo!"

"Can you get me a Tylenol?"

"Sure, I'll be right over."

And then I heard a knock on the door. Carol walked in.

"You're working late tonight."

She laughed quickly. "I always work the nightshift!"

"Splendid."

"You just wanted a Tylenol?"

"Yeah. Can't sleep."

"Oh." Carol frowned. "Would you like some warm milk? That might help you fall asleep."

"Yes I would."

"Okay, hold on. I'll be right back."

Carol walked out of the room and then came back a minute later with a cup of milk.

"I forgot to ask," I said. "Do you have chocolate powder?"

"To make chocolate milk?"

"Yeah."

"No," Carol sighed. "We might have some syrup down in the kitchen but the kitchen's closed."

"It's not the same. I used to drink warm chocolate milk when I was a little kid—I just remembered that. It's okay, this is good."

After drinking the milk I inclined the bed and reached behind and pressed a small black button on the wall. The sound of an electric motor hummed and the curtain rose and gave way to the night sky. All around the spread of darkness lay still like a sheet of black ice, and amid the gloom the stark silhouette of each steel structure stood erect in the space not far in the distance. Above the sky had cleared and the moon shone and reflected off the water in the harbor below and this created the most beautiful mångata in Massachusetts. The stars dotted the infinite darkness like distant candles and I enjoy a scented candle. I decided to try and count a cluster of stars and transition into a short but sound rest. *One, two, three, four, five, six, seven, eight. Hey, this might actually work. Nine, ten, eleven, twelve… BEEP!* chirped the noise from the hallway. *Really… This will be a long night,* I thought. *And a long road ahead. A long road less traveled, my friend.*

Chapter 7

The door opened in the morning and my sleepless rest came to an end. The dreamy early morning serenity was over. I rolled over and faced the window. Across the harbor the city stood resolute and the ashen morning light streamed in through the window and gave the room a dull glow. The air felt warm and I groggily rolled over onto my other side. It was Jess, and she walked into the room and positioned her cart parallel to my bed. I looked blearily at the clock on the wall. Half past six.

"Good morning!" Jess said.

"Morning."

"How did you sleep last night?"

"I wasn't able to," I said.

"Oh? How come?"

"For one I couldn't get comfortable. And then there was also this obnoxious beep outside in the hall all night. Will it ever shut up?"

"Was it a screeching beep?"

"Yes."

"Okay, yeah I actually heard that this morning. We'll take a look at it. Will you still be able to do therapy?"

"Easily," I said.

"Great! Well what would you like for breakfast? Today we have scrambled eggs and toast, oatmeal—"

"I'll have the eggs and toast. With salt and pepper."

"Okay…" Jess entered my order into the computer. "Do you want a peach cup as the side?"

"Oh, please. Just make sure—no onions, no questions."

"All right! I'll be back with your breakfast soon."

Jess came back and placed the tray on the table beside my bed. Sitting on top was a plate with eggs and toast and cup of fruit and a plastic pouch of orange juice.

"Thanks," I said.

"Of course. Can I get you anything else?"

"Well. No, I guess I'm all right."

"Okay. I'll write your schedule on the white board. Today you have speech therapy at eight, and then a little break before physical therapy at ten." She grabbed a marker and added my schedule to the schedule board. She smiled. "Enjoy your breakfast." She turned around and left the room.

I grabbed the fork and ate the fruit and placed the eggs between the toast and gladly ate both like an egg sandwich, all in a few bites, crumbs, egg bits, everything. The food was mediocre at best but to me in that moment it was almost gourmet. And they offered it *a la carte!* I ate so savagely as if there was a prize at the bottom of the plate, a golden ticket of sorts, but there was not. It was only a dirty plate that symbolized reality. Soon it would be full, and for now I enjoyed scraping what I could off the face of it. It had been a long time since I had eaten real food, and I'm not talking about the liquid food or ice cubes at Mass General. For the first time in weeks my palate was pleased. I had forgotten what it was like to eat something wholesome, something simple yet something that's almost always taken for granted. I chugged the juice and tossed the pouch into the trash and inclined the bed and lay back, resting my eyes, waiting because waiting for something felt right.

There was a knock on the door at eight in the morning and therapy promptly began. Speech therapy came first and what a bore it was! My therapist was not to blame. She was kind and calm and had an exquisitely soothing voice. My brain seemed to like it—it tingled with excitement! But the problem was simply what we did and how we spent our time. We started with fairly straightforward exercises for memory and attention, and then we moved on to solving basic puzzles and riddles. Up first were the general questions.

"What month is it?" she asked.

"February."

"And the year?"

"Twenty seventeen."

"What day of the week is it?"

I looked at the calendar on the wall.

"No, you can't cheat!"

"That doesn't count—it's Wednesday."

"Yes… What building are you in?"

"Spaulding Rehabilitation Hospital."

"How long have you been here?"

"Since yesterday."

"What was the first thing that you did this morning?"

"It's hard to say. I never actually fell asleep."

She jotted down a note in her file and then asked me to list out loud as many animals as I could in a minute.

"Animals. All right…" I said.

"Ready? Go!"

"Duck, cow, frog, moose, squid, squirrel, shark, sloth. Hold on. Cat, dog, bull, minx…"

"Is that all you've got?"

"Ranga."

This was a strangely hard exercise, and I didn't know what the point of it was and felt like a fool and asked to stop. I thought, *Is there a hidden camera somewhere? No, no.* It was not a game show but rather a type of hospital drudgery. The questions were all vapid and rudimentary and each game was like a test to measure my memory, intuition, retention, consideration, and basically every other highly vital cognitive function to form the basis for upcoming sessions. We continued with the games and questions and quite unbearably the pain persisted. The therapist urged me against lying down in bed, for a reason that strictly had to do with memory and retention, and coincidentally this reason was never retained. I finally told her that I had simply endured enough and could hardly focus and had to lie down.

"That's okay," she said gently. "We're almost done. You can get comfortable. It'll be fine for the next exercise."

My pain must have been almost palpable, and the tone of her voice suggested that she was empathetic toward this kind of hurt, but her soft eyes had a mildly peculiar look of disappointment, as if lying down would disrupt our session, or as though she wanted to see exactly how much pain I could actually tolerate, how strong my tolerance was, how strong of a man I was, and by lying down I was essentially giving up. Pain won the battle this time—it usually does. It's better to be friends with something that's perceived by the mind, rather than enemies, mostly because you will feel much better when it actually presents itself rather than feeling vulnerable or threatened. I told the therapist that to lie down was absolutely necessary, and then fixed the pillow and followed my words, and simultaneously her satisfaction dissolved.

It might be that many a woman live by masochism. Pain and suffering, beginning to end. Every month living under the sign of the moon and flooded with blood. The sole law of their expansive multiverse. If woman could, she might devour man and his soul completely. And in the end, it's a fact, she always triumphs.

What we did next was elementary, seemingly childish. Maybe she had given up on me, but she was not that type of person and we carried on with the session regardless. I worked diligently on puzzles and riddles, like I said, on a piece of paper until we were finished, and frequently I appeared to be struggling, and just when I was about to stop a lightbulb went off in my head and I figured out the problem, as if the answer hadn't already been in there all along. With this she responded well, enthusiastically, and wrote positive notes in my file. That's how the session ended, and then she gave me an array of homework problems stapled together in a little booklet to work on overnight at my pleasure. Quite a thick packet of cognitive exercises! I thought, *What is this turning into? Reading a book would be better.*

By the time physical therapy started I had finished the packet of exercises. And for the remainder of the short break I rested my eyes, never dozing off to sleep but instead lying comfortably at the cusp of unconsciousness, imagining vividly a sunny day on a warm beach by palm trees, knowing that someday at some point I'll find this spectacular place.

When the physical therapist came into the room she wasted no time and led the way down to the gym on the first floor. Something was wrong with the wheelchair and it wouldn't roll straight. Every time I cranked the wheels the wheelchair veered off to the right, and no matter how many times I readjusted the chair it always veered off to the right again, into walls, steps, doorways, doctors, pictures, plants, tables, chairs, et cetera. It was frustrating and tiring and it hurt like hell to sit in the wheelchair without any narcotics. I bit my lip and embraced the pain. The hurt was unbelievably strong and naturally it sucked the life out of everything else. But when I wheeled into the gym I was truly amazed. It was a large wide-open facility with floor-to-ceiling windows along every wall. Natural light filled the great room like an atrium and a number of therapy tables lined each wall and window, and in the middle of the room were dozens of exercise machines and equipment laid out in rows eight deep along the linoleum floor. But of course they weren't for me to use. The therapist brought me straight to a therapy table and I lay down and found relief from the pain for now. I first started with stretches—calves, quads, ankles, and hamstrings—and then the therapist made me perform a combination of stationary exercises for both legs until the session ended and we left. My right leg was weak and painful but I powered through. And it was the same issue with my left leg too, probably because I hardly ever walked on or even used it for that matter, but its weakness paled in comparison to my wounded right leg. I performed straight leg lifts and side leg lifts and for hamstrings I carefully rolled over and on my stomach I bent my knee up toward my ass and slowly lowered it down to the table. Ten times for each leg, alternating legs after each set. The therapist even strapped a small weight around my ankles for these. For added resistance, I figured, and I calmly powered through. It was like meditating while doing a chore. You don't want to do it but you have to do it and after a while it's not so bad. To finish the session strong I performed bicycles and Fifer scissors to work my core. And after that we were done. I was limited in what I could do and it was smart to be cautious and careful for now.

I had rested my eyes for about an hour after therapy and then I ate lunch, I mindlessly scrolled through the channels on tv but I did not enjoy a single program on that box. Even with a crippled mind you can see straight through to its nuts and bolts. Where was Jess? I would have rather had a conversation with someone. With no belief in the box on the wall I decided to look out of the window, not to meditate, but having nothing better to do, to simply look at a landscape full of emotion. Today was a day in early February and a cloudless day it was. The sky-blue sky of mid-winter and its gusts of wind howled and hissed at the window. Down below an oil barge approached the channel from the harbor, its enormous mass coasting slowly along the shining water. As cold as it probably was it appeared inviting and I thought what a good idea it would be to go outside and breathe a breath of fresh air.

"Come on Andy," Jess said from the doorway. "Let's go!"

"Outside?"

"What? No. The meeting's about to start."

"Not happening. I'm too tired."

Jess grabbed the wheelchair by the door and parked it parallel beside my bed. "You don't have to do anything else for the rest of the day. You can lay in bed all you want."

"And that's exactly what I'm going to do right now."

"But you said you'd go to the meeting. Come on. It won't be very long."

"*WAAAANG!*" the ship's horn honked a long and fierce roar. We both looked out through the window. The ship was dark green and red and it was all muscle.

"Look at that thing, I think it's telling you to go!"

"It's not telling me anything."

"Even if it's not. Let's go."

"No."

"Come on!" Jess said petulantly.

"That's not going to work."

51

"Andrew, come on…"

"Why do you think that I should go?"

"You need to get out of bed."

"No, I like my own bed just fine."

Jess tittered. "I'm not asking again."

"Oh?"

"No."

In the end I scooted off the bed and hopped and sat down in the wheelchair, and then Jess turned it around and pushed me out of my room. Why I was actually going to the meeting I didn't know. I liked Jess and that was probably why, and I wished that she would wheel me past the conference room and loop around the eighth floor and call an elevator and catch a ride to the lobby and go out to her car so we could both drive off and leave all of my problems behind. But that was just a dream and sometimes when you dream enough dreams will come true. The world can work auspiciously, and it can be fair even when its entirety seems unfair. My ache in the wheelchair was hard enough to make a fat lady sing. We arrived on time.

Chapter 8

The conference room was fresh and capacious and abundantly filled with afternoon sunlight. There was a long table that ran the length of the room with desserts and snacks spread out in the middle. I sat at the head of the table by the door and counted only six other people that were present at the meeting and one of them was Chris. At the other end of the table appeared to be the guest speakers: a bald man and an older man and a young woman. They all looked healthy. And for patients there was a distraught woman in a wheelchair to my right and a man with grey hair sitting coolly to my left. It was one of those moments when we were all waiting and we weren't quite sure what we were waiting for so everyone looked around curiously but not at each other and not a word was spoken. What the others were thinking was anyone's guess, maybe about colors, smells, feelings, what's for dinner tonight. I looked out through the window straight ahead and quickly realized that I should've brought a pillow to sit on, anything that could possibly cushion this padless wheelchair. Along with Tylenol, that's two necessities that I had forgotten to bring, and it was already horribly painful.

Chris stood up and walked to the door and closed it. I grabbed and ate a brownie and then moved around on top of this chair that was mostly steel and tried to get comfortable. But with each shift in weight the pain grew worse and I wondered why I had even come. The only attendees at the meeting were me and two patients, three guest speakers and Chris. So much for community, and no wonder Jess had wanted me to go so badly!

"We have a small crowd today," said Chris. "But that will give all of you more time to share."

I tilted my head and looked out the window.

Chris looked at the guest speakers. "Do you want to start?"

"Sure," said the bald man who had a scar below the crown of his head that curved down and around his ear. It was raw and gave him character, and I wondered what the scar on the back of my head looked like, still scabbed and shaped like an X and hidden to the world underneath a coat of hair.

"My name's Mike," he continued. "I was once a patient here on the eighth floor like all of you. Just over three years ago."

"We both were," said the old man.

"Yeah. Coincidently, Tom and I were patients here at the same time with traumatic brain injuries. We've been coming back a few times every year to share our experience."

"We'd come back more if they paid us!" Tom added.

"Now its okay, Dad," said the young woman sitting beside him. "It's okay."

"Everyone, this is my daughter. Isn't she something?"

Tom's daughter smiled bashfully.

"Yes, yes. She is. She's been there for me. I had a bad TBI and she stayed by my side."

"My name's Penny. Yeah, I've been helping my dad. The past three years there's been a lot of ups and downs—three years! You might think this is interesting. My brother made a short film about my father and his recovery and they actually aired it on ESPN."

"We brought copies," said Tom. "They also have copies here."

"Did you get paid?" I asked.

"Well. No. It was more about the network. ESPN!"

I disliked this, and Penny gestured at her father to calm down. "Mike was saying something," she said. "Let him speak."

"Uh, yeah," said Mike. "I still notice abnormalities from time to time. If your brain is injured there's no way to tell how it'll heal. I'd say that mine did pretty well but it's different for everyone. Just right now I forgot where I am and what I'm even doing here."

I softly laughed to myself and so did Mike.

"No, I'm only joking," he said. "But that did happen the other day, and that did happen the other week. I walk into a room happy and I leave very confused. I'm a professional photographer, I take pictures, I don't know what I'm taking a picture of."

"How's that going for you?" the distraught woman asked.

"Oh, fine. It only happens sometimes. I couldn't sleep—this was here—I couldn't sleep and they gave me Trazadone. Now I have the most insane dreams—I love it!"

"I also take Trazadone," said Tom. "And I also have unusual dreams."

"What's Trazadone?" the woman asked.

"It's an antidepressant. Low dosage a sedative. That's why I use it—for its sedative effects."

"Me too," said Tom. "I take one of those little pills at ten, ten minutes later I'm out like a rock."

"We've had to keep an eye on him at night," said Penny. "He's a sleepwalker! That's how he ended up in the hospital. He walked in his sleep headfirst into his bureau."

"I lost everything," he said. "My memory, my car, my mind, my savings…"

I took two brownies out of the container and sadly ate one and set the other in my lap. Almost immediately indigestion set in and whether it was from the brownie or the bureau I did not know. This heavy feeling was quickly masked by intolerable pain and the wheelchair offered only one means of escape. I had to push down on the arm rests and lift my body its entire weight all one hundred and sixty-two pounds off of the seat and hover in the air for as long as I'd like the pain to stop. When I sat on the steel all other feelings were gone. It was basically like a seesaw between the wheelchair and me. In the air every problem seemed minor and in the chair they were all relentless. When I lift my ass off of you I'll get relief and once I sit you'll raise me hell.

And it went back and forth, in the air and in the chair for as long as I sat there at the meeting, and the longer the meeting went on the worse the pain became. My arms were already very tired; they were alarmingly out of shape. I suppose that back at Mass

General my body used the little energy that it had to stay alive and spared nothing for my triceps. There's no better time than the present to recover your strength! If I had been at home it would have been music, but what made it easier here in Boston was the view of the city and the streets of Charlestown. A row of brick buildings stood directly ahead and suspended in the air about a mile away was the Bunker Hill Bridge. At this point the doctors and nurses took the views from Spaulding for granted. Right now it was my motivation. Chris cleared his throat.

"Well thanks for sharing that, Penny and Tom. Let's all share right now. Except for me! Mike, would you like to go next?"

"Sure." He sat up in his chair arms crossed and leaned over the table. "How I ended up at Spaulding. I'm a photographer. The best of the best! I said that, right? I was late for an appointment that I had with a client. On the highway I passed a car. She was driving seven under the speed limit. An old lady, seven under! Wait."

Mike laughed to himself and collected his thoughts and I sat up and lifted my body into the air and out of the chair above the seat and hovered. Tom and Penny looked my way, he confused and she curious. Mike laughed.

"Okay, okay," he continued. "I passed her. There I was—in the fast lane, baby! I dropped the cap to my water bottle and first time I went to grab it I splashed a little water on my shorts. Now I think that the client will think that I wet myself! Well. Second time I went to grab it I got it. I screwed it on and set the bottle aside. My eyes were always on the road. I never noticed anything. I woke in the hospital two days later. They told me a drunk driver swerved across the highway—from the oncoming traffic mind you—and hit the side of my car. I flipped over several times; she barely got a scratch. It was four in the afternoon! Pshhh."

"Good, Lawd!" said the distraught woman.

"Mike almost couldn't walk again," said Tom. "Isn't that right, Mike?"

"He's right. I could but I almost couldn't."

"How did you feel about that, Mike?"

"No workers' comp, no lawsuit, no money. Well I didn't feel too good about it, Chris. No one cares about a victim who's still alive. They just want them dead so they can use them as a prop, an example, so they can make it better for themselves. Those people have never been a victim and almost certainly never will. The real victims are victims at every level, in every sense. Speaking from the standpoint of a victim, Chris, it's selfish and disrespectful."

"Well all right. Tom, did you have something to say?"

"I'd like to hear this young man's story," said Tom.

"Me too," said Penny. "He's cute."

"He looks restless."

Everyone turned and looked my way.

"Well. A couple weeks ago I woke in the ICU at Mass General. The past was all a dream. I was in a coma and had crazy dreams and then awoke to this—being told that I'm lucky to be alive, told that if I move a certain way I could become paralyzed and unable to walk again. Sort of like you, Mike. And sort of like now the pain was incessant. My pelvis was fractured and also my lumbar spine and that's why it hurts so much to sit down—why I've been lifting myself above the seat for this entire meeting. You wouldn't believe it."

"Geez," said the woman.

"That's okay," said Tom. "I just didn't know what it was that you were doing."

"You must have a high pain tolerance," said Penny.

"What happened? I mean how did all of that happen?"

"I don't know. My memory was wiped out. I know that I was at a friend's apartment and late at night I walked home and that's when something happened. I was dropped off of a train trestle. I haven't said that out loud—it's only been resonating in my mind. It really does sound bad to say out loud. I had many wounds and scars, bruises a black eye. Foul play was involved, and like Mike I was also a survivor of something. I don't know what—they're still investigating…"

I had clearly caught the undivided attention of every person in that room and this I liked, and yet disliked. With every wide-eyed gaze I shrunk further into the wheelchair and the reasonless pain was winning the battle. It won.

"Excuse me. I have to leave. It hurts too much to sit down." I peeled away from the table and wheeled toward the door. "I need to lay in bed," I told Chris on my way out, and then my wheelchair veered into the wall as I left the room. I thought, *Oh, Lawd!*

Chapter 9

That night was my second night at Spaulding and the second night in a row without a wink of sleep. The reasons for this were almost exactly the same as the first night—the collar, my beard, the pain, the itch. Cannabis would have solved this problem once and for all and with that I would have been a thousand times happier amid the opioid withdrawals, but for reasons that even amused me every doctor at Spaulding was against it. I knew why; I knew too much but never enough. I wanted what I couldn't have.

In the morning Chris asked how I had slept and I told him that I hadn't.

"Again?"

"Yes."

He seemed disappointed, and he told me that with a brain injury you need a good night's sleep, and he said that he would try me out on Trazadone—as a sedative. He asked. "Do you remember that a couple people from the meeting take it for sleep?"

"Yes," I said.

And that night I tried the little ball of poison and finally fell asleep, if you would even call it sleep. I woke the next morning more tired than the night before. I will say that I dozed off almost effortlessly. One moment everything that was visible was black and the next moment it was a dreamlike landscape, journeying through the unconscious mind and in and out of its every thought. Good, bad, evil, angelic—who has only one kind of thought? It's normal to have a wide range of thoughts, and under the spell of a serotonin antagonist all sorts of thoughts and

59

bizarre projections arose during sleep. Dreams are good, but aspirational dreams are better than unconsciousness dreams, and I feel best in the morning without any dreams.

In that case, that's another reason why cannabis would've been much better—you sleep well without any dreams! My mother had told me that she had read a study on the effects of cannabinoids in your body at the time of a severe brain injury, and she said that it can give you a much greater chance of surviving and recovering. I believed it, but even so, the doctors paid no mind to this and were set on their conservative ideas. Prescription drugs, which they may or may not have been compensated financially by pharmaceuticals for every prescription or pill that was administered, was their only logical solution—for anything. The Trazadone produced what I didn't want—those unconsciousness dreams.

The first place that I was brought to was a place in which I'd be glad to live and die. A private beach with the finest sand that felt like powder and the only sound was the sound of the surf. I was joined by three girls who each strut across the beach to my secluded spot. "Are you ready for your massage?" the head girl in charge asked.

"Yes I am."

I suddenly appeared in a hammock and arbitrarily leaned up, and then lay back. Now feeling very good, the light breeze, the sun, the hands squeeze, the girl in charge, she mounts the hammock and then my lap. What's that? A pair of hips swaying gracefully to their own soundless rhythm, the skin smooth and golden, gleaming as if acceptable. The ocean waves slowly move in and then pull away to the glistening sea. A dream as clear as day is a great escape. What separates a dream that feels real and reality itself is only a very thin line. The watch on my wrist tells no time, I wear no watch, and the sun keeps shining and the breeze keeps breathing and with the softest touch I happily close my eyes.

Possibly what's next is a dream within a dream. The alpha and omega. A black and empty nothingness. An intermission within the mind. A break in inner thought. A sweet silence. I lay aware but unaware.

Then suddenly I appeared outside in the dead of night, running faster than real life, moving so fast no sound could be heard and in the dark not a single leaf stirred. And then there was light, and it flashed like a strobe light on the ground ahead, on the road to the right, off the building to the left. I followed the bend in the road and the flashing light stopped and darkness returned and I turned the corner and a thousand feet ahead a gas station stood. Lights were on inside and out front by the pumps and I ran in its direction and stepped on the ground and slid on top a patch of ice and fell back and hit the ground. The stars in the sky and the moon above blurred into nothing. I heard a voice from somewhere deep in the labyrinth. "Where'd he go?"

"I don't know, Sheldon. Maybe if you didn't have a fat ass you had to carry around you would've seen."

My vision gradually returned to normal and the stars in the sky spun slower and slower until all were still. The air was cooler, vision clearer, dogs barked, a clinking collar.

"Shut up, Eddie!"

"Quiet. Let's go this way!"

I reached behind and felt the back of my head and warm and wet hair and glanced at my hand that was red with blood. I sprang to my feet and off I went and on the ground not a trace of snow. What's a frigid winter without snow? A lucid dream.

A few people were standing inside of the gas station and they all looked crazy and it seemed as if one unfortunate fellow had four arms. He stood behind the front window that stretched from floor to ceiling and picked a bottle of wine and held it out in front of his face. And then from the road behind, piercing my eardrums like flying projectiles cutting through time, I heard the violent crack of gunshots and the night air shattered like glass. I heard a bullet tear through space and the front window shattered and dropped to the ground. The unfortunate fellow dropped his wine and what's next is the bottle burst on the floor and he stiffly fell amid a growing puddle of gas station red. Without control I took off for the store and hopped through the window and over the fellow now red on the floor. I went out back to the bathroom and locked the door, and inside the light was both dark and bright and all around it was hard to see. But was there even anything to see? The one window sat high on the wall behind the toilet and I reached for it to see if it would open. It did.

I climbed atop the toilet and punched the glass and through the screen and cleared a hole and felt nothing. I went through and in the air I flipped and landed on the grass out back. The light that blinked and streamed from the bathroom window illuminated a swamp a hundred feet south.

I lay hidden behind a cluster of frozen cattails and peered through the stems and glued my eyes to the store and the space on either side. A twig snapped, and a solid thirty seconds of silence elapsed and then came back. Even in a dream time stood still. Cold gusts of wind erratically shook the leafless trees and a bough above stood all but still as a figure leaped and flew smoothly into the moonlit night. The world was quiet and a strong gust howled and what cut through the lonely cry was the last snap of a twig.

Riveted by fear I lay flat on the ground and unable to move my vision dimmed to a clouded blur. Everything was silent, everything was dark. At once a change that would change the course of this dream occurred. All that was frozen instantly thawed as if all life had been resuscitated. I picked my head up off the ground and a boot swung down and the world went dark.

Both eyes opened and there I was in the bed at Spaulding. It was too late for a Tylenol and too early for coffee. I rested my eyes and faced the window until Jess came in and offered me breakfast.

Chapter 10

My second night at Spaulding was the first time in my life that I'd had wildly vivid dreams, and these dreams continued every night until I left the hospital, and as time went on they slowly became more and more controllable and by the time I left I could basically decide my dream in the moment. Not knowing what would show at first was half the thrill! And as strangely entertaining as these lucid dreams were, the quality of rest was well below par. Each day was slow and dry as dust. Each day I fell deeper and deeper into distress. The nurses disliked this. On Valentine's Day they were extra nice but they could sense that I was missing something. Well of course I was!

The Trazadone was ruining who I was as a person, my spirit, my love. Chris said that as soon as I got home I could discontinue the use of those chemicals, and after this and all along the holy herb was on my mind. All that really happened for my entire stay was therapy and on one day an ice cream party. I ate a loaded bowl of chocolate and strawberry, whipped cream with sprinkles. One of my therapists helped me shower every other day. To be honest I didn't need the help but help was offered and when it is it's hard to refuse. After Valentine's Day my physical therapist opened up ever so rapidly. Time and again I hopped around the perimeter of the gym as fast as possible as she stood aside and timed me. She was very kind and encouraging. We even had something unusual in common: we were both from Maine. If and when you get out of that state, and especially out of New England, it's very rare to meet a person from Maine. If I didn't grow up in that isolated state I'd probably wonder if people actually still live there. And what is up there, in the top corner of the map, in a state where little lobsters dominate people 250 to 1?

Portland and its surrounding areas in southern Maine can be kind of charming on a good day, and that's where I'm from, but further north there's not much of anything. The girl was from Bangor, and now she's a therapist at one of the most prestigious rehabilitation hospitals in the world. Amazing! Every time coming back from the gym she offered to push me up to my room, and every time I accepted and embraced the pain in the wheelchair as always. And then as soon as I made it back to my room and into bed and under the sheets I rested my mind for the rest of the day.

One day I woke early, remembered that I didn't have therapy, then rested my eyes until Jess delivered my morning coffee and cathartic, then ate breakfast, then went to the bathroom to relieve myself. When I was washing my hands I heard a knock on the door to my room and the door pushed open. Footsteps walked in. I turned off the water and opened the door and left the bathroom. I turned the corner and in front of the window wall stood a familiar doctor. "That's a nice view you have," he said.

I lay in bed and from behind I could tell that it was William. I looked out through the window. The sun sat high in the sky and the water and windows on each building shone like grass on a clear spring morning. "Yeah," I said. "It's much better than my view at Mass General."

"I'd say, sure better than mine!" William turned around and slowly walked to the side of my bed. "I came by today to make sure that your pelvis is healing properly. Do you mind if I take a look?"

"No, that's fine."

He first pinched each of my hip bones and then pressed inward one side at a time. "Can you feel that?"

I said, "Yes."

And he pressed harder and asked, "Does that hurt?"

"No."

William then pushed down lightly on the bone below my waist. "This is the pubis ramus," he said. "It might feel tender right now, and you can see that it's protruding slightly against your skin. This is normal. It will heal into place over the next few months. Did I tell you? Maybe I told you when you were back at

Mass General. If not—your pelvic fracture was quite complex, requiring extensive attention. It was what we call a vertical shear fracture—rough!"

I silently arched an eyebrow.

"But it feels a lot better," he said as he stood up. "You're not as lively as you were at Mass General."

"I'm having withdrawals from the drugs. That pain medication you fed to me like Skittles."

"Well. Would you have rather not had anything?"

"I'd rather continue having them here. You say the fracture was rough—here it's been rough. I wouldn't be on them long term and it wouldn't hurt. When I get home I'd just have my weed and then I'd stop—no withdrawals."

William laughed softly. "Don't let these doctors know about that. They won't let you leave!"

"I know…"

"Okay, now I have to check on the scar. It's just above the pubis ramus."

"All right."

"Can you—"

I pulled down my shorts with one hand and left the band just below the scar. It was alarmingly long for a scar and at first in the shower I was slightly self-conscious around the therapist. It made no difference to her. The thing extended across my pubic bone and only the end beside my leg had scabbed.

"It looks good," William said. "Soon the scar will hardly even be noticeable."

"Wonderful," I said.

"What, you don't think the girls will like it?"

"I don't know."

"Well you should be proud."

"Yeah, okay."

"It healed well after we took out the staples."

"What staples?"

"The staples that we used to seal the incision."

"Oh. When did you take them out?"

"Back at Mass General. Here, let me see." The doctor quickly looked inside of the file folder. "Okay, they were taken out on your eighth day. Remember, you were awake."

"Yeah I know. I was awake on the eighth day I remember that, but I don't remember the staples."

"You had just taken a round of narcotics, that's probably why! You were funny on those…"

"I've heard. Can I pull up my shorts now?"

"Oh, yeah. Well yes, everything looks good, and it looks like I should to get back to Mass General."

"Can you say hello to Alfonso for me?"

"Yes." William turned around and left the room.

I looked out through the window and then at my scar and soon the day passed like sand in an hourglass, and then the next day and the next and so on. Pretty soon every other day had gone the other way.

All in all, my time at Spaulding was better than my time at Mass General. I thought about how strange it was that I was even there. This was one place where I can now say that I would have never imagined I'd live. It made sense to think this way and I thought that life is like a dream and that like a dream the good can be good and the bad can be bad and from time to time it won't make sense and when you know it shouldn't it somehow will.

I accepted that what had happened and the luck that I was given was more than I needed to know. Divine! I began moving on to different issues, and frankly there were many issues that lay ahead. Problems with court, friends, sleep, health, et cetera. But not food! I'd have thirty-two problems but good food and cannabis would not be one. And I'd think, *It's time to go home!*

Before I knew it I hopped out of my room for the last time and in the elevator beside my parents I slouched and stood between the crutches. Had I stayed at the hospital any longer my mind would have melted like wax. I hopped out of the vator and through the doors and like a free man I smelled the air for the first time in a long time and what a fresh smell it was! All that was left was a two-hour drive home.

Chapter 11

I thought that the meeting at Spaulding was bad; I had no idea what I was in for on the drive home. Compared to this the meeting felt like a brief walk in the park. After what should have been a two-hour drive that turned into almost three hours, and because for the entire length of this prolonged journey my seat in the car was nearly unendurable, with good reason I wanted to be alone. I hopped inside and through the kitchen and then in the foyer my mother stopped me.

"Andrew, no. You're not going down in The Basement. Are you crazy?"

"Everyone's crazy."

"You can't go down those wooden stairs on the crutches."

"Yeah? I practiced on wooden stairs at Spaulding."

"The Basement's concrete. It's all cluttered! No, you can't hop around down there—you'll trip and fall! Wait until you're off the crutches. Yes, go up to your room."

"I'm going downstairs."

"If you fall—if you get hurt, you're on your own."

And that was enough for me to rethink The Basement. She was right, and where would I go if I was on my own? Nobody would open their arms for a cripple, and Doctor Trey surely would have been displeased with my choice. If once again I ended up in the operating room, that's at least ten hours of his time from the actual surgery gone to waste. It had been almost exactly four weeks since I was last there. In doctor time that's short.

"I'll go up to my room," I told my mother.

She smiled. "We've set up everything for you. We even put the tv from downstairs on your bureau."

I laughed. "My bureau—better hope that I don't sleepwalk into it!"

"What are you talking about?"

"They made a documentary about a sleepwalker sleepwalking into a bureau. You wouldn't understand."

"No, you can go up and watch tv."

"No thanks. Tv is not for me."

I hopped over to the staircase and crawled backwards like a crab using both arms and one leg. That's how I went up the stairs. I had done this before for a month straight after I tore my ACL playing football. It was the same deal—I was unallowed to bear weight on one of my legs—just this time it was the opposite leg. My parents watched their crablike animal maneuver the stairs unusually. My mother followed me into my bedroom.

"Set up everything, huh? What the hell is going on here?"

"Oh, your bed. I washed your blankets before we got you. I'll put the dryer on right now."

"Why is it so cold?"

"You know how your father is. It's always cold in this house."

"Yeah, that is something that I did not forget."

"I'll put the dryer on. You'll have fresh warm blankets in just a minute!"

She left the room and I sat on my bare mattress and thought that this was not nearly as great as it was previously anticipated. My thoughts drifted for a long while, mostly about everything bad and nothing good. I ate up a large chunk of time doing this, and what brought me back to the present moment was the thought of my cannabis. That will absolutely make the situation better, and what a simple and effective remedy it is! Cannabis is like love: it can help lift you up and out of the ditch, make you feel what is then unfelt, and in that case it can also be like a puppy from hell.

My parents had even tucked my bag of cannabis against the side of my bureau and on the ground to the right stood my water pipe. "The Goldstein" was the pipe's nickname, and inside of its base sat dark yellow water and along the sides stains of tar and resin soiled the glass. I grabbed its neck and sitting on the edge of my bed I set its base between my feet on the floor. I took a small nugget from the bag and as dry as it was I used my fingers and ground it to a powder. I stuffed the bowl and grabbed a lighter. I thought, *It's been a long time coming!*

I sparked the lighter and took a hit, watching the entire time a surge of bubbles percolate from the base of the pipe and with the smoke it rose to the mouth of the tube. Clearly I should have been paying closer attention—my intake of smoke was far too much for a pair of highly sensitive lungs. I coughed and wheezed and shook my head as if the smoke was all de trop. It seemed as though my lung collapsed, or as though it had already been collapsed and the other lung was working overtime. Then suddenly all thoughts and all stress stopped. Every limb on my feeble body tingled and soon disappeared into an independent dimension. Each extremity was there but my mind had set them free. The sensation was incredible! What first came to mind after a short period of disbelief that even right now I could feel this way was a memory, and this projection unrolled from the depths of amnesia like a movie on replay. The first time that I had touched the holy herb.

It was when I was just a boy, still genteel and generous, and in those days only slightly aberrant. One day my day one friends and I made an apple bowl after school and then rode our bikes deep into the woods all the way out to a private campsite under massive pine trees and threw our bikes down in a bed of pine needles. We sat on a log and packed the bowl, carved out where the stem used to be, with herb. With a pencil we had stabbed a hole in the side of the apple to inhale through. It was easy to figure out, and the oldest trick in the book.

"I feel good about this," said Sean.

"Me too," said Ricky.

I held the apple; I was up first.

"You got this, T."

"Cheers," I said.

I took a hit and both of my lungs were immediately greeted with a burning pinch. I knew very well that it had worked, and then after coughing a violent spell I passed the apple to Sean. He went, and then Ricky, and then I, and after that, we suddenly stopped. We set the apple aside and Ricky grabbed it and kept it close to his spot on the ground. One minute earlier I had found a dry spot and lying amid a pile of leaves I looked at the sky through the breaks in the trees, and metamorphosed and reposed, I watched the world above spin and shine in very slow circles. The trees were the sky and the clouds and I were one. Magic! At once the entire macrocosm in which we lived became perfectly clear, and though my eyes were squinted they had all but completely opened.

"I think I'm in a different dimension," said Sean.

"I'm right there with you," I said.

And Ricky replied, "Hey."

"Yeah?"

"Are either of you going to eat the apple?"

"What."

"The apple."

"Geez, Rick."

"Are you?"

"No."

Ricky reached down and picked the apple off the ground. "Well then," he said. "I will eat it!"

"Do that!" I said.

Ricky took a selfish bite and all around a beeping rang and caused a rift in his face that spread and split the trees and sky and sun and clouds and the ground before me and with the blink of an eye I was once again in my bedroom in the pits of reality. The beep signaled the end of the cycle; the laundry was finished.

Softly my mother walked upstairs and then opened the door. "Room service," she said as she dropped my bedsheets onto my bed. "Well now I think that you'll finally feel better."

"The drive home was rough."

"Oh." She frowned. "I know you were in a lot of pain."

"Yeah, I'll make my bed."

"Do you want something to eat?"

"Hash browns."

"Hash browns? I'll have to see if we have any."

"If not, a bowl of ice cream."

Under the covers reality felt almost heavenly. Sudden warmth can cause a quick change and good change can beget a renewed vitality. I wondered where was this on the ride home as I spooned the chocolate ice cream into my mouth. Somewhere early on the road a harsh torment arose and grew as the car drove on. That's all there was, almost three hours of solid pain in my groin, and my mind could not see or focus through the fog clearly. That is, until I told my parents about my plan for university next semester as long as no other roadblocks arose from now until then. It was just about six months away and more than you'd expect can happen in half a year. Without any kind of aid on the drive home I could clearly feel the presence of every injury, but at this point I was only aware of less than half of the whole set. My first truly conscious day at Mass General was the only day that I was informed of any damage. I wondered about Doctor Trey and about the surgery; he did a fine job! What else was there, and why did it have to be so painful to simply sit in a seated position? I badly needed something to dull my firm assache in the backseat of the car!

What really ground my gears was the pit stop that we had made at the liquor outlet in Portsmouth, as a final farewell to Spaulding I suppose. We were only halfway home and as the car was stopped and free from progress the pain was there and that's all there was. My parents had gone inside and then came out and walked my way, a box filled with bottles of who knows what in my father's hands. My mother liked her spirits but whenever she drank a change occurred and a grim coat fell over her common spirit. Because of this I found solace in seclusion at home, and as time went on and through bouts of heavy thinking and introspection I myself a young boy then began to develop. Not physical features, even though I had developed at a very early age, but reason and rationale. Back in those days might be when I developed the patience and appetite to sit and write. Yet I was rarely ever in the house, and normally when I was she was a wonderfully caring woman with motherly instincts and an altruistic generosity—a very uplifting spirit! But after one cocktail at night some sort of chemical reaction occurred and triggered a polar opposite change in her mood. I loved her, and I always will, but for her alcohol may have been a crutch, and some crutches are also detriments and can misalign the balance. For me, since I had been fourteen years old and since the day in the woods with the apple bowl, cannabis had been my primary crutch. And oh how I wanted that crutch in the car and just what I wanted I couldn't have!

My father put the box in the trunk. "Let's get this show on the road!" he said.

"I forgot to tell you," said my mother as she turned around in her seat. "Robert moved the court date back a month. It's on April fifth now."

"Ooh," I said.

"It'll give you time to get used to the crutches."

"It's not that. It's just that the court date didn't really feel like a next week kind of thing—it felt like a next month kind of thing."

"You know I was feeling the exact same way," she said.

"How you doing back there?" my father asked.

"Not good."

"That's another thing. Hopefully by next month it won't hurt so much to sit down."

"Yeah," I said. "But until then..."

I pressed down and lifted myself above the seat. It was no use; the hard ache only became worse. I had some experience but like I said the meeting at Spaulding paled in comparison. Slowly we were getting there.

"I had some time at Spaulding to think," I said. "Remember in high school I wanted to study civil engineering? I reconsidered my education—I'm going to change majors to civil, and if it's easy to do I'd like to transfer to UMaine."

"That's a great idea!" said my father. "Sure, I bet transferring's easy to do."

"No, are you sure?" said my mother. "Engineering's very hard and you're recovering from a bad brain injury."

"Yeah I'm sure. My memory's been coming back half-assed and I remember that business was not for me—studying it at least. I'd rather be among the bricks of a different wall—engineers, that is. And even—maybe even break through the wall with writing. You told me that I told Alfonso that I'd write about my time at Mass General. Well now I have all of Spaulding too. A little bit more and there's a book."

"Oh, I've always loved writing!" said my mother. "I can edit for you."

"No, I'll do everything."

"Wait, did you say that your memory's coming back?"

"Bits and pieces, yeah."

"What about the incident?"

"No, there's nothing."

"I just hope that you'll have the memory for engineering."

"Well. It's sort of like this. Up until now, after I woke from the coma my memory's as clear as a mirror, but everything that's there before the coma is like a fogged-up mirror. I think I'll be fine."

That night I fell asleep in an instant and all through the night I slept like a dog. My medicine compared to their medicine. The feeling was incredible.

Chapter 12

My birthday came and went three days after I got home. Twenty years earlier at twelve past twelve I took my first breath. The day was February twenty-fourth, and complications almost kept me out of this world but strong will and good fortune saved the day, leaving me only slightly scathed with a case of bad asthma. Twenty years of life on earth is a milestone and each lap around the sun is a gift in itself. Only when I was younger did I really care about material gifts, and now at twenty the greatest gift to ask for was a day of solitude, and I got it. I could make up for lost time and lack of events later on, as long as everything goes well, I told myself. The situation at home with broken bones and restrictions might seem forlorn, but it was a perfect time to be alone, nearly carefree and free of most responsibilities. I consumed cannabis copiously and this stopped my mind from ruminating most of the ordeal. At the time there was nothing there except the pain and I indulged in bad food to fill the void and to try and satisfy my insatiability. My mother asked if I wanted anything for my birthday and I readily replied, "European Bakery." And with that she went to the bakery and bought a box of cupcakes, brownies, and puff pastries. The most beautiful cupcake that I had ever seen was in the box and standing erect and straight from the frosting was a single candle placed in the middle. I ate it in a few bites, I ate everything else in just a few more bites, and it's true that those deserts were a great satisfaction. The excessive amount of sugar that sat in my stomach caused immense indigestion. *Me no worry*, I thought, and I grabbed The Goldstein and packed a bowl and hit it, and I didn't just stop at one. It was my twentieth birthday; I went twenty for twenty. My mother walked into the room as I exhaled a cloud of smoke and coughed. She coughed too, but as a joke.

"You're still going?"

"I don't stop. I might even have a collapsed lung."

"Well actually you—"

"No, you."

"Andrew, you should take a break."

"I what? No, I shouldn't."

"You can't study engineering like this."

"Study—I don't study to begin with!"

"Hey, is that the bakery box? It's empty!"

"Yeah, they were very good."

"You even lit the candle on the cupcake. I didn't get a picture!"

"I don't like pictures."

"Well did you make a wish?"

"Yeah."

"What was it?"

"My dream to come true."

"Well what's your dream?"

"If I tell you," I said. "It won't come true."

She reached down and grabbed the box and closed the lid and checked again. Perhaps to see if the laws of the universe had been defied and what was gone had reappeared. "What am I going to do with you?" she said and then left my room.

There I was alone in the small box of a bedroom on my born day. The past twenty years of life was not your ordinary twenty years of life and on this day my body and mind were older than that. Part of this had to do with the walker that stood on the floor beside my bed, and the other part had to do with the feeling of decay after being constantly confined to a bed. Mixed into this was of course a lack of vitamin D. Sun through a window is not the same as it is fresh on the flesh and only sometimes my blinds were open. Now they were closed and my room was dark and however stark I vaguely remembered the decades past. As the next thought succeeded the last thought each memory appeared most clear, and what my mind went to was back in the day when

I carelessly played in the front yard. Baseball had been the sport of choice and that's what I remembered more than anything else. Almost daily as long as the weather cooperated my father and I played catch in the front yard, and it was now my birthday and my father had sired me so why not recall that distant memory?

All memories make up who and what we are and essentially what is. Everything there is and everything there will ever be. The things that you touch and the sights that you see. All the smells you smell and the people you meet. They're all that's there from start to finish and alone in the moment the past just is. It felt good to reclaim a suddenly purged period of time.

In the early years when the sun shone bright and the time stood still I was usually outside. As a kid I was always active and playing sports at home was something to do. Then cannabis entered the picture and consuming that became the thing to do, and it was great because unofficial sports and cannabis mix very well together. But before any substance got involved, if the weather and air felt right I would lie in the grass and watch the tree and its thick canopy sway in the breeze and beyond this lay a deep blue sky and a lustrous sun. I contently waited for my father to arrive at home from work and while doing this I'd throw the baseball up in the air and then above my face I'd routinely catch it. My father was punctual—he was rarely ever late.

When I think of him I think of a good man with a great quality: his sincere unselfishness. He prioritized the interest and needs of others before his own and for better or worse he offered a helping hand with anything to anyone. By nature he was a family man and simultaneously diligent and devoted. If something needed to be fixed, he'd fix it. Had a problem, he'd probably solve it. To most young boys whose father stays around their old man is like a god, who seemingly knows everything, up to a certain age.

There was one day when I lay flat on my back on top of the grass in the front yard. This was well over a decade earlier when my concerns were like concerns from a widow of ten, and while I patiently waited for my father his tardiness arose an uneasy feeling in the pit of my stomach. He was late from work and my innocent mind predicted the worst. Off in the distance an ambulance rang and I wondered was it for him? I hardly knew what to think and seriously startled I threw the baseball into the canopy of branches and it hit a twig and the twig snapped off. My mind was elsewhere. My father turned the corner and pulled into the driveway. The twig fell directly onto my nose and pretty soon it was a bloody nose. I ran inside and snugly stuffed both holes with a tissue and then went out and pitched to my father.

He both caught and called either balls or strikes, the catcher and the umpire, a man of many trades. Three strikes was an out, three outs to an inning, and four balls for a walk didn't happen often.

Fourth inning. Six strikes. Two outs.

"Last out," he said.

I threw two curve balls in a row: strikes. I had a good curve ball as a kid, probably because I went through puberty at a young age and the art of the curve peaked in adolescence just as I turned away from baseball. A hiatus of sorts for one year to run track instead, to stay conditioned and to focus on football, which coincidentally happened to be the season that I blew out my knee. In any event, my curve ball in middle school had some heavy movement, and in games they'd be heading straight toward the batter and just as the batter ducked down to the ground the ball broke away and swiftly slid across the plate. Out of my basic three-pitch arsenal I certainly used the curve most often.

"I know what you're going to throw next," my father said.

He thought he knew. He thought that I'd throw another curve ball. He always used to tell me: "Dad knows everything."

Everything? Not everything.

I pulled the tissues out of my nose and tossed them aside and with my knuckles I gripped the seams and threw a knuckleball. This time without the slightest spin the baseball moved and danced in the air. In motion it was unmoving. Right at my father—his glove remained unmoved.

"Nice pitch," he said and then stood up and stretched.

"We're done?"

"Yes. I'm done for the day. You should pick up those tissues and bring them inside."

With that, I walked away toward the door.

"Hey, I'd like it if you got the tissues."

"Oh, yeah. That's right." I went to the mound and grabbed the tissues. "That's what I *should* have done. I'm sorry."

And nearly a decade later I thought in bed, *The fogged-up mirror is finally clearing.* I aptly rolled to the side and hobbled to the window. I opened the blinds to the past and let the light in.

Chapter 13

It was a rough time of year to live in New England. For over three months we had been living through very short days and long nights with frigid temperatures, and after getting home from Spaulding a few weeks earlier it didn't seem as though things would thaw. I was confined to my bed and hardly left the house, and my walls and windows were thin and the cold air easily penetrated through. My house was always cold—mainly because heating it was expensive and Maine winters are brutal! But like most physical troubles there was a natural solution: cannabis. And I consumed it often just to stay warm and comfortable, and also because there wasn't much else to do. Mostly I read or meditated, watched tv or played Xbox, and only occasionally got out of the house and went to outpatient therapy. The setup in my room was great and not one change could have made it a better place to recover. All that one really needs for a successful recovery is a comfortable bed to recuperate in and all else might be a luxury. Under my bed I had plenty of books to keep my mind active and expanded. When no one else is there books are always there. And reading them was sort of a privilege, considering that my mind would have been like stale soup if I hadn't been so fortunate, and studying their diction and symbolism, meaning and message, form and structure or lack thereof, made me seriously consider creating my own one-of-a-kind book someday. And one day it would be worth the effort to sit and write and try my best to get it right. But of course you leave the best events out. I believe that it was Hemingway who once said, "Write hard and clear about what hurts."

Three weeks after arriving at home it was spring break. Up until that time I ate horribly—ice cream, brownies, hash browns, fast food, none of it concerned me. Food at home was one thing that I anticipated more than anything else in the hospitals, and after my first home meal I voraciously took full advantage of the free food. That, cannabis, and books all had one common similarity: they kept me occupied during the sweet solitude. Three weeks elapsed very fast. Spring break arrived quickly and so did a few friends at their leisure.

Sean stopped by on a Saturday at midday in mid-March and just then Mother Nature seemed to be warming this lonely state. I was thrilled to see a good friend after two tautly long months and had proactively rolled a pearl for us to split. Sean knocked on the door below my room.

"Come in," I yelled from the warmth of my bed, feeling like an entirely different person. "I'm upstairs!"

Earlier that morning I had taken the cervical collar off for the first time and what a fantastic feeling I finally felt free! My neck and jaw were certainly better off without it, and from day one it seemed as though that would be the case. The doctors said that after two months I could take the collar off and that was less than two weeks away. *Better start getting used to it now*, I thought. *Enjoy the liberation!*

Sean opened the door and made his way to the staircase and up the stairs and into my room. We greeted each other with a dap and followed through with a hug. He was tall and tan and the details of his appearance had been partially lost deep within my convalescing mind, but I remembered a few of his attributes and now I want to expand on them.

Sean was smart. He was well-bred and he knew which side of his bread was buttered. He lived almost conservatively and tried to lead a faultless life, but at the same time he knew how to have fun and he did whatever served his best interest. For as long as I had known Sean, and that goes as far back as kindergarten, he was very popular and respected by everyone, girls, guys, adults, teachers, rivals, and so on. They all enjoyed his presence, his calm, cool, and collected demeanor, and I was no exception! He might have been a natural born leader, because people listened to what he said and imitated what he did like proper followers so often do, but I was not one of them. Good friends don't follow or lead one another but rather feed off of each other's ideas and energy mutually. We had been friends for years and of course got into minor mischief along the way, but we focused in school and had our minds fixed on the future. Sean took advanced placement classes in high school and went on to study engineering in college. We even had a couple classes together, and though we both did well what separated us in class was our study habits, or for me, a lack thereof. Sean studied nightly, and I did not—ever. Mostly because it was all common sense and still only high school, and everything that needed to be learned could be learned in class. But this prideful habit of mine soon stopped just as college started, not because I actually had to study, but because others struggled in class and either asked for my help or I was bored and freely offered it. We took many study breaks and all of this extra effort undoubtedly helped. I even made dean's list once—almost twice—out of three semesters enrolled at UNH. Sean, I know, had to study tirelessly for engineering exams, quizzes, labs, the likes. That's what separates studying business from engineering, and boy was I ready for it.

Sean glanced around my room approvingly. He sniffed the dank air and smiled. "How's everything going?" he asked.

We sat down on the edge of my bed. "All right," I said. "I'm still in pain but even that's better than it was. Still kills to sit upright though."

"Was it bad in the hospital?"

"Was it bad? It was bad."

"Damn," said Sean.

"Yeah."

"Did you get bored?"

"Not really."

"What about here—don't you get bored here? Or lonely?"

"Yes and no, Sean. Only boring people get bored. But lonely: well I know that the strongest men are often the most alone. I'll say this. It can get hard—being bed-bound and all!"

"Yeah, wow. That's true."

"It can be."

"So what do you all day?"

"Well, mostly just read and play Xbox, and slowly decay."

Sean laughed and thought for a moment. "You'll bounce back."

"It's these tight walls—they're making me feel old."

"That's understandable, old man."

"Thanks, Sean."

He looked around the blandly small room. "You really don't get bored?"

"Not at all," I said. "If I get bored I'll just have some medicine. Excuse me—" I deliberately coughed "—some weed."

"Oh really? I didn't notice or smell anything."

"Well there's not much that I can do about that."

"No, sadly there isn't."

"How was your bus ride home last night?"

"It sucked. Eight hours on the road with a layover in Boston. What'd you do?"

"This," I said. "And also got slightly drunk. It was *pretty* nice."

Sean laughed. "What? Are you allowed to drink yet?"

"No, but that might be why it was so satisfying."

"For sure. What'd you drink?"

"Well Mack Daniel stopped by the other night and dropped off a six-pack of IPAs—Allagash—I had those."

"That's nice of Mack Daniel," said Sean. "He's a good guy you know, a good local guy."

"Sure is," I agreed. "But my mom caught me trying to sneak the six-pack upstairs on the crutches. She freaked. She said that I can't drink yet. Told me that it's bad for my brain injury and she took them and put them in the fridge."

"She's probably right," laughed Sean.

"Oh, definitely is. But I still had them. I got them from the fridge downstairs after she went to bed and then brought them here and drank them. I watched *The Godfather Pt. II* buzzed."

"That's a good movie."

"Yeah, it was an all right time."

Sean smiled for a sudden second and then his face went bare and straight. Mine mirrored his.

"I can't believe I'm talking to you right now," he said.

"I know…" I expected to hear something different. "It's—well it's tough to grasp the whole ordeal."

"Yeah, man."

"Basically I just try not to think about it and weed helps a lot." *Especially with the pain*, I thought, and all trivialities aside, I was very grateful for that.

"Did you have beef with anyone at UNH?" Sean asked.

"Not that I'm aware of," I said. "Beef with me is rare."

"Was that a pun?"

"Yes it was."

Sean looked at the joint lying on my bedside table and his foot began tapping the floor perpetually. I picked it up and held it out. "You looking at this?"

"It's kind of hard not to."

"Come on, let's treat ourselves."

"Los gets!"

This was all there was to do. Normally we'd go to the gym and play basketball but that was out of the question—for months! And besides, I was feeling generous as usual. But generosity and friends don't mix if it's one-sided—then it becomes expected.

Sean walked downstairs and waited for me at the bottom of the staircase. "Go ahead," I said. "This might take a minute."

I hopped very carefully down the stairs, each step placed with utmost delicacy, thankful that I no longer had to navigate the stairs like a human crab. I was very agile on the crutches and used them with ease, but I consciously chose to reside in my room for now. My room was my room; The Basement could wait.

I met up with Sean outside on my driveway and we shared the pearl and hardly talked. The birds chirped and the sun shone and a thin line of smoke diffused in the air above our heads and vanished at once in a gust of wind. It was a beautiful day and the fresh smell of snowmelt filled the air with the joy of spring. Then Sean said, "I have to go get lunch with my grandparents. They want to see me before I leave."

"All right," I said. "Later."

And that was that. Something had felt off but why question it? I hopped back inside and upstairs to my room and closed the door and slid into bed. My neck felt excellent. I kept the collar on the floor beside my trash and crushed inside were the empty beer cans of Allagash. I noticed them and thought, *Good choice, Mack Daniel. A good local choice.* Allagash is a fine craft beer and after the movie I finished the pack and recalled the night that I had many a drink, resting my head on Ashley's wool socks, the smooth material, those petite feet, that bona fide queen type. And I can't forget, that first time, that rough next morning!

That was all that I could recall. I now felt great and wanted to read. In that case, I reached under the bed and grabbed *Think and Grow Rich.*

Chapter 14

Sean and a few other friends had gone to the Caribbean, and after our brief get together I didn't see him again until summer, and even then we hardly saw each other. He had already gone back to school in New York and he was either studying hard or hardly studying—perhaps jet lagged still with an ongoing spring break mentality. My mind stayed occupied reading books and this delighted my mother, and that's just what I was doing when I finally got a text from Ricky. His spring break was the week after Sean's, and his initial text read, "Coming over in a few. You good to chill?"

I set down the book—*Point Counter Point*— and then undid and took off the collar and leaned over in bed to avoid the pain. It was not exactly terrible to sit in bed right now, but anywhere else it was. I replied, "You bet. Let's go Rick."

Like all human beings on this planet, Ricky had a handful of great qualities, and debatably his best quality was that he was never sorry. When we were together, even if he knew that he was wrong he maintained his position and was not afraid to argue. And in Ricky's presence I was the same way—even when I knew I was wrong I made sure to get my point across. Most of the time I was peaceful but something about Ricky brought this stubbornness out of me. Maybe it stemmed from our naturally competitive nature—the typical I'm young and I know everything, and I'm right and your wrong kind of attitude—which is not a rare quality and which both of us possessed equally. It was a two-way street and it greatly built our camaraderie. We were similar in many ways but also very different. Normally I was reserved, but at the same time I thought that a good conversation was great, probably because everyone is different with a separate perspective and behind those eyes there's a story that's rich if looked at through an observing lens. Ricky was loud half of the time but he enjoyed the sound of silence as much as any real discussion. He was a contentious person and also proud and defensive and smart but at times a bit unkempt and vacuous. We had been great friends for a long while, and we butted heads and locked horns often, which might be the reason why we had such a strong friendship. But one way or another, most bonds like these will eventually break and gradually life will have to go on. Waiting in bed however, through some kind of hazy clarity, I was glad to see a good friend like Ricky today.

I heard his truck, a stick shift clunker, rumble into my driveway and her rich purr suddenly stop. He slammed the door and came inside. I had told him that no one was home and this was usually the case during the day. My bedroom door opened.

"*Wow*," Ricky said. "What's going on in here? I could smell that loud from outside!"

"Yeah."

I stood up on my left leg and dapped Ricky. He's a big boy, over six feet tall and two hundred pounds with long messy hair. He wore a Carhartt jacket and looked huge, and he was desperately in need of a shave.

"How you holdin up, bud?"

"Good enough. Given the circumstance and all."

"Well you look and sound really good—damn! And you're all set up with the reefer."

"Want some?" I offered.

"Hell yeah, brother."

I had saved the roach of a blunt for Ricky to smoke. I got it out of the ashtray and gave it to him. He grabbed the lighter and lit it.

"That's the last of it," I said.

"Really? I'll drive you to the dispensary after."

"That's nice of you, Rick."

"This is some potent herb, buddy. Your parents don't mind you doing this?"

"Not exactly," I said. "Before we leave I'll open a window and air out the room with a fan. After that, spray the house with Ozium. They don't mind because it might've actually saved my life."

Ricky laughed. "What do you mean?"

"Well. Since cannabis is still a schedule one narcotic for reasons beyond me—could really be for political and capitalistic reasons—the potential medical benefits haven't been researched. The surface has only been scratched. But I heard that if you have cannabinoids in your body at the time of a brain injury you're much more likely to survive and recover."

"Woah. Sounds like you've been doing your research. Yeah, no doubt I believe that. You're proof!"

"Sure. My brain injury was so bad. So—" I shook my head. "Yet somehow I recovered from it almost instantly."

"Dude, it's only been what, two months?"

"Not even."

"Remember after Rae's brain injury. He lost two of his senses and it took him *months* to recover."

"And not even completely."

"I wonder how he's doing."

"It's Rae—probably doing great, doing Rae things."

Ricky laughed. "Yeah, true!"

"Anyway, the cannabinoids in my system, I truly believe that they helped me survive the ordeal, and ever since I got home, and since I've been fortunate enough to have weed this entire time, the recovery's been miraculous. I really don't think it's a coincidence. Yeah, I've had to focus and work hard with memory exercises, reading, writing, studying—all on my own too—but I wouldn't have been able to do it with such ease if it weren't for the weed. I can't stand its negative image and connotation within the general public. People will always have their own opinions, and it will forever be highly subjective. But the majority are outdated and new reform is needed now—federally, and maybe even globally. It should be a regulated consumer choice, just like alcohol. God, in the hospitals I was in pain, anxious and depressed. Greatly, like you wouldn't even believe. And if I couldn't have any weed here that's exactly how I would feel right now. I mean how could anyone be happy in a situation like this without some sort of assistance?"

"They couldn't. That's impossible. That's like death. Bro, I bet you were dying to have some in the hospital."

"You have no idea…"

I got out of bed and faced the fan toward the window and then I sprayed the room with Ozium. I was leaving the house; I had to fasten the collar for my own safety. One more week and I'd be free.

"You ready to go?" Ricky asked.

"Hold on, my jacket…"

"I'm waiting."

"All right, los gets."

We got inside of Ricky's truck and drove into Portland and up the hill to Congress Street and took a right and parked in the lot behind the dispensary. On Forrest Avenue where I used to dream and talk with you—not Ricky. He had to wait inside of the car, and as pleased as he was he was slightly upset. Only people with medical cards were allowed inside, but he told me to get him a few things and surprisingly he handed me money, which he never had.

"What do you want?" I asked.

And he declared, "I don't give a fuckaroo!"

With that, I stepped out of the truck and hopped inside. Being inside of a dispensary can make you feel like a kid in a candy store. There were so many choices, and everything looked so good, but purchasing power was limited. Decisions, decisions…

Twenty minutes later I hopped out of the store and through the lot and writhed my way inside of his truck.

"Crutches. Are. Fucked."

"What'd you get?"

I gave Ricky the bag. "Check it out."

Inside was a quarter-ounce of Cookies and two cookies for Ricky and a quarter-ounce of Glue for myself. He was thrilled and so was I. Mission accomplished, and now it was time to reward ourselves! We left the dispensary with high spirits and smiles and in the air the smell of victory. On the drive home we stopped at the Audubon for old times' sake.

In high school the Audubon was a very popular spot to go to whenever we had the time. Very few people knew about it, and many times the entire place was vacant except for us and whoever we were with. There was a big open field with tall grass and weeds that grew wildly tall and wide in the summer, and in these months my thoughtfulness always ensued after a leisurely smoke, and I'd find myself examining the wildlife that surrounded and grew within the reserve with great curiosity. The ocean inlet, when the sun had set and the sky glowed amber was a fine sight to see, but the Audubon had much more to offer. Each flower, and tree, or weed, or leaf, was like its own world in and of itself. I examined tiny microcosms in every habitat, worlds that many different life forms of all shapes and sizes and compositions inhabit, much like everything living as we know it does to Earth. I knew that Earth was a microcosm to the universe, and I wondered if something huge out there with a real conscience, like some sort of giant that we can't see, was inspecting us just as I inspected all of those tiny plants. Mind-fucking! And boggling! And that's usually where the profound thoughts stopped. But nonetheless, being highly buzzed on potent herb those were my random streams and tangents at the Audubon. I was in my own world, and even with Ricky or anyone else it was me against the world. It was wild!

Now that it was the tail end of winter, of course Ricky and I were the only visitors in sight. The ground was frozen which made it easy to hop around on crutches. It worked out perfectly for the situation. But first I had to roll a pearl.

We had decided on the Glue, and as soon as I got to work Rick asked, "So how *was* the hospital? You were there for a long time."

"I was at two hospitals you know. Mass General and Spaulding. Two weeks in each."

"How was it?"

I shrugged. "It sucked. You wouldn't have lasted a day."

"You're a soldier."

"No, that's not what I am."

"Well I can't even imagine…" Ricky sat still for a moment lost inside of Ricky thought. "Actually." He laughed. "I imagined that you were like the villain in *Spider Man*."

"Why?"

"Because something bad usually happens to them."

"Well, Rick. The difference is I actually plan to make an asset out of it."

"How?"

"At some point I'll write a book about it. A little glimpse at life through my lens. A farewell so to say, to the first twenty years."

Ricky watched impatiently. "You want to write a book?"

"Yeah, I have something to say."

"Why not say it on social media?"

"No. I'm too much of a perfectionist. But a little promotion on it, that'd absolutely be permitted! And gladly appreciated!"

"Well you know that a lot of people want to write a book but can't follow through with it. You need a story to tell, and yeah you have one but it's not easy. Not after a brain injury."

"You're right, I don't believe it will be. Especially doing it as my debut. But that makes it so much more—almost alluring. Stories within a story, mi hermano?"

"Yeah, but not a love story."

"Well. Maybe they'll love the author. Maybe that'll be the new kind of love story."

"I love it!" And then Ricky looked at me skeptically. "But you'd really put yourself out there like that?"

"Yeah. Are you kidding me?"

"That takes balls."

"Look," I said. "The way I see it, if you don't put yourself out there you're hiding your balls from yourself. Either they're there or there's nothing there. My flaws and setbacks, those make up just as much of me as the good qualities."

"Flaws and setbacks," repeated Ricky.

I licked and wetted the paper and then folded the top edge over and in. "It's character development, baby."

"I couldn't imagine this—any of this."

"You couldn't—I couldn't."

"I think that it's perfect for you."

"Well. That's what happens when you have the time to think about things."

"So you want to be a writer?"

"That's the dream," I said. "Preferably something."

"Good one! I mean you look and sound so much better than I imagined you would."

"Thanks." I twisted the tip of the pearl. "But you imagined that I was like the villain in *Spider Man*. I don't know who that is."

"The octopus guy."

"What?"

"Well that was only while you were getting surgery."

"Ricky, why would you think that?"

"Because when he was getting operated on he went crazy, and then his tentacles came back to life and killed the doctors."

"Jesus, Ricky."

"I don't know, bro. I thought it was funny."

"Well my mom told me that I was incredibly restless, always jerking around, couldn't stay still, and I even fell out of bed. So apparently they had to strap me down just to keep me orderly. I was told that it can happen after a brain injury and that it resolves itself in time. Luckily for me it happened very quickly, and I believe that was because of the cannabinoids you know? Not everyone is nearly as fortunate. I wasn't conscious yet, or lucid, but I remember thinking that a nurse was trying to steal my pain medication and I called her a bitch several times. You know how bitches can brew. But this was only up until I became semi coherent. Then after that I apologized and we had a good laugh."

And Ricky had also been laughing and then at last he settled and said, "Dude, she probably was. Sneaky little nurse. But when I came over I didn't know what to expect. I was kind of nervous."

I tilted my head. "You doubted me."

"I mean, I didn't know what to expect. But look at you—the same old T still rolling pearls. It's actually incredible."

"It's something," I said.

"You should write about it. Seriously, you were like a genius."

"I don't know about that."

"No really, you were."

At this point I had become sidetracked by the conversation and stopped working. "Well it takes a genius to know a genius."

Ricky laughed. "That's *fantasteek!* Just keep it real and watch out for the critics!"

"No. Their job is to critique the genius, not be the genius. You can only hope that those who read it will appreciate it."

"Then try to make it better than anything else out there."

"That'll be the top priority. Celiné said, 'To be a genius you have to first be scared shitless.' Yeah I was scared when I woke in the hospital, and yeah most geniuses have that in common. But here's the issue, and it's mostly with putting yourself out there. When your truths are told there's no way to tell how others will respond."

Ricky seemed almost amused. "Who's Celiné?" he asked. "And bro, who cares?"

"He was a French writer. I've read only one of his books—his first."

"Is he your favorite writer?"

"No."

"Who's the best writer?"

"One of my favorites and the best is Cormac McCarthy."

"You should've said that you are."

"No, I'm not that conceited. Yet maybe I am."

"You should still write about it."

"That's a good idea, Rick. But enough of this 'you should' crap. I'll do it. It'll be fine." And then I quickly looked out through the window and didn't look back. "There's another issue though."

"What's that?"

"I don't know if the world will be ready for it. I'm a little afraid of what I'll sound like on the page. When you're writing you're a very different person than the person when you're not. I've been reading a lot and that's one thing that I've noticed. You don't know which direction your subconscious will go or how it'll start or finish or roll through a stream of ideas. It's just like right now—I start a sentence and I'm not sure where it'll end up but it's usually better than where it began. You can't take everything that a writer writes so literally. Words are relative."

"It sounds like you're already thinking like a writer."

"Well that's where it starts."

"And I was just thinking," said Rick. "Maybe what happened to you happened for a reason."

"Now you're talking. Everything happens for a reason, and it's fair to say that what happened was something only a miracle could let me escape. You know, save me from the grave."

"You can be hard to keep up with," laughed Rick. "But you're right, it's one hundred percent a miracle."

"Could be fate. Or," I said as I looked at the pearl. "Destiny. Don't ever underestimate her goodness."

We made our way to the nearest trail and went down the path far enough to get out of sight of the parking lot. Across the field and through the trees the ocean could still be seen. Breaks of pale blue water and scattered grey trunks with their bare branches, and the spring sun high in the sky above the sea, but there was not even the slightest glisten on its surface. After a few minutes, and after we began to feel elated, Ricky asked, "Have you seen any of the other guys?"

"Yeah—Chuck, Cole, Sean. And Mack Daniel stopped by the other night and dropped off a six pack."

"Mack Daniel! What a guy."

"He knows what's good."

"He still go to UMaine?"

"Yeah. I told him that I'd see him up there."

"You'll see him up there—when?"

Ricky passed the pearl, its perfect cone no more.

"Good looks," I said.

"Wait a sec—no that's right. You're switching to engineering."

"Yeah, how'd you know?"

"Sean told me."

"Yeah?"

93

"You know you won't have much time for writing."

"Look, Rick. I'll work through the night if I have to."

"That's dedication. But If you're a writer, and I mean if you start writing books, you'll have to use social media… Posting pictures, promoting, all that."

"If I make it, I will."

"And now?"

"Rick, you already know that I'm unphotogenic and hardly take pictures now—candid only."

"Yeah, I don't take or post pictures either. It can be a good tool though."

"No doubt, and one day maybe I will. But first, gotta make it. Otherwise—I have next to no so-called followers right now and any post that I make would feel like I'm just letting the few that I do have know that I'm not dead."

"So that's a perfect reason for you to use it!"

"For now Rick, I'll write."

"Just watch out for people copying you."

"It's the other way around, Ricky. People will steal my words, ideas, style, and they won't care to give credit. That's stealing from me."

"That's not good."

"No."

"What will you do about it?"

A cold breeze passed through the air and sent a shiver toward the water. I thought for a moment and gazed at the open ground ahead and then the sun in the sky above. "At the very least," I said. "Kiss their baby."

Ricky laughed. "Okay, Ochocinco. And what about the very most?"

"I don't know. Hemingway must have thought about it all the time—the most imitated writer of the twentieth century."

"It's nothing new."

"No. They'll take a fat bite out of my writing style. You know this. People have been stealing *mi estilo* since day one. Leeches *divertidas.*"

"Wait, you speak Spanish now?"

"Mi hermano. *¡Eso Es!* Get it? SOS!"

Still laughing Rick said, "I'll admit, I've learned a lot from you."

"Thanks! See I would really like it if people gave me that kind of credit. And my broge, you haven't seen anything yet."

"My doge, you just don't believe in people. It'll happen."

"I believe in people who believe in me. Respect them freely if they respect me. And if it does happen, Rick, I might cry."

Ricky laughed and somewhere out there a compassionate soul understood my quiet frustration. "First make sure that you put all you've got in your writing."

"I will. Even if it takes two three times. You can't expect to get it right the first time—for writing a book, for anything. It's all in the attempt."

"In the attempt?"

"Yeah," I said. "If you really follow through with it, and you do everything on your own and steer the wheel yourself, that's pretty good. It has to be authentic. These days too many quote unquote authors get help from someone else and that someone else basically writes their entire book."

"There's a name for that. What's it called?"

"Phony."

"That's not it," laughed Ricky.

"Line editor, ghostwriter—call them whatever their title is. But what I said is entirely true. There's no artistry, no personality, no individuality, guts or emotion. And then what's actually published just sounds like all the rest, and people naively buy into it!"

"*Blah!* Sounding like the rest—not like you. Yeah you do naive things but you don't buy into phoniness. Just keep yours real, and like you said—"

"Authentic."

"That's right—authentic."

"Yessir, my mind is mine and I own it."

"Your mind is your mind. That's true," said Ricky. "But that's about all you own."

With that, we went back to the truck and drove off, stopped at McDonald's and went through the drive through, parked and ate and went to the bakery. Oh, we were bad.

And ten minutes later it was the end. I felt disgusting and so did Ricky. He said that he'd have to go to the gym and workout later, but I could not. I couldn't even walk or fully workout and this was very sad. The only physical activities that I could actually do were the leg strengthening exercises, lying down on a table in physical therapy and that was all but it. The crutches were at fault but not all of it was bad. Doing nothing extra had its perks. It took little effort and energy, and best of all it was most sustainable, but it was similar to being stuck on the sideline and I forgot what it was like to be in the game with something to do, to be occupied one way and strengthen the other and this became very comfortable and pretty quickly a very bad thing. I couldn't wait to get rid of the crutches and dump them like a drawback and never look back. For now, the agenda was simple: do nothing but lay in bed all day and round out and wait as if that was all there was to do. And that's exactly what I did after Ricky dropped me off at my house. I didn't see him for a while after that. A long while.

Chapter 15

Goodwill NeuroRehab is where I went for physical therapy. The gym there was adequate for the few exercises that I could actually do, and I even thought that the place was very cozy, like something that might resemble your home, but it was practically small change compared to the highly regarded gym at Spaulding, and that was fine by me! I actually enjoyed getting out of the house on a regular basis, having the interactions, conversations, laughing and making others laugh. My therapist was relatable. She and I were close in age and we both enjoyed the outdoors when the weather and circumstances allowed it. Time progressed steadily and so did the recovery. At this point in late March the cervical collar had come off for good. It was a small step to freedom but it was progress nonetheless. You can't expect freedom to happen instantly—there are steps and levels of progression, the same scenario with physical activity. For now I was restricted to stationary movements and exercises, lying curbed and immobilized on a therapy table and this constraint would not be lifted until the doctor cleared me to come off the crutches. After that, I could walk, I could put weight on my right leg and build its muscles, tendons and ligaments, all of which had been dormant for far too long, but this was only one part of the progression and for at least three months after being cleared I wouldn't be able to perform high-impact activities of any kind. The injuries were critical and to make sure that everything really healed properly, patience was crucial.

For reasons that were in a way out of my reach my mother still drove me to therapy. I sat quietly in the passenger seat, listlessly gazing outside at the morning fog and springtime dreariness. I told my parents that I'd be able to drive just fine, but they didn't think so. They argued that after my brain injury it was too soon to drive, but once I stopped using the crutches, for some reason they would then allow it. With that, I was vexed! Only a month from now I expected to come off of the crutches, and as far as my brain injury was concerned, it had practically healed immediately after waking from the coma, or inside even! Everything was and had returned to normal, and my mother knew how badly I wanted to drive and that I probably would have driven just fine, and maybe it was by virtue of her sincere sympathy she occasionally brought me to the dispensary after.

Today was one of those dreary days. While driving through the fog my mother said, "You remember what next week is? It's your day in court!"

"It's only the arraignment."

"I'm worried."

"Don't be. Save your worries for when they're needed."

"I'm your mother. It's my job to worry."

And that's how it will always be. Outside it was utterly grey and how practically addictive it was to look at.

"Do any of your friends know about it?" she asked.

"The arrest?"

"Yes."

"I haven't mentioned it to anyone, no one's asked about it."

"Me neither. I'm just glad that it wasn't in the police beat—*our* police beat."

"You were worried that it'd be on the news. It wasn't even in the paper!"

"Have you checked the internet—on Google?"

I took my phone out of my pocket and within seconds I said, "Yeah, it's there in the Forecaster."

"Oh no… What about what happened to you?"

"Nothing. They left no trace."

Five minutes later we arrived at therapy. I hopped inside, and my mother went to a coffee shop down the street and waited. I went into the elevator and up to the third floor. My therapist stood laughing beside the receptionist and then she looked at me.

"Hey Andy, are you ready?"

"Yes I am."

"Great!"

My therapist's name was Claire and she made her way around the desk and into the hall. I hopped beside her.

"You look good without that cervical collar on," she said. "How does it feel?"

"Amazing. You wouldn't believe it."

"I'm glad! Well that means I'm going to work you hard today."

"All right then, let's go."

We made our way into the gym and went to the table in the far corner. I balanced my crutches against the wall. I lay down flat and started stretching, strengthening, going through the motions. Even these simple stretches were a great pain. But when it's necessary to do something, and it seems as though it might be a total waste of time, act it out, go through the motions. There was only one thing to do at the moment and that was stretch. Up first were hamstrings.

"When's your next appointment at Mass General?"

"April twenty-fifth."

"Hmm. That'll be three months post-op—you should be off the crutches after that!"

"I hope so."

"Aren't you excited?"

"That's about a month away, Claire. I'll be excited once I'm walking again. Not hopping."

"Oh shoot," she perked up. "I forgot your file in my office. Do you remember the rest of your stretches?"

My right leg hovered an inch in the air and I set it down on the table. "Yes."

"Finish stretching on your own. I'll be right back."

Claire walked off and I looked around at every other patient in the gym, drooling, meandering, struggling. It was obvious that they had all suffered a brain injury at some point, recently or long ago, and I felt like the only blessed individual there, and then I even felt bad for them. Why can the world be so cruel? Maybe it's because we treat and do her wrong, and then when she finally has enough and strikes back with plague and disaster only a handful of people are affected. They get the dirty end of the stick, so to speak.

The therapist walked back through the gym, skimming through the the contents inside the file folder. "Which knee did you have surgery on in high school?" she asked.

"My left knee."

"It says your right knee in the file. A torn ACL and meniscus on his right knee."

"Well the file is wrong."

"You're right. I remember you said that it was your left knee when we first started."

"Yeah. That was the first thing that you asked me about—any prior injuries. I remember these things."

Claire rolled an exercise ball from the corner of the gym beside the table and sat on it. "That's good, your leg strength should even out now!"

"Yes it should."

"How did it happen again—during football, right?"

"Yeah."

And by now I had moved on to leg raises. I held each leg in the air for a count of ten Mississippi, and after the first set I decided to elaborate and tell Claire how. "It was pretty unlucky," I said. "It's one of those things that will make you think of a million ways you should've something differently after it happens. All I did was go in to make a tackle, and I sort of hyperextended my left leg before making contact. I planted my foot on the ground far out in front of my body and it stayed there. Then we collided head-on and I twisted and brought him down—you know when I should've kept my legs pumping and my momentum moving forward. But my left leg stayed planted on the ground, and at the same time it followed and twisted with my upper body at the knee. It was that simple. There was a subtle pop like a rubber band snapping, a muffled sort of pop. It was much more of a feeling than a noise—that feeling that something was wrong, and certainly something was."

"Could you walk on it?" Claire asked.

"It was inflamed and weak, but yeah, somehow I could. Then I got surgery and couldn't walk on it for maybe a month maybe two, and now it's stronger than ever. But not my shoulder, that's still a bitch!"

Claire laughed and then shuffled through the file folder. "What happened to that? I don't see anything in here about a shoulder injury."

"I separated it mountain biking."

"Oh, I love mountain biking! Last fall my friend took me on some really nice trails in Falmouth."

"Where?" I asked.

"It might've been somewhere off of Blackstrap Road—I don't remember. But they were the kind of trails that are smooth with no roots—lots of fun!"

"Sure they are."

"Luckily I was wearing a helmet. I almost fell!"

"That was a good call, Claire."

"Do you wear a helmet?"

"Mountain biking I do. But never when I'm skiing."

"Why not?"

"Skiing without a helmet is probably the closest feeling to being free that I've ever felt in my life."

"Well you'll have to wear a helmet now…"

"Some freedoms we just have to give up."

Claire pursed her lips. "Maybe I'll try it."

"I'll go with you."

"Hmmm. You can't ski right now—you need to recover!"

"I know…"

"What about when you separated your shoulder," said Claire. "Were you wearing a helmet then?"

"Yeah."

"That's a good call." She laughed. "Did you get surgery?"

"No, it wouldn't have been worth it."

"Oh, why not?"

"Apparently the success rate is low, but mostly because I didn't want to be sidelined again."

Now Claire laughed amiably. "That makes sense…"

I raised and lowered my leg and then moved on to heel slides.

"Well how'd it happen?" she asked.

"The separated shoulder—well the story is sort of similar to the football injury. Different event, same takeaway. I was on a rugged trail at Bradbury Mountain with my friend Rae. He brought me there that day, and he's the type of person who is very good at anything he does athletically. It was truly a gift, and it might have been one of his best attributes, and mountain biking was probably his favorite sport. He rode the trails with such ease and a natural finesse. Rae was one of my favorite friends."

"I'm sure that he'd like to hear that," said Claire. "Did you see him over break?"

"No."

She pursed her lips again, and I continued, "So Rae was flying down this trail in front of me and I was trying to keep up with him when all of a sudden I hit a stump and flipped over the handle bars and flew through the air and crashed—hard, Claire, hard. It was a complete shock and another time when you might think of all the little things that you should've done differently. It's like playing a game of ifs—if I had done this differently or that differently I'd probably be fine right now. But that's nonsense."

"Oh, yes it is!"

Hearing her say my words sent me straight up and into cloud nine. I thought about Rae, and then the crash appeared inside of my mind almost like it did the day after it happened. A daydream from a blissful conscience.

Rae was slightly wild around friends and this made his presence wonderful, and whenever he did something questionable Chuck would ask for my opinion as if addressing some type of wise oracle. Whose reason was esteemed. I had just seen and learned a lot from experience and experience comes from circumstance. Most kids that I grew up with were very privileged, had many luxuries, and were fortunate enough to live in congenial and unified homes. My circumstance was different and so was my perspective. This seems to be true: when all aspects of life are aligned good things happen, but if one area is out of order or defective everything can suffer. Maybe that's why I constantly suffered injuries and many times fell on the wrong side of luck. And maybe it was this set of unfortunate circumstances that formed a deep coherence and gave weight to my reason and opinion. Others valued my input highly and rightly so. But it's much easier to make sense of everything at a young age when reality hasn't quite set in and become so harsh—yet harsh enough to develop a thought process that's above the standard.

Rae was wild on a mountain bike, but a magical kind of wild that he dexterously controlled, and this made it hard for anyone inexperienced to keep up with him. The time that I crashed was my first time on a mountain bike in years. Rae led the way down a trail on a steep hill and the top had been mostly smooth, with patches of grass on either side of the main line, packed down with soil and flat rocks which made it easy to glide along. Then about halfway down the hill the trail changed and became uneven and rough and I looked ahead to see exactly how Rae was dealing with it and which line he had taken, and sure enough he was riding wildly along the trail about a hundred feet ahead and it didn't appear as if he was following a particular line but rather making adjustments and dodging obstacles as he went. I looked down, and about ten feet away in the middle of my line was a fat stump sticking out of the ground like a makeshift tombstone. There was no time to swerve off to the side or bail. Instead, I strictly prepared to meet death and watched my front tire hit the stump and then abruptly the whole world rotated and spun and then *thump!*

I was alive, but badly hurt. My vision blurred and everything whirled. The canopy of trees and the blue sky above both blended together like acrylics. Sunlight streamed through this marvelous world and glowed golden in color like something in a dream.

Slowly my senses came back, and I lay sprawled in a bed of dirt and rocks twenty feet down the trail from the stump and stood up. "Damn," I said as I brushed the dirt off of my shoulder and bitterly winced. "Fuck a duck. Rae!"

The adrenaline quickly wore off and the pain took its place. I thought that my collarbone might have snapped and grisly images of compound fractures reeled through my mind repeatedly. There was no protruding bone, only a tender lump beneath the skin, and the excruciating pain. "Child please!" I cried out with joy. "Where are you, Rae!"

"Hello?" I heard Claire ask. "Andy?"

"Hey," I said.

"You okay?"

"I'm fine. Just had a daydream, a flashback so to say. I've been having them a lot lately."

"Well I could tell," she laughed. "I asked if your shoulder had ever been diagnosed by a doctor. Has it?"

"Yes, it actually has been. It's a type three separation."

"Does it still bother you?"

"Only sometimes."

"During sports? Or—"

"No. Only if I do pushups or really any chest exercise. And it's weird, because I used to put up two-fifty on the bench press when I was sixteen—way back in the good old football days—but now I couldn't give a damn."

"Oh no! Let's work on that while you're here," said Claire. "We want you to be your best self."

I agreed and told her that she's smart, and by now my focus had dwindled and I performed each monotonous exercise dully. It'd be good for me to vary the routine with shoulder exercises, and soon we did, and soon after that the strength came back, but of course I greatly favored my unscathed right side. For now and for the rest of this session I was somewhat lost. My mind was elsewhere. The arraignment in court lay just around the corner and inside of my mind and toward the back this upcoming day had a very special spot. Where what's dreaded is stored to contemplate. It's very easy to access this part of the mind, and it's very hard not to.

The session ended shortly after the clock struck ten and then I hopped through the hallway and into the elevator and down to the first floor and out to the parking lot. My mother was waiting to pick me up, one tall half-caff soy latte with an extra shot and cream placed in the cupholder. I opened the door and got in the car.

"How was therapy?" she asked.

"Well. I'm not feeling so good."

"Would you like to stop at the dispensary?"

"Yes I would."

"What will you get?"

"Just some cookies."

"Oh, I've had those. They gave me the best night sleep!"

"I like them. Now let's go."

We drove down Washington Ave and onto Congress and made our way to the dispensary. The clouds were gone and the sun shone bright. I ate the cookies immediately after I bought them; It was ten in the morning.

Chapter 16

The arraignment went as expected but time in court passed very slowly—a total drag! It was not my first appearance in court but this time it hurt terribly to sit on the bench, waiting impatiently for my turn at the stand. Just like the meeting at Spaulding, and many times while riding in the car or sitting in waiting rooms with my mother, I repeatedly pressed down on the seat and lifted myself in the air for a brief moment of much-needed relief. It went on like this for a while and flashing in and out of my mind for the entire session was "Get Down," and by the time that it was my turn at the podium the song had changed to "Heaven." The first and last track on *God's Son*, one of my favorite albums. Finally my name was called and I hobbled across the aisle and behind the lectern I stood supported between the crutches. Just about one minute later I left. It was that quick. I had sat through grim pain the entire morning for one minute in the spotlight—only to plead no contest to the charges—and I wondered why I was even there when people were walking free after what had happened two months earlier. But then I realized that it's all pretty simple. No one cares about a personal tragedy; the machine must go on. My fate, and really my freedom, would hopefully be decided by the end of that summer. The next proceeding was scheduled as a preliminary hearing and until then Robert said that we'd keep in touch and figure out a plan. I liked that.

But there was much more to do and things actually seemed to be looking up. Shortly after the arraignment the pain dwindled and my energy soared. I had been slightly testy since the hospital days, and then after this sudden shift toward wellness I began to test my luck. I would lightly bear some of my bodyweight on the ground with my right leg, just enough to get a feel for it, then gradually I increased the pressure, then soon went about walking around the house fluidly with the crutches lodged into position to fall back and hop if I had to. But there was no need to. The pains and problems had apparently left for good. It practically happened overnight, and when it did every ache and cramp vanished into thin air like guilt. After this my optimism grew as the first follow-up appointment approached. And then at last it arrived.

It was the end of April and we drove down to Boston and crossed the Charles River and pulled into the parking garage across from Mass General. A bittersweet feeling arose in my bowels as we crossed the bridge and passed Spaulding, and it stayed there until I hopped through the doors and went inside of Mass General. I had never even seen the lobby before and at first it kind of reminded me of a crowded airport. But instead of going away on vacation, some people were going away for good, and this realization was reflected on many faces. The whole hospital was busy with visitors, patients, doctors, nurses, and it seemed as though there might have even been tourists! I avoided the crowds as much as possible and this was not an easy task. Because the surgeon Doctor Trey hadn't cleared me to come off the crutches, and because my parents were present and watching like hawks, I still had to put up a front and use the crutches like a proper cripple, and then I stumbled into a bathroom and properly relieved myself.

Up first on the agenda were the X-rays. I lay flat on a plastic radiographic table and a large specialized camera arched down and over my torso and took pictures of my lower back and pelvis. The nurse seemed to be in a hurry, and as soon as she had taken the necessary images she ushered me into a separate room and in there I had a CT scan of my head and neck. A quick but claustrophobic experience.

There was a short intermission before the appointment with Doctor Trey and we went to the cafeteria to pass the time. Just as my father had mentioned months earlier the food was actually pretty good. Hospitals tend to have a poor public perception and why that is was recognized while living in the ICU. There were many reasons for this. The level of noise, number of germs, total expense, and lack of privacy were all a problem. And then another reason made it certain after checking in for my appointment with the surgeon, and this would be the wait. I was stuck in the waiting room for hours on end and it was absolutely unbearable! That's what happens when you're cared for in one of the best hospitals in the world. There's no rose without a thorn, so the saying goes. I began to read lyrics on my phone out of boredom, and my mother and father briefly walked around the second floor and again went down to the cafeteria. An hour later they came back with snacks, cookies and granola.

Finally a nurse walked into the room after most of the day had passed. "Andrew Terrio," she called. "Andrew Terrio."

I stood up and then stood before her.

"Doctor Trey is ready to see you."

"Great!"

She turned around and I casually hopped beside her. "He's been very busy today. I think you'll be his last patient."

"Lucky me."

The nurse showed me inside of an examination room. "Take a seat wherever you'd like. He should be with you shortly."

"Thanks," I said and hopped in. My parents followed behind.

I sat on the examination table and scooted back and allowed my legs to dangle over the edge. The crunch and crinkle of the table paper and sitting in a room beside my parents waiting for a doctor was vaguely evocative. My youth was full of situations like this. But then you grow up and you find yourself in the same place as if time elapsed but you went nowhere. How will you know where to go if you don't know where you've been? Mischief and asthma led me into the doctor's office on many occasions, and this time I looked down and flipped my wrist and saw the scar and what came to mind was the time that it split open, going to the doctor's shortly after, and ultimately from a deep vexation the mishap caused an asthma attack that led me straight inside of a hospital. And here I am now, sixteen years later, back inside of a hospital.

Forty minutes went by in limbo, and then I heard talking in the hall outside of the door and the talking grew louder once the door had opened. Into the room walked two doctors. The man in front, the leader, said, "How are you, Andrew?"

"Just fine," I replied. "Thank you."

The other doctor looked familiar, and I quickly realized that he was William.

"Good!" the leader said. "I'm Doctor Trey."

"It's very nice to meet you," I said.

"We've met before. Just briefly, but you must not remember."

"No, I don't."

"It happened shortly after the operation, and I have to say, you look much much better now! How does everything feel?"

"Great actually."

"And around your pelvis?"

"That too."

"Very good. Is there any pain?"

"No, not anymore."

"When was the last time that you experienced discomfort?"

"About two weeks ago. And then it suddenly stopped and now everything feels normal."

"Well," said Doctor Trey as he glanced and nodded at William. "That's what we like to hear."

William agreed with a nod of his own.

"You know—and Doctor Koch may have already mentioned this—some people experience pain that will never go away after suffering a pelvic fracture. They will feel it in their lower back and bottom, and often it's most noticeable when sitting down."

"I know exactly what you're talking about," I said. "But it feels fine right now."

Doctor Trey smiled. "You're very lucky. There are some things that doctors can't control or fix. We like to think that we can, but we can't. These outcomes might already be decided."

"It really is something," I said.

"Yes. Now you said that you're no longer in pain, but are you still using pain medication?"

"No. I stopped a long time ago—at Spaulding."

"You were here for two weeks?"

"Yes, I stopped thirteen days after the surgery."

"Very good. That's impressive."

"See," said William. "I told you he impressed me. You should have seen him back then. His mind is gifted."

"Yes, I know. Right when I walked into the room I could tell. Us doctors know these things."

"Good hunch, thank you."

Doctor Trey sat on a chair with wheels and rolled himself beside the table. "Okay, now let's get into why we're here. I had a chance to look over the X-rays earlier…"

"And?"

"Everything is healing per the usual."

"Wow," I said. "*Per*haps I heard that you were busy today."

"It was just another day." Doctor Trey laughed. "Slow, yes, but that could be the fact that I have next week off. I'm going back to England for a funeral."

"I'm sorry."

"It's my aunt-in-law's. I'll be happy to have some time away from here."

William smiled and gravelly laughed at this.

"Why don't you stand up," said Doctor Trey. "Let's see how it feels under the weight of your body."

"Well." I stood up. "I already know that it feels fine. Once the pain stopped I started testing my luck around the house."

"Mm-hm. Now go ahead, walk around."

And that I did and around the room I picked and stretched my knees and legs and then proudly sat on the table and allowed them to dangle.

"That looked good."

"Well I've been practicing."

"Mm-hmm. Okay, I think that it's time to retire those crutches. What do you say?"

"Absolutely."

"Excellent. Dad, that means that you get to carry the crutches on the way out."

My father laughed at the joke, and Doctor Trey looked at his watch and then stood up. "Well it was a pleasure to see all of you, but I have to get going. We'll meet again for a follow-up in three months, and remember, Andrew, there's absolutely no high-impact activities until then. And please don't practice or test your luck."

"I won't," I said.

"I want you to have a successful finish to your recovery. We all do." And with that, he followed William out of the room and left the patient and parents inside.

"He's a good doctor," said my mother.

"He's a veteran!" my father replied.

"I'm sure he's seen it all."

"Yes, and you heard him—no testing it out!"

"How long have you been walking around the house?"

"Not long. Gradually over the past couple weeks. But you see, my intuition was right."

"Well don't try that again. And no funny business. We've made enough trips here over the past few months."

"Hey," said my mother. "Do you want to go to the ICU? I bet they'd like to see you."

"All right," I said.

"Make sure to grab the crutches," my mother said to my father.

"He can carry them. He has two arms and two legs now."

But when we left the room I left the crutches behind and this was strangely satisfying. Those crutches controlled three months of my life and held me back and now they're gone. My parents didn't seem to notice nor care if they did. I had been fed up with those props from the start and I finally felt free and walked around with an easy gait without them. We made it to the ICU and across the hall a familiar nurse sauntered into a room.

"Do you remember that nurse?" asked my mother.

"No."

"Really? That's the nurse that you kept calling Aunt Barbara."

111

"Well she doesn't look anything like Barbara now."

"You had a bad brain injury…"

"Yeah."

"I'm just so glad that it's healing well."

My parents sat on a bench and I confidently walked around the ICU, coming off as a visitor with a purpose or plan but really I had neither, like some sort of inept wanderer. It felt sort of strange to once again be among the revenants. Nothing seemed the same or familiar and what was hard to grasp was the fact that I had spent two weeks of my life in this factory, all cooped up and stoned on a surfeit of assorted narcotics. I turned the corner and there he was, the man who I came to see, Alfonso.

"My man," he said. "You're walking—looking good!"

"Look at you. You're fly as ever."

"Tell me, how've you been? What have you been up to?"

"Not much of anything really."

"You look like you're up to something."

"You're thinking of your kid. I just retired the crutches, and no wheelchair—maybe that's what looks different."

"That's amazing, my man. I can't believe it."

"I never thought that this day would come."

"How was everything after you left us?"

"Spaulding was all right and home is home. It's been good and I can't complain—but I can!"

Alfonso laughed his seallike laugh. "Does it still hurt? My man, it hurt me to see you hurt."

"No, that stopped earlier this month just after the arraignment in court."

"Arraignment, in court?"

"Yeah," I said sheepishly.

"What for?"

"The arrest."

"You were arrested, when?"

"Back in January, like a week before I ended up here. I thought that you knew. Didn't I tell you?"

"No, you never told me."

"Oh. I was on so many narcotics…"

"You were funny, my man. You were on a lot! But what was it for, weed?" Alfonso laughed excitedly. "You wanted to toke your weed in here!"

"No," I smiled. "I don't really want to get into it right now."

"It's okay, my man. We don't have to talk about it if you don't want to."

"That's a deal."

"You must still use your weed—do you? You told me it saved your life."

"It seriously might have. Well a lot of things might have. But yeah, I still do. It's been a major key to my recovery."

"A major key, my man!"

And as Alfonso said that suddenly the halls began to fill with hospital personnel and patients and like a circus they bustled about and we may have both been in the way. It seemed like Alfonso's help was needed elsewhere.

"Just look at it in here," I said as I glanced around. "All at once too. I should probably get going."

"Ey, it's always like this at this time of day!"

"Oh, I'm sure!"

"Well listen, it was good to see you my man!"

"You too!"

Alfonso went one way and I went the other. My parents stood up from the bench and we called the elevator. Inside I immediately ate a few treats that I had brought from the dispensary and on the ride home their effects began and what a fine drive home it turned out to be. Much better than the previous drive!

When I got home I stopped in the kitchen and grabbed a box of cupcakes and walked downstairs to The Basement and sat on the couch and commenced to indulge. The place was a mess, just as I had remembered it, cluttered with boxes full of dormant junk that were used just once and never again, a large and promising wasted space enclosed by walls that wouldn't stop talking if they could. My secluded area—complete with a couch and a rug and a chair and tv—sat nestled between the junky jumble and this makeshift space was still bigger than my room!

I turned on the tv and then the Xbox. I took a big bite out of a cupcake. Now I was relaxed and after leaving the crutches behind I wanted to relish this step toward freedom in a way that made sense. I didn't get far before my mother opened the door and then walked downstairs and the fibrous wood creaked and groaned step after step. She grabbed a bottle of wine from the trunk and then looked at me, and then at the box of cupcakes sitting on the couch beside me.

"Hey, you already had cookies earlier today!"

"So," I said.

"So, you'll get fat if you keep eating like this."

"Me, no. I'm only out of shape."

"Oh, Andrew," she sighed. "You know it can happen fast."

"But it won't happen to me."

"I think you should slow down."

"Slow down, hell. I'm finally off the crutches."

"I know, but you kind of let yourself go while you were *on* the crutches."

"Well now I can actually exercise."

"Okay. It'd suck if you threw away your whole recovery over junk food."

"'Tis true."

"You remember what Doctor Trey said…"

"Yes."

"No high-impact anything, and no testing it!"

My mother walked away and went back upstairs and with each step the stairs creaked underneath her light frame. *Maybe she's right. That would suck. But maybe it's better to enjoy the moment. Whatever…*

Chapter 17

When I was sixteen it took me three attempts to finally pass my driver's test. Maybe in a strange kind of way my study habits in school translated onto the road. I hardly studied for exams, rarely practiced behind the wheel, and both seemed like a waste of time. Why study for something that you'll likely forget tomorrow? But of course these were two completely different types of burdens, each one demanding its own discipline and brainpower, one being conceptual and the other practical, and that's probably why I passed one kind and failed the other. My mind could think logically and in school come test time it always had the answers and almost always did well, but this was not exactly the case on the road. The first time that I took the driver's test my nerves were on edge, mostly because I was so eager to drive alone at last, but very quickly this test ended in disappointment. I made a big mistake early on and after that I knew it was over. The instructor said, "Why don't you turn down the one-way street," and that I did, but it was in the wrong direction. Back then this blunder was slightly embarrassing but now it seems almost funny, looking back at it, that my mind and even more specifically my subconscious could solve problems in school with ease yet choke over the practicalities of a driver's test. Normally I'm a fine driver, but back then it took me three attempts to pass the test! And with that I ask, where is it now, this subconscious of mine, and what is it doing?

The answer is in the gutter and hardly much of anything. After the appointment at Mass General I promptly started driving, and those deeply ingrained instincts came back easily like riding a bike, but at the same time I was quickly failing a different kind of test. Instead of driving to the gym—to exercise and lift, strengthen and workout—or even stepping out of the house for a morning walk, I continued to eat greedily and live sedentarily despite the dire need to make a change. And as a result of this negligence I put on a few extra pounds yet didn't seem to notice or care and merely brushed it aside as tomorrow's concern.

And then tomorrow came and at therapy something seemed off, vitality was at an all-time low and the patients looked at me with the same sort of exhaust and pity in their eyes as they did each other, which I had never experienced before but which happened to be a strange kind of wakeup call. I had become enervated, and I moved around on the table languidly, sweat profusely, and after the session ended, realized the need to hop on a scale immediately.

And when I got home I went straight upstairs and stepped on the scale and waited. The screen blinked three times and measured the force and displayed the number and disappointment set in. The scale doesn't lie. *204, Christ!* Flashbacks of a blurred past, repeatedly calling Danny Boyd Santa and pantsing him in class. A disgusting feeling arose and then wondering how this could even happen. The mirror said it all, and the answers were all there. Now that I wasn't sucking in like every other morning in front of the mirror, I saw what I had become after getting home, being on crutches critically injured and eating like a dog. I could now see that I was one step away from having a dadlike bod. Work had to be done!

Later on I started lifting weights in the garage, trying to make things right and get back on track, and then my mother arrived at home and I went inside behind her. She had the mail and laid it out on the counter.

"I saw Mrs. P at the Y today," she said.

"Okay."

"She asked how you were doing, and I said really well!"

"Thanks." I thought about the strange day that I'd had but I didn't want to and didn't know what else to say. "Well guess what? I had an uncanny dream in the coma and Mister P was in it."

"Hmm. Uncanny. What was it about?"

"No much, yet a lot. We stood right over there in the foyer and briefly talked. He said that George had gone skiing in the alps and then *poof*, he was gone."

"Hmm," she said again. "You know that George did go skiing in the Alps over spring break?"

"Yeah. He told me when he wished me a happy birthday."

"Oh, that was nice of him. You should see if he's around."

"He is. I asked if he wanted to workout or maybe go for a swim but he didn't respond, and I didn't do either."

"Oh well. Anyway, you know how Mister P went to see you at Mass General?"

"No, I don't."

"Didn't I tell you?"

"No."

"Well excuse me. I thought I did. He was at a conference in Boston and he stopped by Mass General to check in on you. It was early on, and you were still in a coma and hooked up to a bunch of machines."

"Okay."

"Okay, so maybe he talked to you," she suggested. "And maybe somehow in the coma you could sense his presence and your mind kind of... um..."

"It projected what it sensed."

"Yes! What it sensed."

"Probably," I said. "The subconscious is very smart. Well mine can be when it wants to be. But I mean when I woke up I honestly thought that the dream had been real, and for a while I was very confused. It was like an out-of-body experience."

"Comas are awfully strange, aren't they?"

"Yeah."

"Well we didn't know what you'd be like when you woke up. Or—"

"Or if..." I said.

"Exactly. Or if."

"Some get lost and never find their way back."

"You know, I read that some people have come out of comas speaking fluently in other languages." My mother laughed. "Could you imagine…"

"*Yo puedo. Hablo inglés y español también.* But Mandarin would've been something. I could put that on my resume."

"Absolutely! Doesn't George know Mandarin?"

I shrugged, then opened the fridge and grabbed the orange juice and poured myself a glass and nostalgically thought about George. As friends we were a great match, and our minds and hobbies and interests were equally compatible. The interminable discussions we had on various subjects, and whether they were either intellectual or metaphysical, biological or scientific, random or profound, they were always intellectually stimulating and distinctive from a typical conversation. It's strange—even talk can be exciting if it's with the right person. I learned a lot from those conversations with George and it's safe to say that he did too. To learn and gain knowledge starts with a good conversation—with someone who knows much more than all that's said. As youngsters we were both athletes and hopeful intellectuals, and we competed graciously on the field or in thought, but at times our minds clashed from abstract or creative differences. Like most people with a great mind, George had many artistic qualities, a deep curiosity, self-realization, expression, and among several others, a slight yet controlled madness that set his thought process and personality apart from others. If George ever became an artist he'd probably be an eccentric avant-garde type, and I'd probably become a pensive writer type, and secretly that's what I dreamt and hoped would happen. But George was studying astrophysics, and for me it would soon be engineering. The future told by the past. I took a hit of orange juice.

"You know I was just thinking," said my mother. "It's too bad that you weren't able to go to Colorado with Sal over spring break."

"Beaver Creek—I know!" I said. "Well look, that's just the way she goes."

She sighed and then went through the mail on the counter and opened an envelope. I grabbed the glass of orange juice and walked downstairs and thought about the strange dreams in the coma and speaking fluently in Spanish and had it been Mandarin and I tried to make sense of everything. Comas are peculiar. Who knows what the subconscious makes sense of in dormancy? Even though the brain is inactive and basically moribund this inner self endures the pain and remains engaged. It works hard and well when nothing else is and this work that it does should not be overlooked. Like a cosmic committee organized inside of each mind the subconscious knows and dictates what we will say and do before we even know. It's almost like God in that way and it has the answers to questions that have yet to be asked or even realized. Any test can be passed but this is strictly left up to us. Every answer lay in the mind and the mind makes you. I thought that maybe my subconscious knew the who, what, when, where, why, how. But it hardly made sense to think about it now when the memory had either been misplaced or even erased. I sat down on the couch and drank the juice and cleared my mind and opened a book.

Chapter 18

The next week in late May an unexpected letter arrived in the mail and sparked a fire.

Wisely, in the time between the first weigh in and now, after stepping on the scale and seeing the numbers *204* starkly appear on the screen, feeling the disgrace, the slight self-pity, realizing that a change had to be made, I stopped eating unmindfully. It had only been three months and a week since the scale had read one-sixty at Spaulding. Back then I was very thin after fasting and starving for most of my stay at Mass General. The only exception to this were the ice cubes and toward the end an occasional chocolate Ensure, those liquid meals in a bottle, which were surprisingly delicious at the time and which made me think of Kanye West. But fairly poor habits and a few months can certainly change a human's body composition. In other words, things will go astray if you let them. Basically all of my muscle had lost its strength and converted to fat from excessive inactivity and lethargy. It was time to use the fire and to fuel the flame I would blast my music and lift my weights in The Basement. Poor results gave great urgency to get back what I had lost!

At therapy Claire had added a few new exercises to the existing routine, and after performing these I got on the bike and pedaled in place for anywhere between ten and thirty minutes—depending on the day's agenda. This was about all there was to do for cardio. Variation was limited under tight restrictions. And there comes a time when a line has to be drawn in the sand, when repetition has become so habitual and somewhat second nature that the coach is no longer needed. At this point I could do everything on my own with ease.

And that's where the letter in the mail becomes relevant. But it was hardly much of a letter. Receiving a letter in the mail these days is very rare and sadly, pretty soon it might become a bygone and never so much as happen again. But I happen to think the world of letters! They're much more thoughtful than anything electronic and their language is too. When's the last time that you've received an unforeseen letter, and a thoughtful one to say the least? It had been a long while for me, but like I said, this time what came in the mail was not exactly a letter. It was a big fat bill for five thousand dollars!

"You've got to be kidding me," said my mother. "They assured us that they were in-network! I figured it all out while you were at Spaulding. Remember how long you were there—two weeks! I was on the phone for hours and hours and spoke to place after place. *This makes me mad!*"

I couldn't help but laugh inwardly.

"I even called the insurance company and they assured us too. Oh, oh, you know how insurance companies can be. They answer promptly and then put you on hold for hours—five or six hours at a time! Finally I spoke to a representative and they checked and even double-checked to make sure that Goodwill was in-network. This is what we get, huh? *Aargh!*"

The problem was, they apparently weren't checking the right information. Someone had haply mishandled the situation and forgot to plunge the toilet properly, and there was not a janitor on our side to help us clean the mess. The fire had been sparked and there was no extinguisher to put it out. Money doesn't grow on trees, someone has to pay and get paid, Claire has to eat and rest under a roof, and one way or another the five thousand dollars has to come from somewhere—our pockets! The truth is, we had the money but not for what should have been covered. A dollar saved is a dollar earned. The big boys just love to get the most out of you. But without them what would I be? They covered every hospital expense, room and board, surgery, narcotics, therapy, ambulance rides, doctors' time, everything. And this ongoing list of expenses all amounted to a sum totaling five hundred thousand dollars and some change. Without them there would be no me, my or I—just a complete blindness, an absolute blackness, and when it's all said and done, the delight.

My mother was not happy about this, and for good reason; they had broken their word. "I'm not paying that bill," she said. "Don't you worry, after we get this figured out we'll find you an in-network physical therapist."

"No," I said. "We won't."

It was my time to take charge and carry the fire myself, and it was absolutely necessary to accept this responsibility and handle it good and proper. Even if it's not your fault, it's your life. Follow someone else, or intuitively guide yourself. Why wait for someone to tell you what to do when you can do it on your own? Now that therapy at Goodwill had been cut short, I thought that Claire would want me to recover this way, my way. She seemed like someone who would respect a person fending for themselves and recovering of their own accord. But only if the fruits of their labor turn out to be favorable in the end. This wouldn't be easy, the injuries were critical, things had been shattered, and to lose about fifty pounds with those injuries and this soon after would be an arduous task. Surely an uphill battle with winds strong enough to extinguish the fire. But it was time to rise up to the challenge, knowing that those who rise to the top often get hurt the worst, and by falling so low they can then rise to a spot higher than ever conceived.

And then a few days after receiving the bill from Goodwill Rehab, as if the gods had expressly coordinated these events for my convenience, a package from Mass General came in the mail and I actually learned about every injury, every setback that was currently being faced, the details scattered throughout hundreds of pages tucked inside of a thick manila envelope. This is an envelope that with its contents I will keep forever; it's essentially my backbone. My mother read just about everything inside but all that I needed for now was a single sheet of paper from the top of the stack that sparsely listed each injury. And what a surprise! Here I was thinking that I had only suffered a few fractures and a brain injury—if only! But after reading this list I finally grasped the severity of the entire ordeal. Further into the file my head began to whirl and reel in its extensive details.

At the top of the page in bold lettering it read: "Trauma burden and current status." Below this was a long list of injuries in fine print with few details. Many words were written in Latin, and these were mostly parts of the human anatomy, but it was easy enough to follow along and I will try to convey it simply and in a way that's not overly degrading. Sometimes it is, and that's all right.

First on the list were the head injuries and apparently many skull fractures. One was on the back of my head and extended inward through multiple bones, all of which were naturally listed in Latin like the foramen magnum, the occipital condyle, the occipital bone, the hypoglossal canal. Implicatively, this fracture and the X-shaped scar on the back of my head were linked. And there was a separate fracture deep inside of my nasal cavity that bordered my brain and spread between and throughout the ethmoids, sphenoid, and sella turcica.

Next on the list was my brain injury, and as doctors had put it, a severe TBI. With extensive bruising and bleeding throughout the right cerebral convexity, right lateral ventricle, right frontal white matter, right anterior and temporal lobes, it was indeed severe and seemingly worse on the right side. The scar on the back of my head was on the left side; most of the damage was caused by brain to bone impact. The projection of my mind displayed in my mind. Amnesia came as no surprise.

And then the list scantly mentioned a cervical spine injury on the C7 vertebra, a sprain to the ligament at the C1 through C7 level that had cautiously been addressed with a cervical collar. But it did not mention a fracture and for a moment I thought about this and then moved on.

Next the list mentioned a collapsed and lacerated left lung with extensive bleeding and near drowning. This was suspected at once after I had arrived at home from the hospital—having a collapsed lung—but nearly drowning from this injury seemed quite ghastly. *Drowning in your own blood—Christ!* And I thought that maybe it was caused by the displaced fracture to the left eighth and tenth ribs and one end of one bone punctured the wrong side of one lung. But I was beginning to speculate and speculation is cheap.

From this point onward this concise report covered the entire page—there was a lot to say with very little room. My lumbar spine had suffered considerable damage: transverse process fractures on the left side of the L1, L2, L3, and L4 vertebrae, and a fracture on the right side of the L5 vertebra.

But my pelvis was evidently the worst. There had been a vertical shear fracture and more specifically multiple fractures to the left superior and inferior pubic ramus. There was a dissociation of the pubic symphysis and to the right hemipelvis a superior dislocation. On top of that, there was a comminuted and displaced fracture of the right sacrum that expanded into the pelvis and the S1, S2, and S3 sacral vertebrae. With that I thought, *No wonder it hurt so much to sit down!*

Clearly I had been crushed, annihilated, very nearly wiped out as a human being. All perceptions, perspectives, thoughts, actions, habits, emotions, temptations, cremated. All means of fundamental life had been fully destroyed. But for one to be born again as an individual, set apart and singular, he must be beat down to his knees and rise above the ashes on his own. All accountability falls within, and this is where the true self can be found—within. It's a kind of transformational process and everything seems new and nothing is quite the same as before, not one's beliefs, desires, pleasures, joys, habits, conscience, aura, and self. It's a shock at first, freedom and liberation next, and after that it's up in the air. The documents in the file all blatantly painted the picture, and there were many more injuries and details that were listed and hidden inside the rest of the pages in the envelope. But it was too much for me to bear to read any further. There was nothing between the lines and to read it to the end would have been a battle. The diction and doctor talk was hard to understand even though I understood enough to know that I shouldn't be alive and to amply appreciate a miracle when one actually happens. And this was all perfect motivation to move onward and recover from every injury and detriment and whether minor or major it had to be done.

All right, I thought. *Time to burn the weight and carry the fire and rebuild the frame and recover completely. With no help, support, or care; it's all on you... Now what?*

That's right. It won't be a picnic. Remember that advice from earlier and before? Sometimes you need a good kick in the butt to wake up and make a change. Y sí, estoy hablando conmigo. Ahora, no leche, no queso, no bolonia, sin basura. Capítulo nuevo, vida nueva.

Chapter 19

The fact is, all along I had been caught in a vicious circle. After my birthday I ate very poorly because I hurt and couldn't walk or exercise ably, and the more I ate the more weight was gained and energy drained and this made it especially hard to walk and exercise once I finally could. It was not exactly physically difficult, but over the past few months all motivation to voluntarily recover had been lost. That is, until the letter and the file arrived in the mail. Those two deliveries sparked the fire and mining great motivation from music kept it burning. When exercising strenuously good music is necessary. It might be the only way to distract yourself from fatigue and pain and keep you rolling in motion through their spells, and after being terribly injured and excessively inactive, these spells can be quite cruel.

I worked out hard and often now that I was on my own in the good fight, and I took this time to find myself and I took it very seriously. But I was restricted to low-impact exercises, and even though they quickly became tedious, for now they were my limit. Learning about every injury rightly nipped the urge to test my luck in the bud. For once and only once it seemed smart to follow the progression or curriculum—I had promised myself that I wouldn't end up in the operating room. In that case, I had to get creative with my low-impact activities. First I either hopped on a bike or swam in a pool or rowed at the gym, and then I went home and dumb crawled up and down the driveway through the scorching sun. This was quite the unorthodox workout that I had created on account of the weight-bearing restrictions. To put it simply, they were bear crawls with dumbbells. And believe me, they were tough!

Summer lay just around the corner and at the gym in early June I almost literally ran into Mack Daniel.

"Hey Terr," he said.

"Mack Daniel!"

"Are you leaving? You look like you're in a rush."

"Yeah—going to do dumb crawls at home."

"What? Why?"

"The workout is not over."

"You didn't do enough here?"

"With what I can actually do, not even close. It's too easy to fall short at the gym and I like to finish at home."

"Oh yeah, that's true. How is everything?"

"Well," I said. "It could be better."

Mack Daniel laughed.

"I got up to two-o-four—pounds. Dead weight."

And Mack continued laughing. "No way, I don't see it."

"Well. The scale said otherwise."

"What'd you say you're going home to do?"

"Dumb crawls."

"*What* are those?"

"They're hard to explain, Mack."

"Terr, you can do it."

"All right. They're like bear crawls but with dumbbells—it's that simple. You get down on the ground and hold the dumbbells and crawl like an animal. Crawl till you drop, baby."

Mack smiled and laughed.

"That good enough? I'm not very good at explaining myself."

"Yeah, it sounds intense!"

"It's something. They're fast and fluid when you're doing them, and they put up a very good fight. You're in for a helluva time."

"Word, I might give them a try."

"At your own risk, Mack."

And that was that for now. Mack laughed and I told him that it was time to go and that I'd see him soon.

"All right," he said. "Bye Terr."

"Later Mack."

Ten minutes later I got home from the gym and inside of the garage I grabbed the weights and faced the driveway and dropped to the floor in a plank position. It was an unusually hot afternoon for early June and the sun beat down and a soft breeze blew and one thousand and one cicadas synchronously buzzed through the air like an electric razor. I listened dreamily for a moment and then picked up my left foot and then my right arm and carried the weight and swiftly took off. Each time that I pulled the weight from beside my waist and into the air I jolted it forward and with momentum the ten-pound weight slammed against the pavement beside my head. My legs pumped and arms pulled and weights dropped as I crawled the driveway and at the end I turned around and crawled back. In this direction the driveway was slightly sloped and seemed as though it was twice as long as crawling down. I made it back to the garage rather unspent and turned around and started down for round two.

After several rounds of continuously crawling up and down the driveway to my displeasure the fire burned out. My head bowed to my chest and I noticed every crack and dip and rise in the pavement and took one, two, three breaks on the last trip and then made my way to the garage and on the ground I collapsed, my chest on the concrete and legs on the asphalt. I lay flat and still, panting for air for what was hardly enough. The spell was strong, and it weighed heavily on my shoulders and around my groin, and this caused me to recall the memories that I wanted to write about but would never get the chance if I never got up.

Like the time at the owner of Under Upper's house on Sanibel Island when I caught a small hammerhead shark fishing from their pier and paddle boarding into the deep blue sea and sticking out above the water was a sleek grey fin and I thought that was it but gracefully she swam right by like a friendly dolphin so often does and the thrill and relief and then later that night the crimson sun sinking below the horizon like a ball of fire and all around sat a calm sky painted orange and red like oil on canvas and soon the twilight and then the darkness but still the warmth and after all this time I can still feel the powerful Florida sun on my skin and the humid air expand each lung on the first day that I woke in paradise and since that time every sole experience and sight seen and smell smelled and mountain climbed and water trod and storm chased and veiled underneath a layer of awareness that slice of existence will fade away like condensed air from a wet breath on a cold day as new juice as fresh as an uncorked bottle of crushed grapes fills the vacant space.

Nothing triggers memories like hard work and hurt. And it's true that you can lose yourself and your way whirling between the shadows and shades of your past; but doing this can also rapidly restore your creativity and vitality.

I got up and walked inside and down the stairs and into The Basement. I sat on the couch and took a hit from The Goldstein, settled, felt good, loose, revived, and one more hit unexpectedly did it. Vividly my mind and vision descended into slow motion and like a daydream went through a cauldron of acute senses. I sat on an examination table beside the apparition of Doctor Trey. He was in a good mood and he dangled his legs and swung them back and forth in the air.

I dipped my head. "Doctor Trey."

"Andrew, how are you?"

"Good. But I've gained some weight—gotten a bit husky."

"Husky?"

"Yeah, unfortunately."

Doctor Trey laughed. "Well. You were just on the crutches and stuck in bed for four months, survived and beat the odds and did what had to be done. Who cares if you're a bit husky?"

"Look," I said. "I do. That's just not like me."

"Then change the way you eat—start by going on a diet. See, diet and nutrition form the foundation of wellness. Have you ever heard of the old saying 'you are what you eat'? Well, that actually goes without saying."

"Sure, that makes sense."

"So if you want to lose weight, go on a diet, make a change. It's really that easy, and you'll feel great! But first, it'd be a good idea to weigh yourself. See where you're at and then go from there."

"I can do that," I said. "Right now."

"Right. Now."

With that, my eyes gained focus and I sprang to my feet and went upstairs and stepped on the scale. There was one blink, two blinks, three blinks, four: *200.* *Well*, I thought. *Better go on a diet.*

Chapter 20

My instinct told me to intermittent fast but my conscience decided and tried a ketogenic diet. For the first two weeks it went pretty well. This was a budding diet and online at the time it hardly had any information, and then eventually the mainstream press caught wind of this major breakthrough and among the masses it became a popular success. (And candidly I hoped that that would happen to this book someday soon—if it actually gets published!) For now I had the time to focus on myself and the diet and that's just about all I did. I was very lucky for this and these days back then might have been the very best days of my life. I knew that an authentic ketogenic diet consists of seventy percent fat, twenty-five percent protein, and the rest are those unwanted carbs. To realize these daily percentages is one thing and to maintain them was very hard. I did the best that I could do but without a caloric calculator that's all it was—my best attempt. For breakfast I ate eggs, lunch it was chicken and cheese and for dinner it was trouble. Whatever these dietary percentages calculated out to be, what I ate seemed to do the trick. I felt lighter and stronger, mobile and energetic.

Much of this vitalic and physical improvement was owed in part to frequent long hikes at Knight's Pond, a nearby nature preserve with an interspersed system of trails. It's strange how refreshing it feels when the high sun shines down on your skin among wildlife compared to open areas or among concrete or through a window. Through and through I enjoyed every second of it. What a perfect place to clear your mind and meditate! The dumb crawls had been short-lived; hiking trails and lifting weights was my new routine.

The trails at Knight's Pond were brand-new. Some were still under development and I was probably the first person to regularly use them. And in that case they would have been great for a tough run, with an abundance of roots, rocks, dips, hills, and obstacles, but I wisely resisted the urge. I'll stick to my word, I told myself. There was no need to test my luck.

But often, as I made it to the end of the access trail strewed with leaves and noticed the dark blue pond through scattered trees and the high sun sparkle on the rippled breeze—and off to the left lay the land bridge that connected trails on one side of the pond to other—I considered smoothly escalating my pace from a walk to a jog or even a run!

The days were now very long and the earth and water warm and many animals flocked the land to enjoy the fruits of late spring. One afternoon, after seeing a local acupuncturist for neck and ass pain and then stopping at the theatre to watch a matinee, I went to Knight's Pond and walked along the access trail and then the land bridge and raptly absorbed my surroundings. To the left on the edge of the pond stood five or six miniature turtles perched on logs that shot out above the water like stilts, gently still. They solitarily bathed in the shade, made by a row of coniferous trees along the edge of the trail, and life for them seemed sweet and serene, slow, meditative, dull. That was likely all that they would experience in their short lives and they were absolutely content. I was envious, and then I walked across the land bridge and into the forest where verdurous leaves dripped wet in the humid air.

The temptation to run was strong and it takes a very strong will to resist temptation. I thought about it, and then thoroughly about the few times when I had skied just four months after knee surgery. Recovery for a torn ACL is very prolonged, and coincidentally just about the same timeframe as this recovery. Six months without any sort of high-impact activities, *and then* you'll get tested. If you pass, you're cleared; if not, you're doomed. I chose not to wait the entire time, four years earlier when I was sixteen years old, and skiing was almost perfectly fine. Except for that one time—and there's always that one time—when the winds were strong and the air lay numb and I carved the trail and wove in and out of the glade and between the trees on the right side, and then there it was, a small jump with a smooth hump formed from a stump covered in snow, and I went at it fast and rash and then flew off. And into the air I soared. And like a wild beast trapped in a cage the wind roared and whisked me further down the trail and what felt like a minute was less than a second. I hit the ground with a thud, completely crouched against my ski boots. *Oh, Christ!*

There was a sharp burst of pain and a deep unease inside of my knee that spread and swelled around the back. Pain is a shock at first but the panic of an injury after is worse. In any event, it's all mental, and I thought that my ACL and meniscus had both fully retorn. But I skied on and by the end of the day it was only sore and back to normal the next. The only sensible explanation for the pain was scar tissue, and I did not want to run and find out right now if I had some. So I gladly hiked along the edge of the pond and past the intersection and up and around the long meandering trail to the top of Bruce Hill, and then down and off to home I went. Altogether, the trail was about a three-mile loop. That's all.

The first order of business at home was to step on the scale. Was I making progress or wallowing in what is better known as nothing? *Well okay*, I thought. *195's not bad.* But after two weeks of calculating nourishment and lifting weights and hiking trails the difference should have been greater than five pounds. It was mostly water weight that kept the number high in this very moment, but something more had to be done, something that without much effort simply hit me. A three-mile hike around a small hill was not nearly enough but up a mountain would certainly be something. I wondered, *But is it too soon? Not at all!* Skiing on a mountain four months after surgery had been fine for the most part, and I figured that hiking a mountain would probably be the same. *It's not even a high-impact activity. Should be a breeze. Tough, but a breeze.*

And then instantly Tumbledown Mountain came to mind and this was no surprise. There's a pond at the top to swim in! How many mountains have a body of water to swim in at the summit? The answer is not many.

The weather app forecasted rain for the next four days—your typical blow—and I decided that I'd go the next day there was sun. I walked downstairs. My parents were both in the kitchen.

"I'm going hiking," I said.

My mother smiled. "That's great! Right now?"

"No. The next sunny day."

"Today's a really nice day. Where are you going?"

I filled up a glass with water and drank it. I set the glass on the counter. "Tumbledown Mountain," I said.

"Oh, no. I don't know. It's too soon to be hiking mountains."

"Not too soon," I said. "But too late."

"Leon?"

"I like Tumbledown Mountain," said my father. "He'll be fine. Just be careful and take it slow."

"Of course."

"We don't want another call from the hospital."

"Yeah, I know."

"Why not hike a mountain a little closer to us? Oh, what about Pleasant?"

"It's too easy."

"Too easy?"

"Yeah."

"But you're recovering from serious injuries," said my mother. "Hike an easier mountain."

"I'm strictly hiking Tumbledown. It's that or nothing."

"What would Doctor Trey have to say?"

"Be careful—it's not a high-impact activity."

"Well you can't hike that hard trail," my mother said and then she looked at my father. "What's it called?"

"The chimney trail," he said.

"Deal. I'll hike the trail that I did as a kid. Remember that?"

"No, you did that with my sister Lisa—camping."

"That's right. Well I'm glad that we're on the same page."

"Just be careful, please!"

I turned around and filled another glass with water and thought about the other plan that I had in mind. The chimney trail, which had logically been forbidden to hike—also called "the loop trail"—was exactly the trail that I had in mind when I decided to hike a mountain. It'd be a challenge and that's just what I needed to burn the extra weight. In the good old days, even after every setback and mishap, a naively audacious rationality stood behind many of my own decisions. Every time one of these choices went awry their boldness grew—so often as it does. Most risks will pay off but a chance has to be taken. You'll find yourself on either side, reaping the reward or learning a lesson. And with that, I went down in The Basement to lift weights and after that to read, exercising body and mind consecutively, and then happily collapsing on the couch. In the end I slept.

Chapter 21

One morning the next week I woke and yawned and smiled at the pale sunlight that streamed into my room between the blinds and through the window. Nature's daily alarm clock. I rolled over and got out of bed and went to the bathroom and then the kitchen and poured a cup of coffee and drank it, looking outside at the front yard and the street and the golden glow all about. I said to myself, "It's a good day."

Upstairs I packed my backpack with water, peanut butter and jelly no bread, a towel, a lighter, a pearl, a hard-boiled egg, *The Sun Also Rises*. The epigraph in Hemingway's first novel is candid, deep, and simple. Every quarter century it stands closer and closer to the truth. "You are all a lost generation."

I quickly took a shower and planned to leave immediately after. Tumbledown Mountain was a two-hour drive north and this really made you get up and go. Leaving early meant beating the crowd and scaling the mountain in peace, and then swimming in the pond and atop the rocks, meditating at ease.

The drive was uneventful save for one near mishap when the car swerved on the road and slightly went off the side, but we got back on course and the rest of the trip was smooth. I arrived at the mountain and pulled into the parking lot and what engulfed my car was a cloud of dust as thick as a sandstorm. Small particles of sand and mica stagnated the air and in the sun they all glittered. I could hardly see through the haze. It cleared. Only one other vehicle. A Volkswagen van. I put my car in park and stepped outside and into the lot, spreading my arms wide, stretching, yawning, and smiling, I inhaled, exhaled, and thought, *Is this real? What a fine day!*

The trail first started off flat and very gently inclined and wove between birch and pine and oak and hemlocks and gradually rose its way through the thick forest to the base of the mountain. Along the side of the trail and burrowed underground between exposed tree roots were small holes uncovered, gateways to the world above and the ground below, narrow nests where cleaver creatures softly rest. And there off to the side one sat, a small squirrel with only her head poking out and above the ground, tentatively looking around, thinking about God knows what. I stopped walking and stood still. The small creature cautiously hopped out of the ground and came closer, as if looking for attention or simply out of intrigue. Then the sensibly sensitive soul stopped and sat upon her hind legs and looked at me and into my eyes. We had a moment.

Through a large treefall gap the mountain peak jutted out into and above the clearing and stood enormous. Soon the trail climbed rapidly through the spine of the mountain. The ascent was tough and that was good. Hiking the trails at Knight's Pond had been a perfect stepping-stone for this kind of exercise, and then came the boulder fields.

I scrambled tirelessly from rock to rock and carried the fire and without a rest the excess bodyweight. Sweat poured down my face and from my nose it dripped like a leak from a spigot. It seemed to be working. With each step I felt lighter and each breath I wheezed louder. Like a bad asthma attack. And old memories of the early football days with spells of asthma arose. My first year in the first grade I quit, and right now I wouldn't dare to. You don't give up, and you don't stop short. I'll admit, a couple of times I stopped to dry heave and once I nearly vomited. I chugged a bottle of water and washed it down and carried on. And then a weakness in my legs settled in like some sort of dull polio. The markers were hard to follow at times and it's fair to say that my instinct led the way. At every twist and turn in the trail ahead on the path sat the past.

Quickly I made my way through perpetual boulder fields and then I heard a faint whisper from somewhere ahead. I looked up: bright sun and large slabs of granite rock and densely packed trees on either side. I looked back: a painful death. Past an extended bend in the trail and a narrow catwalk above a small ledge and a vast openness of boulders stood a large rock face and a group of hikers at its base. In the middle of the trail stood an athletic man and a pretty woman, maybe three years older than I was—but's it's hard to gauge a person's age. Most people initially assume that I'm at least three years older than I actually am, and then one time on the street a girl thought that I was her age, three years younger than my actual age. No doubt this couple standing in the middle of the trail were both older than I was—not by much, and not that age matters. Off to the side stood their friends—three men no more than boys. One was quite short and large around the waist, arms, legs, neck, in all the wrong places. The other two were skinny and pale and each wore a silent smile upon their icy face. I continued climbing.

"Get out of the way," said the large one. "Let him go first."

The athletic type caressed the girl's lower back and then man and woman stepped off to the side with the others.

I studied the precipice from afar and looked at the group. "This the chimney?"

"Fat Man's Misery," the athletic one said. He punched his large friend in the upper arm who then became tense and all about him a melancholic shine.

I walked past them and approached the vertical rock and faced the entrance to a small cave. There was a miniature granite ledge that protruded out from the wall of rock and stood as an obstacle to get inside.

"We need to watch you do it first."

"I'll see what I can do," I said.

On the side of the rockstacle was a crack for support and that seemed to be all. It worked and I mounted the rock and stepped into the mouth of the fissure.

"How is it in there?"

"Good," I replied.

The dim space at the base of the fissure was limited, cramped, fresh, entirely welcoming. In its rear ran a small stream that along the back of its figure dripped and gushed water through the cracks on the boulders and the wall of rock above. Marvelous!

And then arose broken chatter from down below and outside and all along sweet feminine laughter.

"You—"

"No you—"

"He—"

"Go."

"Made it look easy."

It was spacious enough for only one in this crevice and then claustrophobia began to set in. The only source of light other than the entrance from which I came came from a narrow egress in the rock above. Quickly I made moves to get out of there. A few iron rungs were lodged into the rock on either side of the fissure and led up to the exit. Beyond the opening, blue sky and not one cloud or disturbance. But then there it was, dangling down toward me. I stumbled back and got out of the way. It was a spider. He dangled from his string and fell to the ground. Perhaps me and that spider were alike. Slightly reclusive, curious, defensive, edgy, and utterly harmless.

I grabbed a hold of the rock wall and stepped atop the bottom rung and grasped the rung on the far side with both hands. The iron was wet from condensation and mountain runoff. I stepped on the rung above and moved slightly too fast and my foot slipped off and I cleverly held on, heart raced, heat flashed, time stopped, on the ground, the spider dead. My foot had found the rung and I recovered. Below at the entrance of the fissure the pretty woman climbed inside and only the top of her head was in sight. I moved on up and out of the chimney.

I drank a bottle of water and then climbed atop a pile of rocks beside the fissure and sat and leaned back against a boulder. The southwestern views from this spot on the shoulder of the mountain were rich. Bright green hills dense with trees undulated as far as the eye could see. Past the valley on a grazed ridge stood dozens of wind turbines spinning methodically in the susurrus breeze. And somewhere far off in the opaque space sat bone white the cap of Mount Washington. Like the pale snows of

Kilimanjaro. The sky and the earth all but one. I breathed in a long and deep breath and thought, *My boy, we made it.*

Chapter 22

Peace and freedom had never felt so real, so tangible, so close to my fingertips. Mountains are sacred, gifts. What an incredible hike, and this my legs rightly agreed with! I had made it to the summit and breathed the unbreathed air and took mental shots and scarcely thought and then hiked along the trail atop the mountain's crest. I absorbed the view, energy, sun, sky, warmth, liberty. A few clouds drifted overhead and appeared far too close to be real. Or was I just closer to them, to something heavenly, divine, true, *The One*?

I made my way over a mound of metamorphic rock that then sloped down to a pool of water nestled between two mountain peaks. Tumbledown Pond. The wind blew from the south and I followed its flow and down the slope to the pond. I dropped my bag and then undressed and sat for a moment. This very act I have to endorse to any convalescing being. You will feel what you have never felt before—real. I walked over to a rock ledge on the edge of the pond and looked down at my reflection in the water. My ugly mug bobbled and stirred in the small ripples on its surface. I stood mesmerized and out of it as if a pendulum lay swinging in front of me. What swung wasn't a ball; it was the past.

Looking back, I was as much of a city boy as I was a mountain boy, but most of the time I sat somewhere in between. Something about a mountain creates rich memories. Maybe it's either the smell or just the call of the wild. First what came to mind were numerous times on a pair of skis or snowboard, mostly at Sugarloaf Mountain, plowing through powder on unmarked trails and dodging trees and creating new tracks.

There was that one time with George and Nate and Late the Great. We all got lost from a wrong turn made and found ourselves deep in a valley and far out of bounds off of West Mountain. How this happened—poor judgement. But what an experience it was getting out of that ditch! We had skied off into no man's land and kept going, plowing, thinking that we'd end up on a trail but we did not. We finally stopped when the snow was too deep to continue and there was nowhere to go. Further down was the bottom of the valley with a frozen river sitting still, and further up this valley sat chance and hope but nothing definite. No phone service, we were stranded. We took off our skis. There were trees all around and the snow stood four or five feet deep. When you stood up you did not touch the forest floor. It was like treading snow instead of water. In my mind, and probably the other's too, a simple thought arose. *We could easily die out here.*

But we trudged through the terribly deep snow and traversed the steep valley and crawled closer to dehydration and fatigue, and then after hours had passed and the sun went down we finally made it to a neighborhood absolutely spent. We stayed away from West Mountain after that.

And another time on a mountain when I was still a boy I will never forget—that's the power of a scar, a reminder that the past is still present. I rode a snowboard in those days and was on a trail that crossed another trail which created an intersection of trails. I passed slowly along the intersection and looked up at the cross trail and twenty feet away a child from hell wildly skied directly at me. I yelled, "Watch it, prick!" but it was far too late. He barreled down the trail and crashed into my left leg and I fell over. And he fell too, the little bugger that he was. And then I raised my head and glanced ahead and a few feet away slid a novice rider and she tried to stop but she couldn't stop and then *THUMP!*

Maybe ten seconds later I regained consciousness. In front of my face a concerned father couched and bawled, "Get off my son! You're bleeding all over him!"

"What?"

"Get off!"

I rolled over and raised a fist and then its middle finger. He had already scooped his son off the ground—who I had actually been launched onto after the novice rider and her snowboard slammed into my head—and then he set him down and they skied off and continued down the trail. *Puck you*, I thought. *With a P!*

Other skiers and riders nonchalantly passed by. My head rung and buzzed like a high white noise. I was bleeding badly from the mouth. I took off my gloves and underneath my chin I placed my hand. In seconds there was a small puddle of blood sitting in the middle of my palm. I wiped it off on the snow and then drew my hand up to my mouth and felt around. My upper lip stretched over my top teeth and slightly off center to the right my pointed canine stuck through its flesh like a thumbtack. At the time of this incident I was eleven years old and like a grown man I yanked my lip from the tooth's pull and spat blood and phlegm on the snow. At that age in the sixth grade, and starting much earlier in the fifth grade, I had armpit hair and shaved my face almost daily. It was very well admired or ridiculed by the boys, it reminded the little girls of their dads, and in gym class it was talked about often. At the time I was slightly embarrassed. But it's much better to be talked about than to never be talked about at all. In the best case you'll feel good and the worst case you'll grow thick skin. That all ran through my mind after regaining consciousness—gym class, early androgenic hair, what people might think, what I might look like, what the hell had just happened—and indeed the crash and aftermath were talked about in school. But those that sung did not see it happen, no one did, except for the girl who crashed into my face and left the scene. She happened to be a classmate and she denied this incident for years until one night when we were alone at a party and I casually called her out and she finally admitted it. She could blame it on the alcohol; I was thoroughly satisfied. The blood dripped from my lip like water from the tip of an icicle. No pain, all shock. And then I felt a gap between my front teeth and back then right now I'd think, *Fuck a duck!* My front tooth had been knocked out for the third time and there was not a chance that I'd find it in the snow right now. I paid the medical bills. You win some and you lose some.

Over the years, one adverse event after the other caused me to develop a certain type of protective coat. It's basic biology, and it's better to be warm and prepared than bare.

The water in Tumbledown Pond sat still and clear and fresh as day from summit runoff. The reflection of my face wobbled on the ripples and a shoal of large minnows swam uniformly in the water below. I stood on the rock ledge and spread my arms and jumped and dove into the water above the school of fish. It was amazing—the cleanest, purest water! I stood up on the sand and sediment and a few fish astutely swam back. They nibbled at the dead skin on my legs and feet. A placid solitude, magically still.

I waded back to the shore and climbed atop the granite ledge and up the rock to my folded clothes. I dried off and dressed and on a flat rock meditated next to a small cairn. The mountain, pond, wind, trees, sun, sky, I, space, all fell silent, connected. Celestial poles in polar motion. The cosmological eye in the sky. Stillness of time and life. I opened my eyes and heard a soft voice. If not the voice of God, it was the group of hikers from the Loop Trail. They walked by and found a spot by the pond and set their gear down. I stood up and packed my bag and searched for the trail.

The hike down the mountain was rough. The rock scrambles had to be maneuvered carefully, and when you're recovering from injuries and doing something that you probably shouldn't be doing your nerves are on edge. At times my legs shook so much that my hands began to shake. They were strengthless and they had effetely wobbled from rock to rock like stilts. So be it, it was all still a thrill! I quickly pressed on down the mountain and went through the fissure and then the boulders and crossed a stream and then a campsite and walked along the trail through the forest and back to the parking lot. The final stretch is always the worst. So close yet so far away. So often the case.

I entered my car and reclined the seat and rested my eyes. Had I not been in the middle of nowhere, and had that not weighed heavily on my conscience, I would have soundly fallen asleep. But it was not the time nor place for rest. The mountain welcomes you; you don't sleep on it.

On the drive home I thought about little of anything, and then from the shallows of my mind arrived a short conversation with my mother the day before yesterday. A packet of police reports had come in the mail. She wondered if the suspicious footprints leading down to the river and onto the ice next to my body were from the anonymous caller.

I said, "That's not something that I'd like to think about."

"There were two sets, it says. And the call was untraceable."

"Okay."

"This is not a pleasant read," she said.

"You think?"

"Yes."

"It won't be very easy to make it pleasant in a book. Let alone profound."

"What?"

"I said tell me more. I need a glass of wine."

"Well I guess your shoes were missing," she said. "Or maybe they weren't. It's not clear."

I opened the fridge and poured a generous glass of red. I said, "Those were a pair of raggedy-ass shoes. I'm not sure who would even want them."

"But that nice jacket you had—where was that?"

"You're the one with the information. I don't have a memory of it."

"It's vague," she said.

"Vague. Okay."

"You won't learn a lot from here. Not much was done about it. I mean, there was no surveillance, leads, clues, lab work, anything, I guess."

"Laziness," I said and slammed the empty glass on the counter. "I guess my life just doesn't matter all that much to them."

"Oh, don't say that. I spoke to sergeant Carejo many times on the phone."

"And who knows what he was feeding your ear."

"Andrew, you don't need another."

I poured a thin glass of red and sipped it this time. I said, "It's strange—because I'm white and enrolled in college."

"Well you can talk about that at the meeting with Kenneth Conrad."

"Yeah, okay…"

"That's coming up you know. July sixth."

"I know."

At that point the conversation faded. I fiddled with the volume on the radio and drove along the open road unbothered. Kenneth Conrad was a specialist that Robert had spoken to and then set up a meeting between him and I. We would discuss the arrest and he would write a report on what had happened but all else was up in the air. I wasn't worried. What person doesn't enjoy openly talking about themselves? Well, it depends how much of themself actually gets opened.

Chapter 23

It was July sixth and the last time that I had seen or talked to a friend was at least a month earlier. But before their summer break started in mid-May Cole had actually stopped by The Basement a handful of times, and once the boys came home from university, Sean a few. Ricky was living in Boston, MIA, that jerk. And Rae was either in Laos or Cambodia. They had all gone on with their lives and I was stuck picking up the pieces to mine. But something great had come from this. Inside and out I had learned all there was to learn about myself. This is not an easy quest to comprehend, but it's very easy to go from cradle to grave without a single trace of comprehension.

During this time of solitude I had been relentlessly exercising night and day and thoroughly enjoyed every second of it. The trek up Tumbledown Mountain, I might go so far as to say, was a life-changing experience; only because it had been so soon after being saved from the grave. You appreciate the natural world and life around you much more when you appreciate your own, and you see things that you would never see with a clouded or distracted mind. Try to be conscious of who and what your mind absorbs for food, because once it's consumed that's its food for thought, and most of the food that is currently available is innutritious. You are what you eat.

About a month earlier I lost four pounds from that one hike and to this day I'm uncomplacent and hungry. Nothing was good enough, nothing satisfied, not my expectations—nothing. And the numbers on the scale dropped and dropped like gravity to one eighty-five the day before I had the meeting with Kenneth Conrad. It was like basic physics. The product of work and displacement.

All of this happened unaccompanied; music and intuition were the only guides. No one tagged along for the ride or even checked on my existence. I thought that more friends would have cared, and soon it became clear that people really only care about themselves. The only two people who got in touch with me were Sean and Cole, and this was when they were desperately in need of weed. But I'll be honest, I didn't reach out to anyone—I was too busy getting my life together and back on track, and on top of that, I didn't think that it was my job to do so. Later on Sean simply sent a text that said, "It's a two-way road," and this caused me to hurl my phone at the wall. I thought, *The nerve, you ass! Fine, you can stay on your side of the road and I'll stay on mine.*

My side of the road might have been rough and muddy but at least it was wide open. I figured that these friends of mine had all seen the arrest on Google and wanted no part in my life any longer. Once your true friends are gone very seldom will new friends come along. Their ignorance planted a nice fat chip on my shoulder and perhaps the best way to do away with resent toward anyone is to remember the good times with them when they were great. You can't take back the past—how you act, what you think, what you say and what you do—but you can remember what you can.

Two years and two days earlier a few friends and I had gone up to Moosehead Lake for the Fourth of July. That night we went to a party at a sandpit in the depths of a forest in northern Maine. We traveled there in a loaded car and I believe Ricky and I both had to sit in the trunk. The dirt road was immensely long and we drove along at a steady speed of ten miles per hour. I had never been up to this area of the state, this perfectly isolated wilderness with endless hardwoods on either side of the road and dwarfed ferns lining the forest floor like leaves. A deep ditch sat on each side of this narrow road and if another car approached from the opposite direction both would have pull off to the side and drive extra slow to avoid a collision or even worse, slipping into that ditch. With no service, there would be no one to call for help if you got stuck. We drove slow and it took us a long while to get to the sandpit and by the time we did the party was just getting started. No problem, we got it going.

Bill set up the tent on top of the hill and then joined us in a game of beer pong, and then it was flip cup, and then Ricky found a foreign girl's Jell-O shots and happily indulged in many. She was a Spanish exchange student and for some reason she was staying with the hicks of northern Maine for the summer. Of course, she seemed much more out of place than us. She warned Ricky that *los tragos son fuertes y llenos de tequila. Cuidado, muchacho.* He wolfed them down and the night went on.

The stars in a clear and unpolluted sky are timeless where possibility is limitless. Where are we in this intricate vastness? To where does the unexpanded expand? And what are we to do? We do the best that we can with what we have. We live by interest and we don't give up... But what's that noise? Sounds like Ricky.

Later that night after we all got situated in the big tent Ricky obnoxiously entered, gasping, possibly crying, sweating profusely. He told us that he had gotten into a fight with the Gilford brothers and one of those hicks had headbutted him in the face and he stumbled back and fell and hit his head on a metal trailer. I could hear the *ding* of the trailer in his voice as he sobbed. His nose was bleeding and sweat was dripping down his face. "My head fucking hurts!" he said. "The trailer was really hard!" And all that I heard was the high *ding* that his head must have made upon contact. I was quite concerned. Later that night he ranted deliriously.

"I need to warn my mom," he said. "I need to call her! I need to make sure that she's all right. I think she's been abducted by the aliens!" Ricky sat on his knees and covered his face with his hands and then fell and rolled around on the ground and continued, "Oh no, no, no—the aliens, not the aliens! There's too many of them! Where did they all come from? I need to let my mom know now—right now! I tell you, they're coming for her! I tell you! I—oh no. Oh hell. Are you guys aliens? Where are you taking me—where!" Nearly his exact words.

For the life of me I could not stop laughing! That's how I went to sleep, and that's how I woke in the morning—laughing.

Ricky appeared to be missing. Only a dried puddle of sweat sat on the floor where he had slept. I unzipped the tent and poked my head out. "Ricky. Hey, Rick!"

There was no response. The others were still sleeping. And I stepped outside to find him. The sun was rising but the light was dim. A smell of exhaust and fireworks lingered here and there like pollution in otherwise untouched air. I walked down the sandpit, thinking about another time at a party when I had found Ricky sitting outside at dawn on a stump by a fire pit, alone. He sat still as stone, eyes wide open, gazing blankly at the ashed and charred logs.

"What's happnin Ricky?"

He looked almost like a ghost and he didn't say anything. I sat on a chair opposite him and tossed a pebble at his nose and he jerked back and woke up, absolutely shocked. "*Wow!*"

"You okay, Ricky?"

"What?"

"What's up, my dude."

"Nothing," he said, dripping sweat. "I just woke up."

"Just woke up," I said. "Your eyes were wide open. You were sitting like you are now. How's that possible?"

Ricky looked confused and ill. His face was pale and his arms and legs were tinted mauve. "Well it's possible," he said. "Trust me, I just woke up. I had a bad dream."

"Oh hell, Ricky."

"What, I'm serious!"

"Want to talk about it?"

"No."

"It's not a bad thing, Rick. Bad dreams mean that real life is actually pretty good. But when you have a good dream, that means your subconscious is trying to escape real life."

"It was just weird. You wouldn't get it."

"That's fine," I said. "I feel sleazy, wanna cure this hangover?"

"My doge," said Ricky. "Yes!"

And that we did, with a flawless bomber.

And now back at the sandpit I walked across the dune and to the fire and there sat Ricky on a log, apparently slouched over in a deep sleep, unmoving. It was like déjà vu.

And then it was gone.

Chapter 24

When I arrived at Kenneth Conrad's office in Augusta I looked at my reflection in the rear-view mirror and this made me wonder what I'd be doing and where I'd be if life had only been fair and my choices had all been righteous. But that was the past and there was no time to dwell on it. I was running late and didn't intend to keep Ken waiting. I opened the door and stepped outside. In town there had been a variety of deciduous shrubbery and perennial flowers lined along the building fronts and walkways. The grass in each yard was vibrant and lushly green and leaves on vigorous trees swayed in the continuous light breeze. A few clouds drifted in the vast blue sky and far beyond lay a blazing sun. The day was fresh like a manicured lawn and the air was pleasant to breathe. Driving through town many locals and tourists alike moved slowly in the street and walking among them I thought that I noticed William. Could it really be him? But I passed the man fast and didn't make out a clear picture. I had moved on.

Kenneth's office was in an old white building and seemed professional and unpretentious. I had let myself inside and took a seat on one of two leather chairs. To my right in the corner stood a small statue of Buddha and hung on the wall behind him was a portrait of a sailor at sea. He stood on the deck of his ship amidst a storm and the lustrous sky glowed cerise and peach and like a fire the stormy water mirrored this depicted aurora.

Kenneth walked into his office. He was a mature man with a grey goatee and glasses. We greeted with a handshake. He released and said, "It's very nice to meet you, Andrew."

"Nice to meet you too, Mr. Conrad."

"Feel free to call me Ken."

I sat down. Ken had a refined calmness about him and seemed very wise and kind.

After a few minutes of small talk to get acquainted Ken wasted no time and began. He mentioned that Robert was a good lawyer and that he had known him for years and assured me that I would be just fine. He mentioned that Robert served to represent me in a series of charges, and the charges that he named included a count of Class C Burglary, Class E Theft by Unauthorized Taking, and Class E Criminal Trespass. These were brought forth from events that had taken place earlier that year in the Maine Mall in South Portland. After this he said that his role in the case was designed to assist a finder of fact. The meeting smoothly commenced, and Ken started with the basics. He wanted to know more about me and my family.

It was tough to decide where to start but everything that starts has a beginning. And what came next was a loose description of the typical qualities and activities of a suburban family. We went on road trips annually, skied regularly, watched tv, played pool, argued, fought, got along, the usual. Going to the beach or the lake was my favorite and it was a top priority to go often. The waves, the sand, the sun, the fun, all of it was marvelous.

But then unexpectedly and almost at once the tide took a turn in the wrong direction. I believe that it started when I was eleven years old, I told Ken, and my brother got sick. It happened over many years and these affairs hardly concerned me. I was too young, and like many adolescents and siblings, selfish. That was a dismally eventful period of time and an entire book could be written about it. But during its course I had paid it little attention and avoided the drama without a genuine concern. Looking back I can see that this was my attempt at protecting myself from its harsh reality. You're only young once and there is no good reason to grow up fast. Yet sometimes it's inevitable. Times were good before they were bad but sometimes all that you can remember is everything bad. It's a battle with the subconscious and its defense mechanisms.

I remembered one time when he was terribly distressed, I told Ken, paranoid for some reason and we were the only two home. I was downstairs in The Basement watching *Cops* on the tv when the door suddenly opened and he stomped down the stairs—*bohm bohm bohm bohm*—and I thought that the stairs might collapse under the nasty noise of his tramp. And then he reached the bottom of the staircase and turned the corner and looked at me and had my attention. He was breathing heavily like a person hyperventilating, while time momentarily stood still, probably because he hadn't said anything and neither had I. At that age in those days I was the least concerned—mostly I was confused and frustrated. I thought, *Hey, broge! What is the meaning of this?* And he just stood there vexed and cold like a war statue and after a moment of dreadful stillness he turned around and scaled the stairs hurriedly. I sat unmoving on the couch, eyes squinted, brows furrowed, wondering what it was that had just happened and then insouciantly got up and went upstairs to check on the situation. His head rested on his forearms and he sat slouched over the kitchen table, panting for air still. He looked up, and like I said he was very distressed about something. Whatever it was I soon found out, and coolly I told him, "No… Calm down, man. Relax… Breathe… You got this…"

But it took time to settle his nerves, and a lot of consolatory talk, and his flat eyes gave me goosebumps. After all, he had told me to shoot him.

I told Ken that some people will face at least a spell of misery at some point in their lifetime and you figure out a way to handle it. I have yet to find the secret but it starts with being there when no one else is, and I must have been mature for my age to control and ease the trouble instinctively. I was twelve, and there were a number of other instances that were dreary and rainy and all of which made me grow up fast but which later came back to help. Now that I'm facing troubles of my own it's clear how to handle all of them, navigating the rough passage of this ordeal afloat, calm and still like water.

Still water runs deep and flows easily like clouds floating in the sky. Where there are no concerns. A life without concerns won't be very serious, and I didn't take it very seriously; mostly I liked to joke, laugh and play even through all the rainy days. It needs to rain for life to grow; if not, what does manage to grow will probably be dry and flat. Learning to dance in the rain is one of the greatest skills to develop. And it can be fun.

Ken had a surprised look in his eyes as if my family's affairs had been unexpected, and he also seemed eagerly interested to learn more about them. But we stayed on course and he followed up with all sorts of questions, starting with my injuries prior to what had happened in January.

"I've been scathed pretty bad over the years," I said. "I tore my ACL and meniscus. Separated my shoulder. Broke a finger. Broke a toe. Knocked a tooth out. Four or five times. The same one. And probably more. But I'm all good now, somehow."

"You're resilient," said Ken, and then he segued into my arrest history.

"I'm not proud of it," I told him. "I've been arrested three times total. Two times prior to the Macy's incident."

"What was the first arrest for?"

"When I was seventeen I was arrested for an OUI. School had been in session for three days and a group of friends and I were celebrating the end of the summer. We had a little party at the beach and we all hit on beer bottles by the fire. I sipped of course since I had to drive, and from what I remember I only had one or two beers but I still enjoyed the young night, the conversations, the people, the sand, sound of the waves, stars in the sky, everything. I can go on and on about all of the little hidden joys in any given situation, the things that you wouldn't expect to please but rightly do. See, I had a hunch, and there was a feeling in the air, and this same feeling sat in the pit of my stomach, that some sort of trouble was going to happen. Something bad and unfortunate. It was just like the feeling that I felt in the hours leading up to my near-death experience.

"All feelings are highly memorable, and physical feelings are probably remembered the most. Have you ever heard of the phantom limb sensation? It's a strange example, but many people missing a limb feel as though it is still attached, and they even feel

155

pain where there is nothing. This feeling that I had felt before that eventful night is sort of like that. And there's no projected memory of it. It's still lost somewhere in my mind. All that's there is the feeling that something bad and terrible was bound to happen, and I can still feel that I felt it. It was something more than instinctual and that feeling comes back occasionally, and it makes me shiver.

"Now to get back on track. The night of the OUI was a good one, but my hunch was right, and later when I left the party—a few cops had been staking it out and one of them followed me from the parking lot and through the town and got me. I blew a very low BAC—I don't remember the exact number but it was low—and because I wasn't twenty-one years old I was obviously arrested. It was a juvenile offense and the charge was dismissed after I had to jump through some hoops."

Ken had been busy writing notes on his clipboard, and he still was!

"I'll try not to go off on tangents anymore," I said.

"No, that was quite all right—interesting, interesting. What was the second arrest for?"

"Well that one was also quite unfortunate in my opinion. My roommate and I were arrested at UNH for possession of drugs when we were caught in the woods with only a pinch of cannabis in each of our backpacks. I didn't know how illegal cannabis was in the state of New Hampshire at the time—I didn't know their laws. It was only my third week of being there. And I was arrested. Just for having a few crumbs of cannabis on my person. It was very frustrating to say the least, and why that was an arrestable offence I never understood."

Ken said, "Each state has the liberty to govern itself, and many laws are passed to protect other laws and liberties. Usually they're agenda-based, and that's what happens when man takes the sole responsibility of running a society. Somebody has to do this. The criminalization of marijuana may have been in place to protect their liberal gun laws. But to me it's very odd in a way, every one of its bordering states decriminalized marijuana, and I expect that in those states it will soon be legal at the recreational level."

"But that won't help me," I said.

"No, but it might prevent a similar encounter from happening again. It's not always about you—but what's best and fair for the people."

"That's right."

"So what happened with the case?" Ken asked.

"Got dismissed," I said. "I had to do community service at a jail, stay out of trouble, that was about it."

Ken wrote a final thought on his clipboard, and then he looked up. "Now let's get into the arrest at Macy's. You said that it was a prank?"

"Yes."

"It wasn't for financial gain."

"No. It was a prank to stay in the mall overnight, and I know that sounds pretty stupid, because that's exactly what it was. The whole situation."

"How did you get inside of Macy's?"

"I walked right through the main entrance about thirty minutes before the store had closed. I went up the escalator and went to the bathroom and waited in a stall for a long while until I finally ventured out."

"Did a janitor ever go into the bathroom?"

"No. I was actually very surprised about that."

"What would you have done if a janitor *did* walk in?"

"Probably pretend to be asleep on the toilet."

Ken raised an eyebrow and subtly grinned. "That would have been quite the encounter."

"Yeah…" I shook my head.

"That wasn't all."

"No. Then I left the bathroom and wandered around the store for a few minutes. Upstairs first and then downstairs. I tried to get inside the mall but everything was gated off. And shortly after that I went back upstairs to the bathroom deeply regretting the choice that I had made."

I held off for a moment and allowed Ken to finish the thought in his notes and imagined what it might have been. *Choices make up the basis of life. Every day we choose to get up or not.*

Ken looked up. "You had a set of the store keys with you. How did you get those?"

"You're right. The second, and also the last time that I left the bathroom I turned the corner and walked by a desk and noticed the keys on it. I stopped, and even though the lights in the store were off and the store was mostly dark, I still noticed them. And I grabbed them, and then I went to the escalator to go down to the first floor. To open the gate and get inside the mall. But…"

"Go on," said Ken. "Don't mind my writing. I'm listening."

"But," I said. "As I was walking down the escalator the lights on the first floor turned on…"

"Well. You likely tripped the alarm much earlier—probably as soon as you walked out of the bathroom the first time. There are sensors all throughout the store."

"Yeah, I know. But that never occurred to me—just that the alarms were only on the doors. Pretty foolish, huh."

Ken casually shrugged. "I've seen and heard it all. Foolish is a man robbing his own store for insurance money and then getting caught on camera. You're smart, but this was not."

"No, it was not."

"So you went to the escalator and…"

"The lights turned on. And my heart raced, and my stomach dropped, and I slowly walked down the escalator, cautiously on my toes, looking around for any movement, any people, any cops or security or anything. But there was nothing, and I crept further down the escalator—now a bit curious even—and then at the bottom I peeked around the corner opposite me and I saw my life flash. This had happened only one other time on a plane when it seemed like we might go down. Both times I was fine, but it was the canine that shocked me this time. I saw one dog and maybe seven or eight cops at the other end of the store, by the other entrance, and making their way in my direction, fast. And I pretty much knew then that I was doomed. Yet thinking that it was a good idea I dove on the floor behind a service desk, and on the desk was a small bag that I had knocked off and it landed on the floor beside my feet. There I was, laid out on my stomach, waiting, regretting, and then the next minute I was being handcuffed and led out back to the cruiser behind the store. And it wasn't even until a few hours later when they told me the charges in the holding cell in jail."

And I mentioned to Ken that in the holding cell an officer of the law had told me that I was being charged with criminal trespass, which I understood; unauthorized theft, because of the bag that had fallen on the floor beside my feet, and inside were a handful of trinkets, key chains and clearance jewelry; and burglary, because it looked like I had intent, with a set of keys next to me, a hat on my head, the time of night, the whole situation. And when the officer flatly told me that I was being charged with a felony I trembled and practically collapsed, the only good man in that cell behind bars, partially drained from the loss of virtue.

Ken continued to listen and write in his notes. He interjected only when my recount of the event needed to be steered elsewhere, and after every detail had been mined from my memory, I told him about my plan for the future with engineering, and my enjoyment of meditating and reading, writing and wellness, water and food. Ken understood that the event at Macy's does not represent me as a person, nor at that time as a naive adolescent. Normally I showed better judgement but growing up fast can lead to poor decisions when you're still young. The best thing to do is to learn from them, but even if you do, sooner or later they can and will have wretched consequences regardless.

"I just hope that the case doesn't go awry," I told Ken.

"You'll be fine," he said. "I'll tell you how it'll play out in court. There are two possible scenarios…"

And Ken told me both scenarios and we each agreed that the best idea would be to strike a deal early and forego my right to a trial.

"Going to trial would be risky," said Ken. "Yes, there sure is a chance that you could get off scot-free. But there's also a chance that you could be found guilty of some or all charges and have to face the consequences. Now we were all eighteen nineteen years old once. Not everyone pulls off immature antics like this, but you know that no one is perfect, and I would really dislike seeing you get undeservedly punished."

"I agree with you about going to trial," I said. "It would be best to avoid it. I can see myself right now choking at the stand, and it makes me nervous just thinking about it. But as far as a punishment goes, the way I see it, it's already happened."

"What do you mean?"

"Well I've suffered plenty after the arrest at Macy's."

"Because of the assault? Oh, let's talk about that. You indirectly mentioned it earlier. The whole ordeal sounded terrible back when Robert briefed me on it."

"It certainly was," I said. "And very bizarre."

"So it happened just a week after the Macy's incident—where you were pushed from a trestle and fell some fifty feet onto ice?"

"Pushed or dropped. And I know that it sounds so grim to say out loud, but yes."

"It's horrible indeed. My colleagues and I have concurred that this was a malevolent assault."

"Look, I have these scars on my knuckles and hands." I stood up and showed the scars to Ken. "And also these on the side of my chest and near my armpit."

Ken cringed and made a note on his clipboard.

"It's disgusting that I'm going through this legal procedure, and yeah I realize that's completely my fault, but I'm going through the system when hardly anything was done after what had happened. They're walking, I'm praying. Where's the justice?"

"Remember earlier how I told you about the sole responsibility of running a society? That's where it is."

"If man runs it—he knows exactly where his interests lie."

"Very good. Now did the state police ever get involved?"

"I don't believe so. The case is still open, I know that much, but it seems like they were well aware of the arrest, and because it had happened just a week earlier they did their job—well, maybe half-assed. They put less effort into the investigation than what should have gone in. They didn't have many clues or leads or information to follow I was told. No surveillance, witnesses, forensics, nothing. And it's too late now to investigate seriously— too much time has already passed. Any valuable forensics— washed away and gone."

Ken, writing a note on his clipboard, added, "Every day that passes after a violent crime is committed the chances of solving it drastically decrease."

"That's a good point."

"Afterward, how was the support within your community?"

"Well." I didn't particularly like having to answer this kind of question. "I hardly saw any myself. In the coma I dreamt of my friend's dad giving kind words of support, but after that hardly any. A few friends visited over spring break but it felt sort of strange, like they were put up to it, and since then only one has made some sort of effort to occasionally visit. But as far as support goes, none really. To me it seemed like hardly anyone cared, and whenever I ran into a familiar face around town I was blatantly given the cold shoulder. I can only imagine what was said behind my back…"

It felt very uncomfortable whenever I saw people around town, like there was some sort of palpable tension in the air, something disgusting and horribly uninviting, some type of cold judgement flooded their mind and by not broaching the subject it left *my* mind reeling over what it might be, and it crushed my spirit after each time that this happened and then soon I deliberately began to avoid them. A man can only take so much. So in a sense, I was almost forced to stay at home and there I chose to workout, read, write, dream, and plan. Ken asked if I had always enjoyed reading and writing and I told him that honestly, hardly. Circumstance sort of forced them into my life and I'm very lucky right now that I'm still able to do both.

Ken sat tapping the tip of his pen into his palm. "Well, why do you think that is—with your community?"

I shrugged. "Maybe people saw the arrest after hearing about what had happened to me, but whatever the case might be, it all evolves around assumption. People talked amongst themselves but never once to me, and that probably surprised me most. Come to think of it, I was always very kind and respectful to everyone in or outside of the community—all around where I grew up—and also very generous to friends and really anyone, so besides assumption, I can't think of why else that is."

"And people at college?"

"Probably—well, basically it's the same deal. I just haven't seen any of them since. It's pretty much the same deal for everyone that had once been in my life. So that's where I'm coming from."

"How does that make you feel?"

I shrugged again. "Sure it's too bad, and yeah it hurt, but after facing more than enough affliction I don't really care. Ignorance in people isn't worth a given damn."

"That's good. Speak your mind and let it out. It's not good to bottle anything in."

"That's right."

"Are you still living in the same community?"

"In the one that you asked about, yeah. But it's better to live where you're respected than where you're condemned."

"Well you're going off to a new college soon. That should be a positive change."

"I hope so." And then maybe out of resentment I diverted the topic. "But I have to admit that after everything had happened, and after I finally got home and could clearly introspect, I've become far far more spiritual."

"Go on," said Ken. "I'm a spiritual person myself. I regularly attend retreats and meetings."

Ken also mentioned that he was a Buddhist and after this our conversation flourished a bit too much.

"I believe that it all has to do with karma," I said. "And a God of some sort, so to say. And unbelievably bad luck—that was also mixed with very good luck."

I said that there might not be anything in the world as real as karma. Sometimes she gets you and sometimes she spares you. For me, both happened and it was all undeserved. But she could not help the wicked and wild things which had occurred, only that some sort of misfortune was bound to happen by chance. It was unreasonably brutal and the undue pain was utterly unjustified, but just about a week earlier I did commit a crime, and occasionally I wondered if everything that had happened had something to do with karma and a godlike power, and that somehow the fatuous crime made the ordeal justifiable.

It was very rare for me to sit down and think about the ordeal as a whole, or what my life might be like if it had never happened, or if some part of it had happened differently, but every once in a blue moon if I sat and thought clearly, it seemed like *They*—karma and a godlike power—were part of the inner workings that caused it all to happen.

In a way, thoughts have a snowball effect and accumulate and expand as each idea rolls on to the next and the stream proceeds. Usually they're orderless, but when I thought about the ordeal it was best to start from the beginning. Everything that starts has to have a beginning. I was still at my family's house in Maine until the day of the ordeal. The plan was to go back to UNH on Sunday, but then at the last minute I had changed my mind and went back on Saturday instead. It was the feeling in the air that something wasn't right, and knowing that one more day here is one less day there, that's what might have changed my mind to go back a day early, and the rest was swayed from karma and God knows what else.

I hadn't done much of anything all day, but that night a couple of friends from Maine came to my apartment almost unexpectedly at UNH—at around one in the morning I later learned—and they insisted that I go to another friend's apartment across campus with them. I didn't want to, but I did. There was a foreboding feeling in the air, a deep feeling of apprehension and a stagnant shade of hot doubt, and it churned firmly in my gut and this I could remember, but despite my efforts I couldn't muster up any sort of perceivable memory. Was there more to it, probably, but based on what I knew I wondered if *They* had led those so-called friends to my apartment, somehow almost astrally, and then ultimately made me leave. There was no other sensible reason to go across campus that late.

163

Yet I went, and I can't recall any memories of being there, or what time I had left, or what had happened after, but I wondered if *They* had led me to the wrong place at the wrong time on my walk home that night, not randomly but fatedly, causing something like synchronicity to occur. Maybe it was just an accident, but I didn't know, and I didn't really care to find out either. It's one of those things that might be best left unknown.

And the same goes for the anonymous caller who had tipped the police. Whoever it was, they were wise to remain anonymous. But *if* they hadn't phoned law enforcement about my whereabouts and my wretched condition, I likely would have frozen there on the ice, preserved and crushed.

And then *if* the first responders hadn't responded fast enough, and *if* they hadn't all been consciously careful, and *if* I hadn't been brought to a local hospital where I was revived and saved and then swiftly transferred to Mass General, I'd probably be back in school riding the short bus. Imagine that—if I was in fact back in school! The doctors were unsure if I'd walk or talk or function well again, and they were doubtful of my future endeavors, my ability to learn, read and even write, and in their eyes I might have been reduced to a breathing cadaver, forever inept and incompetent. But oh, how the tables have turned! And it all started with their help! Fortunately I received the best care in one of the best hospitals in the world, and possibly the greatest surgeon alive performed the orthopedic surgery, and some of the most advanced technology and modern medicine were being used. It's incredible what doctors can fix and what convalescent bodies can overcome. But the outcome could have easily been a lot worse *if* one thing went wrong or happened differently. Or even, *if* it didn't happen at all.

Playing a game of *ifs* will never help the player, I mentioned to Ken. It won't make the situation better or alter anything at all. But occasionally in life some things happen that can't be explained in a definitive or simple way, so it makes sense to mull over a series of *ifs*. Early on in my days at Spaulding it did for me, and it made sense to do this when a lot of circumstances led me to the wrong place at the wrong time when I never should have been there. And when the margin of error was so small yet somehow no mistakes were made.

"I don't believe that this was a coincidence," I told Ken. "And what I mean is, all of this or anything else."

Most coincidences in my opinion seem to happen for a reason. They seem to be caused by a greater power or energy, something like synchronicity, and it seemed as though what had happened that night and the days that immediately followed was a result of these powers and energies. Whoever it was, *They* subjected me to a major wakeup call, offered a test and I passed it. I was mostly a good kid, but it's the most blest who get tested, and what happened was close to a divine intervention.

Ken sat thoughtfully in his chair as the sun peeked through the windows and shades and filled the room with a golden glow. Like some sort of ethereal space. I felt slightly enlightened, and the only other time that this had happened was in the coma with Mister P. Instances like this are delightful and they're best to be appreciated and absorbed when they can. Many come close but when they're real they're rare. That's when you know that they're the one.

"This room has a wonderfully brilliant natural light," I said.

Ken smiled sagely. "That's why I chose this office space. And it's probably why I've stayed here after all this time."

"Why not," I said.

"Well it's hard to change what you've gotten used to. Plus, it's expensive to move."

"You're right about the latter."

Ken looked at his watch.

"I didn't mean to change topics," I said. "I can get back on track and keep going…"

But the ordeal had already been talked about ad nauseam and truly I'd rather not. When something bad happens it's always talked about, speculated, and you can only hope to never be the subject of speculation. But if it happens that means that two bad things have happened to you, and there are more or less only two ways to respond—learn from it and make an educated change or let the badness steer you into a downward spiral and watch it win.

165

There are two sides to everything, and now I like to read and meditate—a lot. I care about my health, workout and eat well. And I like to separate what I understand from what I preconceive. It's a mindful quality but it's also very uncommon to see in the world today. I try to see something for whatever it is, based on understanding, when most people see whatever is expected, based on assumption. This is not new, and it's doubtful to change.

I told Ken that this is a cliché expression to use, but it's also a true one. You never know how much you have until it's all nearly taken away. Think about it—the ability to walk and talk, breathe and eat, sit and live, and above all—to ruin this syllabic sequence—defecate and copulate. These basic needs and many more were on a thin line but for some reason the gods thankfully, and possibly rationally, spared them.

Ken took off his glasses and set them on his clipboard. In Ken's notes he wrote that I was a young man with a keen awareness of the role of fate in life, and he said that the assault and fall from the trestle was in no way related to the events at Macy's. And it was no coincidence either. All along it had become clear: the power of fate, chance, and luck.

We continued to talk for another ten minutes, and then as if a muted alarm went off the meeting suddenly ended. So fast. Four hours altogether. And during its final minutes I told Ken that I am truly sorry for the events at Macy's, and that this was an unusually asinine choice to make that will never happen again. Ken said that choices in life can have decidedly negative consequences no matter the motivation for the action. Life will be what you let it be. It is; it will always be.

On my way out I went up to Ken to shake his hand, but he said no and offered a very big bear hug instead. That, I didn't expect. Always expect the unexpected. I parted and left Ken's office, the room still fully filled with golden afternoon sunlight, thinking that he was kind, wise, and dignified throughout the entire meeting. I went home a changed person.

Chapter 25

It was a murder, and we approached the Piscataqua River Bridge and the electric chill bombarding my soul shocked my bowels bone cold. The air was warm and in the sky the sun was hot. For now the balance was perfectly stable.

We drove under the green arch and off to the right on the surface of the water thousands of whitecaps winked and bobbed in the wind at once. On either side of the river stood hundreds of happy trees and in the wind they shook and bent and dotted the river along its banks that snaked its way into the continent. Off in the distance and down a winding tributary that dreary picture was taken six months earlier. Everything looks better in the summer.

"It's such a nice day," said my mother.

"It'll be a hot one," my father replied.

By the end of the day I seriously hoped to be cleared for high-impact activities. What a long time coming! I had come a long way in the past six months, that is true. From the dark cloak of death straight to an operating table, reading books in bed to gaining fifty pounds on accident, and hiking mountains in Maine to running the trails at Knight's Pond. Just so long as Doctor Trey gave me the go ahead to run. He was a class act surgeon; I had no doubts.

Hiking was and will forever be pleasant, but after repeatedly hiking the same trails day in and day out it gradually began to lose its spark. Running on the other hand—which I planned to start tomorrow as long as Doctor Trey cleared me today—I believed would refuel the fire. I had all but fully stopped the ketogenic diet. I ate well when I could: frozen fruits, vegetables, chicken, hummus, eggs, and an occasional banh mi. For dessert I ate frozen berries out of a bowl with a spoon like ice cream, and it was delicious! The scale had nearly stabilized, my bodyweight slowly plateaued, but it was nothing that new sweat couldn't fix.

We arrived at Mass General well ahead of schedule and I walked through the revolving doors and into the lobby and stepped on the cracks and breaks in the tiles with the arches of my feet. I went up the stairs and crossed the skywalk and waited by the elevators for one to open.

We rode up to the fourth floor with a group of people and in the air lingered a smell like Portland in the morning at low tide. I checked in for X-rays, and after sitting for a few minutes in the waiting room a nurse entered and called my name. I insouciantly stood and walked up to her. "Come right this way," she said.

She was a young nurse and she wore her hair up in a bun and held it together with a pencil. She merrily led the way to the imaging room, and then we walked through the doorway and blithely she said, "Go lay down on the table. I'll be right over."

That I did, and the nurse walked into a small office to the right that was separated from the room by glass windows. Inside stood another nurse, apparently her friend. Arching down above me like the arm of a robot was a highly sophisticated camera. One day AI will rule the world and we will forever relax and do as we please; they will take over the unnatural machine that we have built and work for us. That is the unbounded power of technology. And then a lead apron was gently draped over my midsection and put an end to those random thoughts.

"Well hello," I said. "That's cold."

"Sorry!" the nurse said. "I forgot to remind you."

I groaned, "Mmmm."

She reached down and lightly patted the apron below my waist, either as an apology or out of affection, and I felt her hand through the lead like soft fingers touching bare skin and pardon me, I got fairly excited. But the superfluous embarrassment quickly brought things back to normal, effectively repressed. This fervid feeling in the first place was rightly inflated by my mind for obvious reasons. I had been celibate for the entire recovery, distracted and empty for all six months but my mind had never felt clearer. My mind was essentially free, and this short tale of affection swiftly aroused some wonderful memories of long-forgotten evenings.

The nurse wagged her tail back to the office and went inside to take the pictures. She said something to the other nurse and then she grinned and with her hands made some sort of measurement, her rosy fingers spread broadly apart. She walked out of the office. "That wasn't so bad, was it?"

"No, it was all right."

She smiled and then lifted the apron and hung it on a hanger on the far wall. "Do you know where you're going next?"

"Yeah, I have a meeting with the surgeon."

"Is it in trauma? I bet it gets busy over there."

"Oh yeah. Last time it was brutal!"

"The rest of my day should be pretty light."

"That's good. Have a glass of wine when you get home."

"Yes, absolutely!"

"Unfortunately I have to drive back to Maine."

"Bummer. Well fortunately I think that your X-rays went really well."

"How'd they look?"

"Oh, I just take the pictures. It was just a feeling that I had."

"Good enough for me. Trust your feeling when you have one."

"My feeling—okay!"

I walked toward the door.

"It was nice to meet you," she said. "See ya."

"Later!"

I walked off with a bittersweet feeling that you might get after connecting with someone but knowing that you probably won't get to see them again. I went down to the orthopedic trauma center on the second floor and checked in at the service desk. The entire waiting room was completely filled with concerned patients. I was lucky enough to find an open seat, but some people that came in a bit later had to stand. Maybe the doctors were behind schedule or maybe the trauma center was routinely crowded. The wait was in fact as bad as it was the first time. I sat unmoved in the chair for three hours, and at one point a man got up and expressed his frustration to a nurse at the desk. He said that his father was in desperate need of medical attention, and she replied that he would have to wait like everyone else. "But my father's a veteran," he said. "Is this how you treat veterans?"

"It's the same for everyone, sir. No special treatments. We don't believe in nepotism."

He seemed upset and walked back to his father who sat stiffly in a wheelchair, noticeably uncomfortable. Thinking back to the wheelchair days, I felt his pain but from a different angle. That is, a generational angle. Beads of sweat covered the old man's face and his son steered him in the wheelchair and pushed toward the door.

"Thank you for your service!" my mother said as they rolled by. Her father Giancarlo, but to me Papa, had fought in World War II. He had been my barber until he turned ninety years old, and he never took a break—ever. He had a tremendous laugh and a pocket full of cash—always.

At last my name was called and I walked down the hall beside the nurse. She showed me into a room and I sat and waited for fifty minutes before a doctor finally entered. It was William. "Hello," he said.

"Hi," said my mother.

"How's it going," I said.

"Good. I had the chance to briefly look over your X-rays with Doctor Trey. To my knowledge you're doing great."

"That's good to hear. Is Doctor Trey coming in today?"

"Yes, he'll be here shortly."

"Okay."

"So do you know what happened?" William asked.

"How all of this happened?"

"Yes."

"Well. It was a—an assault. That's all I know."

"Do you have any memory of it?"

"No, not yet."

William took a deep breath and sighed. "I'll go find Doctor Trey and tell him that you've all been waiting."

He left the room, and then my mother said, "Hopefully he gets here soon."

"Yeah, I have to get back home."

"He'll be here soon," said my father. "See—hear that? I think someone's right outside of the door."

He was right. Doctor Trey opened the door and entered the room with William.

"Hello Andrew," the surgeon said and then sat on the table to my left. "Mom. Dad," he continued. "How is everyone?"

My parents replied, "Good!"

And I said, "Great."

"Have you had any problems, troubles?"

"No, it feels better than ever."

"That's wonderful," said Doctor Trey. "A surgeon loves to hear that."

"It's been fully healed for a while now."

"Well let's take a look at the x-rays from imaging."

On his laptop Doctor Trey opened a file that displayed dozens of pictures from nearly every possible angle. I thought, *Technology is really something.*

"So the fractures have completely healed," the veteran said as he quickly switched from image to image. And then he stopped and studied the screen intently. "How's your walk?" he asked.

"What?"

"How does it feel when you walk?"

"It feels fine," I said.

"Have you been limping at all?"

"No. No limp, nothing hurts."

"It wouldn't hurt. But here, see this?" Doctor Trey circled with the mouse cursor up and around a bright white bone that vaguely resembled an eye socket. "Your right pubic bone has healed slightly higher than your left. It's possible that it happened from excessive force being exerted on your legs. The same amount of force given off goes back. You didn't try any high-impact activities, did you?"

"No," I said, wiggling my toes.

"Do you see that?"

"Yeah, I see what you're talking about."

"You see, it's marginally displaced."

"What does that mean?"

"It means that your left leg is longer than your right. Just *barely*, but enough for me to notice."

"Uh huh."

"Most people would limp. You said that you don't limp at all?"

"No, haven't noticed a thing.

"Well that's good news for you. That means you can ease back into high-impact activities as soon as you'd like. Unless…"

"No unless," I said. "I've waited long enough. I'm getting right back into it."

"*Ease* back into it, Andrew. Ease."

"I've been ready for weeks."

"Well. You're only six months out."

"So does that mean he's cleared?" My mother asked.

"He's cleared to do anything." Doctor Trey looked at his watch and stood up. "You've successfully graduated from Mass General." He laughed. "Congratulations."

"Thanks," I said, and shortly after this we all walked out of the room. William and Doctor Trey went one way, I went the other.

"I bet that's a good feeling," said my mother.

"Yeah."

"No more coming back to the hospital!"

"And no more waiting in those waiting rooms!"

"I'm running tomorrow," I said.

"Oh, be careful," said my mother. "Please ease back into it."

Said like the last words before walking out of those doors for the last time.

Chapter 26

The next day I did as I said and went for a run at Knight's Pond. All along each trail were little stones painted pink or red or orange that were not there before. It could have been that I just hadn't noticed them and that you don't see what you don't look for. After I spotted the first stone I spotted many others, and on the face of each one there was a tidbit of advice written in sharpie. One said, "Love yourself," but I knew better than to set my heart on itself. And another said, "Never stop yourself," but like I've said before, the trails were mostly uphill, notably tortuous, and the pain was torturous. At times it was so bad that I had to stop and laugh. My legs were painfully out of shape. Maybe this harshness came from the fact that I had wisely chosen not to ease back into running; I went straight back into it, no delay, no dogging it. My preferred method.

The first run was very hard but after that they gradually became easy. Strangely enough, what pushed me most was my imagination. In these woods I was not in Maine but instead running through a merciless jungle in southern Africa, or as the locals call it, the bush. Behind me or that tree or around a bend in the trail stood dressed in black a figment of my imagination. The bush will keep you on your toes. Here in Maine though, there was nothing, but the idea that there was something sparked a fire within my psyche, and what kept me and the fire going through the ache and pain was selected music. Soon I ran the entire loop nonstop.

I have to stop and thank a large list of artists for helping me achieve this ridiculous feat. Namely, The Notorious BIG, Mobb Deep, Outkast, Kendrick, Pac, and Pun—to name a handful and one. *The Infamous, ATLiens, Capital Punishment, To Pimp A Butterfly,*

Ready to Die, Me Against The World—these albums were all packed full of great records. I had always looked up to these hip-hop artists and of course there were many others. They gave strength when no one else gave it and support when no one else offered it. But most of this credit and admiration deservedly goes to Nas. See, he was like a God to me who now hovers closer to a hero. He can tell a mean story with precision in a song and that is very hard to do—and with such finesse and emotion! No wonder his words kept me going! In the early days it was he who I had learned my vocabulary from. Imagine hearing every one of his records again for the first time. But every record in his oeuvre is much more than the surface and each time they're listened to anew—with plenty of space and time between each play—they seem to sound better than what had preceded it. As time goes on and the quality of musical output declines, his work appreciates. It's sort of like aging wine, timeless art. By and large, during this recovery he and his work were perfect greatness and highly contagious to those battling with greatness.

I think now is a good time to mention it. I'm not musically out of date or old school; I just love hip hop. The problem was, I felt dumber and duller the more that I listened to some hip hop artists of today, and you only have one mind, and one brain, and that one organ is a terrible system to waste.

In any case, for this run the album of choice was *The Lost Tapes*.

I pulled into the dirt lot and parked and stepped out into the high sun of early August. Cicadas hummed and birds chirped and busy critters buzzed about from plant to plant and foraged for anything sweet. I started down the entrance trail and soon began to stretch with leg kicks, and then after about ten steps I wondered why I had even begun. Very quickly I felt like a fool and stopped.

Further down the trail, there between the trees lay sparkling like a sapphire the water of Knight's Pond. Peace flooded my soul. I walked across the land bridge and lodged an earbud into each ear. Out of routine at the time the first song played was "Victory," and what a great song to run to! I pressed play and

174

then darted off and into the forest. The trail wound around trees of all shapes and sizes and followed the pond into a dense and dark woodland. Around every tree or twist in the trail my mind played a silly trick. Standing there in black was something strange. Was it a Bushman, William, an alien? It wasn't so. I hardly noticed anything, and I ran along the trail relentlessly.

I jumped over a mound of roots and landed and dodged a stray log. A fallen tree in the middle of the trail made for a perfect hurdle, and further along and off to the side I juked around a grounded tree and spun around another. The humid heat sat still in the air, and with every stride and step beads of sweat slowly dribbled into and around my eyes. I wiped away the blur and there they were, walking along the trail toward me, two men and a dog on a leash. About a hundred feet away I squinted and saw their badges, and then they stopped talking and I noticed this and slowed down and removed an earbud. Sniffing the ground beside them was a happy German Shepherd, Max. We approached each other on the trail.

"How's it going?" one officer of the law asked.

"Good," I said all short on breath.

"Nice day isn't it?"

"It's great."

"Stay safe."

"Yessir."

Max said hello and sniffed my legs and wagged his tail back and forth.

"Hey, Max."

"*Woof?*"

The other police officer yanked Max's leash and they all walked off and I ran on.

On the brow of Bruce Hill I slowed down and walked along the pine needled forest floor. I was covered with sweat and panted for air like a wasted free diver. Further ahead the trail led to a dead end. All around stood enormous pine trees that shaded this junction of four trails and their warm smell of pinene made it hard not to feel incredible. This was not the feeling that you get on the top of a mountain, but it was close. Six months earlier while lying in a bed of pain in the ICU, did I expect to run up and down the wooded trails on this hill six months later? So soon and so desperately mind and body heal. I expected it to happen sooner, but it's better late than never.

I jogged over to the trail that led a perilous straight shot down to the pond and then I took off. What momentum! The steepness shoots you wildly down the trail and the hardest part was having to keep up. My only problem was my legs; every kink and cramp from half a year of indolence needed to be worked out. It wasn't Forrest Gump flying down the trail; I was. From top to bottom there were rocks and roots and scattered pools of sludge that had to be dodged or plowed through. I slipped, split, staggered and hastily pressed on. Running this fast down a hill you might look like some sort of untamed wildebeest, but this frenzy lasted at most a minute or two, and then between tree trunks and leaves and branches appeared the crystal blue pond. I slowed down and caught my breath and looked above. The trees shook lightly in the breeze and a small squirrel scurried from branch to branch across its thick canopy. The little creature stopped, ate a nut, kept going.

Back at the land bridge I myself stopped and looked out over the water and at the trees on either side. Above the treetops lay a cloudless sky and a very hot and naturally bright sun. Not long after the run began I had changed my plan and the album to *Life After Death*, and now I heard the start of a mystical instrumental, the final song on the final album, and then the intro and Diddy's hypnotic voice. I shuddered and thought, *Great timing, great song.*

And then I walked across the land bridge and onto the access trail and looked to the left and my mind recapped a drunken night from the past in the old party shack and I reeled and spat and finally sat and the night turned black and nimbly from the left an ardently lustful girl tiptoed across the room and mounted my lap and after that all went black and the night went on and later that day the word came out straight from the horse's mouth.

The squalid shack that stood just off the trail on the pond's edge was there no more. The authorities had gotten rid of it and then turned Knight's Pond into a nature preserve. At best the shack was an eyesore, and now what remains of it is only in memory.

I walked along the access trail back to the lot and got in my car and drove home. Once there I went straight upstairs and stepped on the scale. It blinked twice and I stood there wondering what the last measurement even was, and then it blinked a third time and I no longer cared. This time it read 175. I thought, *Nice! Thirty down, only ten more to go.*

Chapter 27

After going for a morning run at Knight's Pond on the second Wednesday of the month I drove down to Fort Williams.

As a public park Fort Williams was marvelous, and part of its charm and character came from decades of heavy use when it was operated as an army post. It was built directly on a piece of rugged coastline, bedrock and bluffs, and with views worth one thousand words I'd often go there to enjoy the sun and read and meditate, sitting on the rocks above finely delicate tidal pools looking out at the Atlantic. The waves crashed down on the rocks below and the seawater burst overtop and flooded the pools, and before the tide drained the excess water back out to sea, I wondered what would happen if you were to jump into this harsh and frigid microcosmic waterbody. It wouldn't be so much of a swim as it would be a fight, or in the worst case, unpleasant death. For now I simply laid back on the bedrock and let the sun shine down from the sky above. Nothing could break the tranquility of seclusion in that spot, no thoughts, fixations, preoccupations, vexations, anything. And in that case, this quick escape properly numbed my mind from the upcoming court date that lay just around the corner at the end of the month. That dreaded day.

Along with incredible views, Fort Williams also has a famous lighthouse called Portland Head Light, and this is a very popular tourist attraction. It stands red, white and resolute atop a mound of bedrock on the eastern edge of America. And for some reason, every single tourist seemed to crowd its vicinity just as a horde of flies will instinctively flock to a fresh pile of shit. I was wise to stay away from the crowds and lolled back in my spot instead, a flat slab of rock on the outskirts overlooking the Atlantic. It was the most perfect spot for reading and meditating.

But I didn't go to The Fort to read or meditate this time. I went there to meet an old friend of mine, one of my badass roommates from UNH, and when I got there I saw him standing calmly on the shore, a big man with long hair and tourists all about. I parked my car and walked over to the cool dude. "Hey Sal," I said. He turned around.

"Wussup, brother!"

We dapped and followed through with a hug. Sal and I had lived together freshman year in the dorms on the eighth floor. Three of us had to share a small room but somehow we all made it work. We arrived early on the move-in day and immediately rolled a pearl and shared it in the woods behind the Adams Towers and swapped stories and connected, and it was coincidentally in the same spot where we were arrested for doing the same thing three weeks later. Regardless, Sal was impressed with my cannabis and said that it was the best that he'd ever had, and when we got back to our room he raved about it to our other roommate, Gonzo.

Gonzo was a good man and another badass, and he's the only person who ever apologized to me for any kind of wrongness, and that's the sad part of the story. The word sorry, if it's meant and true, is hardly ever used but when it is it will never be forgotten, just as the scars that were made to deserve an apology will never go away. Any man can play off something as nothing, but it takes a real man to realize and admit when he was in the wrong.

Both Sal and Gonzo were great roommates and for the entire year our dorm was open to anyone. People coming and going all day and night, the door hardly ever locked or closed even, and like I said, we made it work, three dudes in a built-up triple. Sal had his own bunk and Gonzo and I shared the other. He slept on the top bed and I slept on the bottom. Everyone used my bed like it was a couch, and that's when I learned that what you think is yours is not really yours. Be that as it may, Gonzo was still a good bunkmate to have. He was a quiet sleeper, unlike Sal who snored savagely, and we even shared similar dissenting views toward college and saw the truths of it early on. I remember one time in the dining hall Gonzo said, "UNH is a joke. They spent seventeen thousand on a dining room table and no one ever uses it. I bet we're the first ones."

I replied, "All universities just spend and spend and spend. They're like a toilet bowl full of money. Watch it flush right down the drain."

"Yeah but you have to go to college to get a decent job."

"Well it depends how you define a decent job."

"One that pays more money," said Gonzo.

"True, and there's more opportunity. But that's just the system that we live in. It's not catered to who's smart."

"You're screwed."

"Financially most of us are screwed from the start."

"It's always about money."

"Right now it is. But one day it won't be."

Gonzo tilted his head. "What do you mean?"

"First there will probably be a universal basic income. But then someday money won't have the power that it has today."

"Then nothing will be worth anything—there will be no value to anything."

"Exactly. That would help mankind tremendously. Think—no greed, no war, no silent warfare, just peace."

"But how would colleges go on like that?"

"They wouldn't. There would be no value to a college degree. This is the future. Nothing will be the same as it is right now."

"Nothing," said Gonzo.

"The world is changing exponentially fast. And it's funny— the only thing of value that I've gotten from here are a few kind words from my English professor. He said that I'm talented. He said that I could be a writer if I want."

"Hah! You a writer. You're playing."

"I'm not. I like it more than any other homework that I have to do now, and that's basically all it is—homework."

"Here," Gonzo offered. "Have some Zhenka."

"I'll pass. I had an aperitif back in the room."

"Writing—I thought you just wanted the most money."

I felt slightly offended. "No, not at all. Money just seems much more important when you don't have any."

"Big talk."

"As fast as money grows, it shrinks."

"You want to know something?"

"What."

"I heard that if you get hit by a UNH bus they give you a year free of tuition. Now that's a lot of money."

"Yeah," I said. "I heard that from Guac. But I bet if anything else hits you they won't give up a dime."

"No, because they need to buy more tables like this."

"That's right. Hey, look who it is."

And then Sal walked over and sat and joined us for dinner at the seventeen-thousand-dollar table. Soon after this Blevin and Miller arrived, and the meal was marvelous. The food there might have been the best thing that they had to offer. I'm serious, it was exceptional.

Sal was very funny in a Sal kind of way. Many memories come to mind, and I'll describe him more in a minute, but I remember on orientation day from our eighth-floor window to the groups and families down below over and again in his jocular voice he yelled, "We want your daughters!" And these days every now and then I'll remember this scene and the voice he used and on the inside have an excellent laugh.

As a friend and a roommate, Sal was wonderful to have around and we were almost inseparable freshman year. He could sway and be swayed easily, and I remembered one afternoon I told him about someone ripping the fire extinguisher off the wall and spraying its discharge up and down the eighth-floor hallway and leaving the entire stairwell coated with residue. This idea was planted in Sal's mind and clearly resonated with him longer than I had anticipated, and then it finally got to him and he tried it out for himself. Close to midnight on a Sunday he went into the stairwell beside our room and removed the fire extinguisher from its cabinet, and as the alarms rang and sang through the building like sirens he sprayed the extinguisher up and down the stairwell from the eighth floor to the ground floor and then finally went

181

outside and waited with the evacuees behind the building. Sal was a good friend, and I'm a simple person, but back then I revealed my complexion to Sal not as frankly as I try to do now, but instead at intervals. "You're like a riddle," he said. And I replied, "I inspired the last of the real." Sal was in a long-distance relationship throughout all of freshman year. His girlfriend lived richly in Manhattan and certainly enjoyed my Maine medical—that top-shelf cannabis—which Sal spoke very highly of.

And that's why we were here today at Fort Williams. Sal was on vacation in Maine and wanted one thing and one thing only: weed. I told him that I'd get him some, and then we figured out a time to meet at this gorgeous park.

"Here, Sal." I showed him the light bag of green and dropped it in his hand. "Take it and don't let the tourists see. They'll flock to you like gulls."

"*Ooh, look at this.* What strain is it?"

"Conceal it, Sal. Conceal it."

"I gotchu."

"It's Rugburn OG," I said.

"Rugburn OG. I don't think I've ever tried it before."

"OG only, baby. No questions, no exceptions."

Sal laughed. "You're funny."

"I truly never try to be."

"Here—" Sal slipped me a Franklin.

"Come on," I said. "I brought a pearl of it. Let's get away from these tourists."

"Hold on. You know I roll the best pearls."

"I know. But it's too windy today to roll one outside."

"I can roll it in my car."

"Come on, let's go."

We walked down a paved pathway with lush green foliage overhead and to the left in a small wooded area. Crowds of people, families and lone adventurers ambled along the path in front of us. They were all smiles and babble and cackle. *Mooove it!* We made it past them and went up the stairs of the old cement barracks that were practically untouched over the years, but still covered in the same sand and dirt as when they were first built.

Over one hundred years of exposure to Maine's natural elements hardly showed. They had aged very well.

As we climbed the short staircase and crossed the roof of the barracks the view of the ocean opened and sat absolutely sublime as we approached the bedrock. The water was dark blue and grew lighter further out to sea and floating amid the waves below the spume shone like fresh snow. We walked atop the rocks and had to hop over crevices deep enough to fall in to never be seen again. We jumped down a ledge and ducked behind cover.

"You have a lighter?" I said.

"No."

"No?"

"Do you?"

"No."

Sal's face turned sharp and serious.

"I was joking," I said. "I have one."

"Damn," Sal sighed. "I thought we were out of luck."

"How many times has that happened—forgetting a lighter, not having one."

"Too many."

"You know it's happened here," I said. "With my friends Ricky and Sean."

"Oh, I think you've told me about them. How are they?"

"Cover me from the wind."

Sal cupped his hands around the tip of the pearl but the lighter would not ignite.

"Let's turn around," I said.

And that we did and I sparked the lighter and lit the pearl and puffed once, twice, thrice, and then exhaled a cloud of bliss. Then Sal grabbed the spliff and took a hit and coughed. "*Wow!*" he said as he cleared his throat. He spat. "Hey, you remembered how I like spliffs!"

"Adding a little tobacco for this occasion—I thought what the hell."

"What strain is it again?"

"Rugburn OG."

"Yeah… OGs… This strain… Bomb!"

With that, I did not disagree. But all that I really cared about lay directly ahead. Earth is full of well untold sights that cannot be replicated by words or pictures but have to be experienced in the flesh. Whether they're mountains or canyons or jungles or oceans or glaciers or even the flow of water over rocks in a river—that wonderfully zenful experience—they're frequently overlooked and depreciated by trivialities. These wonders are free, and not a lot of what's left in the world is free. Here at The Fort it was a perfect day and the sun sat high in the cloudless sky that off in the distance blended together with the water as one. Add to that the soft breeze and the rich smell of saltwater and the soothing joy from a pearl. It was great.

Below in the water the tide perpetually came in and then pulled away to a swell and slowly came back at the rocks full tilt. White water burst and soared in the air like fireworks. To swim in these waters could be pleasant or it could be rough. On any given day the waves might roll across the water calmly and the next minute plow into the first rock it sees. If you're in it, timing is everything. It can get ugly out there, and for now I enjoyed the show from a ledge on the rocks in a safe spot. Cannabis can heighten all five or six senses and also deepen any conversation.

After a long moment of peace and quiet I flicked the roach and spoke to Sal. I told him that I hadn't seen him in about six or seven months and the time elapsed felt closer to a minute. "How've you been?" I asked.

Sal laughed. "Pretty good."

"What's funny?"

"This strain."

"You're right, it is pretty good. Well how was Colorado?"

"Ah, it was all right. The skiing could've been better."

"You're just saying that to make me feel better."

"Damn," Sal laughed. "Yeah the conditions weren't great. But it was Colorado skiing—it was still pretty sick."

"What was wrong with the conditions?"

"The weather was getting warmer—you know spring skiing—and the snow was straight slush in some parts."

"That's no bueno," I said.

"No, no bueno."

"I am the one."

"What?"

"You know," I said. "That's no fun."

Sal looked in both directions, slightly confused. "What about you?"

"What about me."

"Well, how have you been?"

The sun hung high in the sky and shone on the world glaringly. I said, "Great actually. Sliding, staying low-key. You?"

"Not much," said Sal.

"No?"

"Well I'm landscaping and working out a lot."

"Oh yeah, doing what?"

"Actually, mostly just P90X."

I laughed well. "It's working. You look ripped."

"No—I don't know," said Sal. "It's not working that well."

"Hey, anything is better than nothing."

"What have you been doing?"

"Running, lifting, crunches," I said.

"Well that's working. You look like Dan Bilzerian—minus the beard."

"I never saw that."

"Why haven't you grown it out?"

"The beard?"

"Yeah."

"I have, just unwillingly."

"What do you mean?"

"This past winter I had a thick beard and I wanted to shave it but I wasn't able to."

"I wish I saw that," said Sal.

"No, I looked like an alien."

Sal laughed and he liked that.

"It was a strange time," I said. "I was in the hospital, crippled."

"Yeah, about that…"

"You could have visited."

"Well hey, Gonzo and I were going to but we couldn't get in touch with you."

"Nah, a few girls called the hospital one time and got in touch with me."

"Really?"

"Yeah."

"Well we tried texting and calling you but it wouldn't connect."

"That's because my phone was missing. I didn't have anything in the hospital."

"Nothing?"

"No."

"Dude, hospitals are boring. What did you do the entire time?"

"Not much," I said.

"Rough!"

"All I basically had was the tv, myself, my pain, my thoughts."

"That sounds like fun."

"It was, and it got very old after a short while."

"Well what would you have liked to have the most?"

I nonchalantly shrugged.

"Weed?"

"The most," I said. "Good head."

Sal leaned back and shook with laughter and once again I felt superfluously embarrassed.

"It's all so messed up," he said. "But that was pretty funny."

"Yeah."

"No luck with any of the nurses?"

"No luck, no try."

Sal said, "We should've gone to see you, really. But we didn't know what to expect."

"Yeah." I picked a piece of driftwood off the rock and threw it into the spume. Out to sea it bobbed and slowly drifted away.

"Hey," said Sal. "What are your long-term goals?"

"My what."

"Your long-term goals."

"Who are you, Tony Robbins?"

186

"No," Sal laughed.

"Enjoy the day," I said. "Question tomorrow."

We sat on the rock quietly, and for some reason I wondered how these giant slabs of Earth's crust on either side of us were even formed. Whatever the case may be, why would it matter how, and what does Tony Robinson have to do with it? I didn't know, I was quite buzzed.

I looked over to the right by the lighthouse. The water was deep blue and all along the coastline the bedrock jutted out to greater depths and the waves smashed against these slabs of shale and slate and burst into foam. It was truly a landscape nonreplicable, and after a while we walked back to the parking lot and said goodbye. I grabbed from my car a copy of *Ham on Rye* and then went to my spot on the flat-faced rock and thought about the talk today with Sal. He didn't ask about the arrest, the charges, what little of it showed on Google or what even happened. I figured that he was oblivious to it and thus the subject was left unmentioned. But there was a whisper that I sensed, not a word but an unsaid feeling that he knew and looked passed it. *What is understood need not be discussed.*

Chapter 28

The month of August passed very quickly. It was a humid stretch of time and the days were torrid and I ran on the trails and sweat like a spout. This energy was a result of two upcoming events and both fueled the fire but for very different reasons. One was the kick for college in just a few weeks and the other was the continual drive to alleviate my nerves for court. A good run will relieve any angst, and down I ran the days until the time came for my preliminary hearing. The morning sky was clear and then clouded over on the drive to the courthouse. I walked into the lobby and had second thoughts. About what, about things.

I emptied my pockets and placed the contents into a bin and slid the bin down the belt. I said to the guard, "I have metal screws in my hip from surgery. Just letting you know that the alarms will probably go off."

"Step through," he said.

I walked under the framed detector. Nothing happened. I said, "That's weird."

"Let's try this." The guard waved his metal detector before my face like a magic wand. "Step over here."

Again, nothing. "Those are *some* metal detectors," I said.

He shrugged. "It happens. Maybe they could be titanium screws or something."

"Okay." I grabbed my phone and wallet out of the bin and went upstairs to the second floor and sat on a bench beside my mother. Across the corridor was courtroom seven and that's where today's session would be held.

"Oh no," said my mother.

"What?"

"I hope that Robert gets here soon."

I checked the time. I said, "The doors won't open for another thirty minutes."

"Do I have time to get a coffee?"

"Yeah."

"Can you watch my purse?"

"Take it with you."

"I'm just going to the café. I'll only be gone a minute."

She got up and walked down the hall and then came back about five minutes later. She was walking beside Robert Renoffski. They didn't look very serious and neither did I. My mother sat on the bench. I stood up and greeted Robert.

"Hold on," said Robert. "Wait here, I'll see if I can track down the DA to give her Conrad's report." He turned around a left.

"I hope that everything goes well today," said my mother.

"Hope. You and your hope."

"Well I do."

"And it should," I said. "That's why lawyers make the dough that they do."

"You could've been a lawyer."

"The world doesn't need any more lawyers."

She laughed. "You're probably right."

"Yes."

"He's good."

"What did he say in the hall?"

"Oh, not much. Nothing about your case."

"Maybe that's a good sign."

"I hope so," she said. "What do you think will happen?"

"Well. Worst case scenario I'll plead guilty to a misdemeanor to dismiss the felony."

"But I want everything to get dismissed."

"That could happen. Let's *hope* for the best. It'll all work out one way or another."

"You don't want a felony on your record."

"I don't want anything on my record. Period."

"But if it's a misdemeanor—"

"Yeah," I said. "I'll take what I can get."

And then Robert walked through the doors of the courtroom and over to the bench. "I had a chance to speak with the DA," he said as he glanced around the corridor. "Let's try and find an open conference room to talk in."

We went down the hall and found an empty room on the corner and sat around the table. "The DA was able to look at the report," he said.

"Okay."

"She agreed to an eighteen-month deferred disposition but she wasn't willing to dismiss everything."

"Okay."

"Do you know how a deferred disposition works?"

"I do."

"Good. Well I'll explain it anyway—they're all different. The DA offered you what I think is a good deal. If you decline it, we go to trial. But if you agree to the deal you'll walk out of here very relieved. If you agree, all you would have to do is enter a guilty plea at the stand which is very straightforward—you wouldn't have to talk much—and then in eighteen months after you complete the conditions of release the guilty plea would be withdrawn. You'd come back to court and the charges of burglary and theft would get dismissed. However, the trespassing charge would undergo an unconditional discharge."

"And that'll be on my record?"

"Yes, a misdemeanor criminal trespass. It should also indicate that it was an unconditional discharge."

I thought about it. *There they go, countless job opportunities...*

"I tried to get the DA to dismiss everything," said Robert. "But she wouldn't for this case."

"Okay," I said, and that's what I had second thoughts about—hiring the right lawyer. Did he really try his best to get everything dismissed? Who in this world who is on your side can you trust? Hopefully family—if they're on your side.

Robert gently clasped his hands together and laid them on the table. "The two heavier charges will both get dismissed, and all you have to do is enter the plea and follow the conditions. After that the case will be closed."

"What are the conditions?"

"One hundred hours of community service. You wouldn't be put on probation. Have drug tests. Curfews. Fines—"

"Okay," I said. "Sounds like the best outcome I'll get."

"Well look at it this way. You won't have to wait for a trial and have that hanging over your head. You'll be able to go back to college with a peace of mind. But then again, it's up to you."

"Hold on," said my mother, quite overwhelmed. "I just need a minute to wrap my head around all of this."

And we sat and took a short moment of silence to absorb the new information, and very quickly she understood and felt better about everything, and then I signed the document that detailed my disposition and conditions. That permanent brand on my record.

"Engineering's a hard field to study," Robert said. "What made you want to do civil?"

"Well I considered civil engineering before I went to university for business. This was back junior and senior year of high school. I was always good at math and wanted to design things. Anything really: skyscrapers, cars, structures for Mars…"

"Structures for Mars—I was not expecting that."

"I wasn't really being serious."

"But you were good at math?"

"Yeah. When you do something every day you start to notice patterns. I made sense of these patterns early on, and then in the hospital—at Spaulding—when I had plenty of time to think and reflect, I thought, *why is my higher education in business?* That's not something you have to study, that's something you learn through experience. I was only three semesters deep, and I saw it as a good opportunity to try what I first wanted to do—engineering."

"Wow," said Robert. "That's pretty good."

"Just my thoughts and reasons."

"If you first wanted to do engineering, is that what you still want to do?"

"Yeah," I said gruffly. "Excuse me, yes. I'm not having second thoughts about engineering. Yes that's what I want to do. But I'd also like to do something else."

"You'll have a lot on your plate. How are you feeling?"

"Very good."

"You had some pretty serious injuries."

"I know," I said, and I told Robert that everything had healed almost perfectly. I said that engineering might be a hard field to study, and especially challenging this soon after the ordeal and also when I want to write, but it's now or never. He knew that it'd be hard, and my mother was glad that I was giving it a try. We sat and waited to pass the time, and then at last it was finally that time. The doors opened and the session began.

Chapter 29

The air inside of courtroom seven felt the same as it had felt five months earlier, stagnant mixed with victory and defeat. I sat on the front bench and waited quietly for the session to commence. Judge Johnson seemed to be running late; it was just another day for him manning the system. Then we were ordered to stand and we rose and stood and then sat down as the judge entered the room. He surely looked like a judge and he sat behind his raised desk and set his coffee down before him. The first case was called and if I'm not mistaken it was for a felony OUI, and the defendant seemed to be only a year or two older than I was and supremely obese, and as his proceeding continued Robert whispered, "I think you'll be called next."

He was right, I was called next, and I walked to the podium and stolidly stood. I told myself that before I knew it, it would all be over and I could then get out of there. That's what I always used to tell myself in unwanted situations, and almost always it would happen right before having to speak publicly—because it made me kind of nervous—but now that I know a few things and have more to say and don't mind the sound of my own voice it doesn't really bother me. This time in the courtroom it was very strange and uncomfortable. I had swallowed a breath of air into my stomach and it sat in my abdomen hard and static. And it was too late now to burp out this bloat. My freedom depended on good manners!

Standing stoically before the judge, mostly distracted by this tumorous feeling inside of my gut, I scarcely heard the discussion and maybe it was this abdominal discomfort that caused my mind to wander. A body to mind and mind to body kind of connection. I had stood here twice in this very spot when I was seventeen.

The venial OUI that I had been charged with was at first arraigned and then dismissed, and now I stood distractedly in a dreamlike déjà vu and remembered the event that led me to this exact spot three years earlier.

My old friend in his truck to the right, and me and two others in my car untroubled. He put his truck in reverse and peeled out of his spot and skid across the gravel lot as rocks flew off in every direction. He abruptly stopped and then slammed on the gas and drove off, leaving in his wake an opaque cloud of dust that drifted stilly through the air in the dead of night. The two others in my car turned around and we watched the peacock pull out of the lot and onto the road and his truck disappear behind a cluster of trees. And then like a game of cat and mouse a dark and disguised car drove lightless through the lot and turned onto the road and stepped on the gas and sped off toward the truck. *And then* its headlights flicked on.

"Did you see that?" asked Bill.

"That was a cop," said Smiley.

"Balls! I barely saw him. He came out of nowhere."

"They always do, Bill."

"He didn't have his lights on. Is that even legal?"

"Does it matter?"

"You think there are any more?"

"No," said Smiley. "I doubt it. He probably got a call about kids drinking on the beach and then waited in the dark until somebody left."

"Boys, that was a good time tonight," said Bill.

"Oh yeah, bud. It's always a good time on the beach."

"Until the cops come after you!"

"Terr, what should we do?"

"Well. We could call and have someone get us," I suggested.

"No, we're fine. Let's just get out of here."

"All right then, let's get out of here." I reversed my car in the lot and slowly drove off and at the exit checked the rearview mirror. Like an abyss it was utterly clear and dark as death. I turned right and drove onto the bridge and far to the left and over the water the lights of Portland shone dimly in the sky. I

194

drove cautiously, and then about halfway across the bridge an array of blue lights flashed through the night like some kind of aurora.

Smiley said, "Nate's screwed," as we drove by his truck.

"They'll getchya when you drive like that."

I looked in the rearview mirror. And at the shape and stealth of a presumed vehicle for law enforcement. The palpitations. "What's that?" I asked.

Bill turned around in the back seat. "I see lights on the top. It's a cop car. One of them explorers."

"Bill, you listen to country music too much."

"What should we do?"

"I'm getting the fuck off this road once we get past the bridge."

"Where?"

"Down a side street."

"No!" cried Smiley. "Follow the car in front of us. You always want to follow the traffic."

There was a car a few hundred feet ahead and I listened to him. *I* followed the traffic! The car drove five miles per hour under the speed limit and really obstructed us kids on the run. In my head I saw the blue lights on the bridge, I wondered about Nate, and I drove as cautious as the sightless walk but soon the cop caught up and rode my tail to the intersection. Like he had nothing better to do. I turned left and drove the speed limit down the hill and just when I thought I was safe…

Nate walked away a free boy; I was arrested and charged with an OUI. In hindsight, some things are so ridiculous that they're funny.

Still standing in the courtroom before the judge I turned my head and glanced to the right. At first I thought that it was William. A familiar man stood erect and off to the side of the courtroom beside the benches. He had just walked in. But it was not William and this man had no legitimate business in courtroom seven—it was a father from my community and with him his big nose! I felt kind of ashamed, and then I wondered exactly how many people knew about the arrest and my proceeding in court right now, but I didn't overthink it.

In fact, it was hard to think about the currently stored setting at all. I tried my best to pay attention but that tumorous lump of air contorted my stomach and it seriously diverted my attention from the discussion. The DA spoke often, Robert seldom, and the judge listened attentively. I heard the DA mention one hundred hours of community service as a condition of my release and once again my mind gladly went into the depths of recollection. Back in time to the community service in Dover and the event that led me there. Sal and I were sharing a pearl in the woods behind Stoke when two campus cops infiltrated our peaceful time of leisure. At the time I thought that they had come from somewhere in the trees above, a guerilla warfare kind of tactic that they were taught to use strictly on newly enrolled students early in the schoolyear. It was only the third week of being there at UNH, and an instinct flashed before my mind to make a break and run, and it might have been wise to do so or equally possible a bad disaster, so maybe my judgement to stay put was right. A typical cowardly surrender. And then after campus law enforcement arrested us we were loaded into the cruiser and brought to the station and cuffed to the bench and waited to get booked. There was a drunk kid sitting next to me and he vomited viscously into a bucket all night. By the end of the night he had nothing left in his stomach to expel but he went on heaving and laughing like a spotted hyena. Sal and I each got our papers and possessions and then left. We copped a fresh pack of mints and indulged in them deep into the early morning hours behind our building and Amy sat with us and shared her wisdom. She consoled us and filled our heads with kind words when she otherwise would have been sound asleep. It was comforting to know that someone cared and was kind enough to show it. Random acts of kindness don't happen often enough.

"Not to worry," she said, and that I didn't.

But like I told Kenneth Conrad, at the time of the arrest it didn't really make sense to me, and I didn't see it as clearly as I do now. Céline had said it best: "Nine lines of crime, one of boredom." The eleventh line goes either way.

The community service was an absolute hassle. We had to convince our friend Abe—mostly with money—to drive us to the county jail in Dover and arrive promptly by eight in the morning. Here we chopped and stacked wood all day, and it wasn't the free labor that bothered me so much—it was being treated like a pet in the chilly and wet November weather that justly bothered me. We worked at a jail, cheek by jowl with an array of serial offenders, and some of them were pretty funny. They weren't the brightest people in town but they could tell a good story! I finished my community service in two weeks, and I bought Abe a large pizza for helping out with the transportation. Without him we might have been out of luck.

After this, my case right now in Portland soon came to an end. Judge Johnson concluded my proceeding with a long list of generic questions that I successively answered yes to—to all of them. What they were I can't remember, but his final words that I do remember were basically a gentle reminder that I would come back to court in eighteen months to resolve my case which ought to be enough time to complete the community service. *No problem*, I thought. *And that's only two days before my birthday. But then what?* And that just might be the thousand-dollar question. When a plan or timeline is followed all the way through and the desired outcome is reached the immediate response is always the same: what's next? Usually it's because the end result is never quite as delightful as it was first expected. Take pleasure in the fruits of your labor, but most fruit will rot in just days.

I looked over at Robert and he seemed to be slightly eager to get out of there. I went up there ready to get out, and our patience would soon be rewarded. He leaned in and whispered to me, "You can head outside. I'll meet you out there in a minute."

I walked out of courtroom seven and felt most elated. I saw the corridor in a new light, and I stood tall and set my shoulders and expelled the lump of air in my stomach out through my mouth in a loud burp.

"Don't do that," said my mother. "Use your manners."

197

Robert Renoffski walked out of the courtroom and found us in the hall. We went to the division clerk's office and stopped in the hallway outside of the door. "This is Kelly's office," said Robert. "She's very nice. Give her this piece of paper and she will give you everything you need to do the community service." He handed me a single sheet of paper and looked at his watch. "I have to run to a meeting. If anything comes up, call me. You have my card?"

"Yes."

"Great. Hopefully you won't need to use it," he joked.

"That's right," my mother laughed.

I smiled and thanked Robert, and so did she. Robert told me to stay safe and to stay out of trouble and then he turned and stopped in the doorway. "Hey Kelly," he called out and waved.

"Hi Robert."

He walked down the hall and I went into the office.

"Hi," said Kelly.

"Hey. Robert mentioned information for community service."

"Hold on." Kelly opened a drawer on the side of her desk and took out a packet of paper. "It's all in here. These are the approved agencies and on the next page it has the steps that you'll need to take to complete your hours."

She handed me the packet and I skimmed through the pages.

"Make sure to send me an email before you start working at an agency."

"Okay," I said.

"Did Robert give you the sheet of paper with the conditions of release?"

"Yes, here."

"I just have to file it," said Kelly.

The sheet of paper listed every charge and condition, the one hundred hours of community service. Kelly disapprovingly studied the paper and in a low voice she said, "This is your one slip up."

"Most definitely," said my mother.

"I know," I said.

I knew that it was big a mistake that I had made but in black and white it seems much worse than it really was. I made a poor choice and that one momentary lapse in judgement will be with me forever. I would like to go back in time and manipulate the past, change my mind and stay at home and go back to school the day of my assault, and in that case, prevent the whole ordeal from happening in the first place; but the point is, the only direction is forward and the least that you can do is learn from each mistake and with it the experience that is fated, and if you can do this, you just might be all right. But it's not always the sufferer who is solely obliged to find the direction on their own; any help from others will truly go a long way. Compassion and consolation will truly go a long way. Being good to them for no reason will absolutely go a long way. I wish that I saw this, but all that I really got from anyone when it actually mattered was undesirable judgement. It might be wise to get used to this kind of treatment.

I said thanks to Kelly and then got the paperwork and walked out of her office and down the hall and out of the courthouse and up to Federal Street. My mother unlocked the car and we both got inside. "I'm so glad that's over with," she said as she put the keys in the ignition. "I was getting worried. I'm just happy it's all over."

"See I told you it would work out one way or another."

"Well *I* didn't know."

"I did," I said.

"But how would anyone know?"

"Well there's only one outcome that doesn't work out and it's destined for everyone."

"Well we really didn't know if it would work out for you."

"Neither did I really. I didn't even know that it happened. One day I just randomly woke up in the hospital—but I guess that could happen to anyone."

"You were in *really* bad shape. It was a friggin nightmare. And look at you now—how you've recovered!"

"Yeah, I know. That's gotta be God's work."

My mother backed out onto the street and drove off.

"Wouldn't it be nice to know how you ended up all the way out in Dover," she asked. "And who did it to you?"

"Yeah. Then it'd be time to do something."

"Andrew, you have to stay out of trouble for the next eighteen months."

"Don't worry, I was joking. The memory still hasn't come back yet. There's no basis to do anything."

"But if there was…"

"I would do nothing. I try to choose my battles wisely. Unless *He* chooses them for me."

"*He?*"

"Well yes. Something that has the power to decide. Something that's already destined to happen—already decided."

"Yeah—yeah, that's right."

"What, you don't believe in *His* power?"

"No, it's not that."

I dully looked out through the window.

"No," she said again. "I think I follow you. There's just already too much of that these days."

"Right. So I try to forgive and forget when there's nothing else to do."

"That's a good way to look at it. And you never know, your memory could come back in time."

"Maybe," I said. "But really I lucked out."

"How?"

"Because memories are strange—the subconscious is strange. What you want to remember will fade away and what you want to forget will stay forever. Why would I want to know who and how? There'd be no peace of mind in that. A little ignorance in this case is blissful."

"Yes, you're right. You're very—" she thought for a moment, focused on the road "—philosophical right now."

"Only after a day like today," I said.

"Well you sound like a writer."

"Okay."

"It's just, you're sometimes hard to follow."

"Here's the thing," I said. "I heard that great writers are not and should not be easy to follow."

"But you haven't started writing yet, have you?"

"I'm getting there," I said. "I'm ready."

"You're ready."

"I was born ready."

"Born ready."

"I'm more than ready."

"Well why don't you focus on engineering first. That'll be hard enough after your brain injury and everything else that happened."

"Okay. And about that—about the ordeal—it is what it is and by chance I was spared and then recovered. And maybe the only way to get closure from a tragedy is to create something from it or get something out of it. In my case I was lucky. The details would only blind and torment."

Now that summer was over it was time. When I got home I went upstairs to the bathroom and stepped on the scale and thought for a moment about the past seven months, that strange chunk of time. The best part of it might have been right now, looking down at the machine measuring my force upon its being, waiting patiently for its reading, for it to say something, anything, or instead, maybe the best part had actually been everything that had happened along the adventure to get here, standing five feet seven inches tall now a partially free man, a changed young man proud to be one hundred and sixty-two pounds. I glanced out through the window and then again looked down at the scale to make sure. On the screen in bold black numbers flashed a big **162**—even. I pounded my chest once, twice, thrice. Running those trails tirelessly had really paid off! I looked in the mirror and clearly noticed the powerful effects of convalescence, and for a surprising change I actually liked what I saw. *Get this man a beer*, I thought. *This man right here, Trifecta T.* The displaced pieces had been all but picked up; I was thrilled for Orono!

Chapter 30

The time had come to head up to college and we drove on the highway and just past Bangor we took the exit and drove through Orono. Along the way I had listened to music and tried to sleep but had no luck and instead gazed out through the window at the ripened landscape. The leaves were still alive and green but in a month they would begin senescence and a month later all fall down. The cycle repeats itself year after year and most of these trees will stand tall for decades. It's all in their root structure, and the strongest, most developed trees will survive the longest.

During this time of observation my mind contemplated the road ahead. For some reason I had grandiose dreams to help the world through engineering and I was very excited to finally begin. If mankind can't help the world then one man can—absurdity! My excitement then diverged into pleasant anticipation. Basically this was strictly about the leisure time in college and the long nights and lazy mornings, lounging in bed as the room spins or turning around and taking position, all well-deserved recreation after months of undeserved pain and prolonged restriction. I clearly went back to school overly optimistic this time around.

We drove past the campus and then the gas station and then pulled into my apartment complex. My parents dropped me off, and I'll be the first to admit it, they're great. If family is perceived as a tree, but if instead of the tree being a family tree *you* are this personified tree, family does not make up the branches of your existence but instead the many roots intertwined at your base. They support and nourish your growth during times when you otherwise might be dead wood. That's your foundation forever. And in that case, I wondered how many intertwined roots I actually had left. How long would I stand?

Had the arrest not happened, life would not have happened. It's the one thing that greatly and wrongly hinders the recovery from being respectable, and it's the one thing that caused it all to happen like falling dominoes. Without it there would be no pieces to pick up, nothing to rearrange, no change of guard. I'm not proud of it, but I like the change that it forced upon me.

I unloaded the car and set up my room and put away clothes and sat on the couch. Two of my other roommates I had grown up with, and coincidentally the property manager chose me as their new roommate. They walked in and out of the apartment, carrying bins and totes of their belongings, tense and hesitant to talk to me.

Gil set a bin down on the island and I got up and helped unpack the kitchenware. Four of us lived in this apartment and together we had one skillet and a spatula and one Teflon stockpot in which we would cook our pasta.

"It looks like we might have to eat with our hands."

"No utensils?"

"That's what it looks like," I said.

"Humph."

"I'll get plastic forks at the gas station later."

"You set with beer, T?"

"Yeah," I said.

Gil started going through the cabinets and drawers as if hidden inside might be a golden spoon.

"What are you doing?"

"Nothing," said Gil.

He seemed neither interested nor like he wanted to talk, and we didn't say another word to each other until later that day. His father had taken my spot on the couch and I took the presence of shared blood as the reason for his taciturnity. Then his mother walked into the apartment and set the bin that she had carried from her car down on the floor and looked my way. "Andrew," she said. "I thought *you* were the sane one."

That was what she said, and apparently the preconception, that bitch. *So*, I thought. *She knows about the arrest. But she doesn't* know *about it.* And that seemed to be the case for everyone. It was right on Google and right in the police beat—just one search away! And that kind of information will spread like an arid forest fire. I could see people thinking: *He* used *to be a good kid, a good local kid*—shaking their heads. People assumed, and by doing so they wrongly reduced me to a soiled ass, themselves included! I wondered what else she thought about—and exactly how bad every other highly caustic remark behind my back actually was— every and all undeserved discourtesies. *The ignorance and impudence!* No one in the apartment asked how I was doing after the assault, and of course there was no information on Google about it; I was basically left for death, and then left to fend for myself, so long as the machine could go on. Many rightly curious people had used Google to find out what might have happened to me and instead of that they found the arrest. It was this along with every other inflicted prejudice that through my lens created such a hopeful outlook.

Aside from the slanderous suppositions, after thinking about it directly, like I've said before, it might be better to be talked about in any context than to never be talked about at all. My response to the insolent comment was honest: I'm actually surprised to still be sane after everything that happened, the near-death, pain, recovery, betrayal, time in the hospitals, all of it. I can't believe it. It's all as though I had actually died and had actually been resurrected, and that alone was an unusually excellent feeling! If this would happen to anyone it would surely be the one and the only one who could rise above would have to be the one. But I have to admit, the arrest was bad, disgraceful, defaming, and what I did was wrong. There's no hiding it, it's branded on my record forever and over time I began to feel as though it's much better to be frank about it. But this time I sealed my lips and swallowed my pride and paid her no more mind than any other scoffer and quietly walked off down the hall and went inside of my room, hoping that I could remove the arrest from Google someday soon and facetiously thinking just how great of a start my return to academia had gotten off to.

Chapter 31

The good thing was, classes didn't start for three days and we had the weekend to do whatever we'd like. This meant partying at night and recouping in disgust the following day. I enjoy a strong drink or two or three and I think that it's very good for the body and soul to get drunk if the drunk can handle it. Of course the setting plays an important role on any occasion of inebriation, and for underage kids in Orono, the only options really came down to either house parties or fraternity parties. I love house parties, was indifferent to fraternity parties. Most of the time you form a circle with a group of friends and stand together casually, but as the night went on it became a challenge to converse coherently over the steady noise of the zoo. I never understood why anyone would want to live in a shared castle whose sole purpose is to house bangers, but it was all part of the brotherhood and what confused me others saw as an opportunity. The brothers understandably would not let you inside if you didn't know one of their own and this really made perfect sense. It was their party and they deserved that kind of authority. Most people had to pucker their lips and plead their way inside, and then once they were in it would usually be a boisterous show of benevolent mayhem, and every guest looked ostensibly happy maybe because they had finally made it in with the in-crowd. Otherwise it was just another weekend night, and the brothers that had opened the doors to their massive abode either flit from group to group or hid in their rooms to escape the madness. If I had chosen to live in a factory like this I probably would've done the latter.

In that case, and this was more or less sporadic, if I decided to go out at night and try and gain entrance to one of these gatherings I would almost always have to walk there and walk home, alone or accompanied. For the first weekend at Orono that's exactly what I did. My roommates and I watched the big fight on pay-per-view between Floyd Mayweather and Connor McGregor and after this we went to a party. We took a shortcut and walked along a wooded path on the edge of a river and a sandpit. Far ahead on the path a feral black cat scurried across and stopped and glared with yellow eyes like a shadow of illusion. The others carried on unmindfully.

We came to a road at the edge of the woods and turned the corner and strolled along a neighborhood. Walking ahead appeared to be Mack Daniel. Zane Brachman and I went up to him.

"Look who it is!"

"Hullo," I said.

"It's the return of the Terr!" said Mack.

"You going to Bradman's party?" Brachman asked.

"I'm heading there right now."

"Same with me and Terr."

"Vamanos."

We walked down the street and at the end stood a decayed house with white paint chipping off the sides and a pile of garbage stacked behind the driveway. This was certainly the house. Music echoed down the streets and there were lines of people at every entrance. We all wondered if they would let anyone else inside. Mack said that he'd find a way in, and Brachman and I knew exactly who to look for. And there he was, standing in the front yard, holding the fort down and clearing out the crowd. Who do you know here? No one? Smell ya later!

My roommate and I walked over and Mack went around back.

"Terrio!" said Bradman. "How are you?"

"Good, you?"

"Good. I haven't seen you in like five years."

"Remember at UNH last fall?"

"Oh yeah, that's right!"

"Yeah."

"Well are you going here now?"

"Yeah."

"Where are you living?"

"Apple Orchard Apartments. It's me, Gil, Brachman, and their friend Joey Calvin."

Bradman looked at Brachman. "Well I gotta get back to work. I'll see you guys inside. Go in through the basement around back."

There were only a few people behind the house, and we went inside through the bulkhead and made our way through crowds of people up to the first floor. The music was very loud. There was slightly more space to breathe and we found Joey and Gil and formed a circle with a group of girls. I looked at the girl to my right and smiled amiably.

"Hi!" moved her pink pillow lips.

I heard myself say, "Hey!" but it was hard to tell if she did.

"What's your—"

"What!"

"Name!"

"Wanna play a game?"

She offered me her beer and I drank it, and then she moved closer and brushed her tail against my leg. Had it not been for what happened next—*¡quiero pasar la noche juntos!* But absurdity always seems to happen at the most inconvenient times. And right then on the other side of the room a girl picked a lamp off the table and dropped it on the floor. The glass shattered. The music stopped. The room cleared out. And I stayed and watched a brother walk up to the vandal. "What are you doing?" he said. "You're cleaning this mess and then you're leaving. Now!"

I briefly looked around and could not find my roommates nor the girls. I went upstairs and walked down the hallway and stopped by a room loud with music and laughter. I walked in and through a cloud of smoke made out about a dozen people around the room and on the bed sat Mack Daniel. He looked my way. "Terr, come over here. There's plenty of room."

I sat on the edge of the bed. "It's hard to believe that someone actually pays to live here. The rent's not cheap."

"I know," laughed Mack. "I really just wanted to smoke and this seemed like the right room."

"Yeah, it seems like it."

"At least they have good music."

"That's exactly what I was thinking," I said.

Mack looked around dazedly. "It's a cloudy room," he said. "A cloudy room…"

"That's about all it is, Mack—a cloud of smoke."

"Word, let's make it cloudier."

And that we did.

The room was now fogged up like a forgotten memory. I sat on the bed in my own world and my mind went back to an earlier time in a room at a party much like this. Except I was alone with a crowd of strangers. One guy sat on the bed and three girls sat by his side and gave him attention. Every other guy in the room looked at him with contempt. They may or may not have been slightly jealous, and then I sat on the bed and quickly realized that the guy was very personable and it made perfect sense why the girls were with him. As for the girls, they each had a good head on their shoulder. Fine women of the Earth.

I asked Mack Daniel a question and turned my head and he was gone. Half of the room had emptied and most of the haze had cleared. Does time elapse when you least expect it? Maybe it's when you pay the least attention. I got up and left the room for a breath of fresh air.

The house had all but emptied save for a few drunks on the dance floor. Soft music came from somewhere but not from the surround sound speakers. I ambled through the living room and looked around for Mack or Gil, Brachman or Bradman, Joey Calvin or the girl with the pink pillow lips. Everyone appeared to be the same, and then I turned the corner and a pretentious boy shimmied backward into me. *Cuidado, pen*—I zipped my lip and pardoned my French and went out back.

After being utterly disappointed I set off for home. It appeared as though two boys were about to seriously square off and fight on the porch but what had looked hopeful turned at most into a light scuffle on the grass. The night was over, I did not anticipate any other entertainment, and I really struggled to find my way back to the Apple Orchard Apartments. Somehow I stumbled across the entrance to the wooded path from which we came and into the darkness I went. These woods at night were not very different from the woods in daylight, yet they were entirely different worlds. There was a pure stillness throughout this moonlit thicket where only nocturnal creatures crept about, and right now I was one of them, walking along this land of calmness, looking at the canopy of trees above for eyeshine in the ghostly dark and wan light. They were there, somewhere, but where? If I could whistle, along this path I would have whistled. How far had I gone, how far was there to go, how would I know that this was the right direction?

Then a cloud drifted in front of the moon and all around it was pitch black. Behind me a twig snapped. Another twig. A rustle of leaves. I turned around and wanted to laugh! There were a pair of phosphorescent eyes that sat upon a dark frame shy of five feet tall. If it was William, that man had shrunk tremendously. This starkly shadowed phantom could east my dust! I turned around and ran through the wood and tripped only once on a fallen branch from intoxication.

Very quickly I made it to an open field and walked through the grass behind an apartment complex. It looked very similar to mine; I was right next door. The moon once again shone vividly pale in the dark sky. In just a few days it would be the harvest moon and somewhere out there the wolves of tomorrow would howl and cry for comfort. I walked inside of my apartment and poured two full glasses of water and brought both into my room. I undressed. I turned the lights off and tonight soundly slept.

Chapter 32

I had never really been the type for going to school and this time around it was a serious wake-up call. The hardest class of all was at eight in the morning and I was out of the house to catch the bus by seven. It's true that the early bird gets the worm, but there's not a single worm to get when everyone else is doing the same thing, searching the same ground, studying the same material. As an abstract thinker just understanding the basic principles in these math-based classes was hard! An intensive study was required but I despised studying, and my previous flair for math certainly helped but only so much. Materials for Civil Engineers was the class that began at eight in the morning and of course we delved straight into the book on the first class. I sat in a row toward the back on the left side of the lecture hall and kept to myself, mainly because a quiet soul is completely full of potential wit and wisdom until his first word is spoken. After that the listener is the judge.

It's possible that the professor unknowingly knew this. He was reserved and affable and down-to-earth. His first words after a brief introduction were, "Strength is power. Strength is a value. Strength is a paramount principle to understand. You will come across it all throughout your engineering careers."

He was right, but what he didn't mention was that aside from a basic principle of science strength in a person is a quality that is genuinely hard to find. And this is true.

Then after he mentioned his introductory statement he turned around and clumsily bumped his desk with his leg and thereupon his mug of coffee fell to the floor. A tan liquid puddle expanded in shape and size on the linoleum tiles and a few drops scattered about like loose paint. He stood there and looked fixedly at the mess that he had made. "Hey Pera," he said. "Do you mind getting some paper towels from down the hall?"

A student in the front row got up and left the room and by the time she came back he had not moved. She willingly sopped up the puddle of coffee and cleaned the floor with a wad of paper towels.

"Thanks, Pera. Now where were we?" And all at once a few pubescent voices toward the front of the room said:

"Strength—"

"Careers—"

"Value—"

"Pera—"

And I had a good laugh on the inside.

"Yes," said the professor. "All of you are right, yes. So how do engineers measure strength?"

"They calculate it."

"No, Pera. That's not what I meant."

Not another guess was given or breath was taken.

"I'll rephrase the question," he said. "*What* is strength?"

Silence in the lecture hall, and not one hand was raised.

"Well. The strength of an object is the maximum stress that it can withstand before breaking..."

That's exactly what he said, and being a living example of this I felt obliged to record it in my notes.

It made sense. I formed an association and for a moment I closed my eyes and daydreamed, thinking about how some things happen that are purely up to fate and based on luck and spine they will make you or break you. I looked around at the other students in the room and didn't think that they had it in them. Misfortunes are relative and everyone has their own but as a whole there's a scale of degree. Some thrive in conditions others couldn't handle and this goes both ways. I could tell that engineering would have its own set of challenges. Both the work and study would soon become progressively onerous.

I only ask for help when I feel comfortable asking for help, and sometimes the answer comes without having to ask at all or even think twice about it. When these aren't intuitive realizations I think of them as gifted signs. They're there, and they will always be there, but you have to pay attention to perceive them.

I was new to this school and my sense of direction was pretty bad. The library was in the middle of campus—my hideaway spot while I was actually on campus—and all around stood many brick buildings that looked the same. During the first week I walked out of its front door in search for Aubert Hall. I had been up since six that morning and went to bed four hours earlier; I was in a testy mood. There was not a chance that I would ask another student or staff member for directions, and I didn't have to.

My ear buds were in and the song on play was "Blue in Green" and the longer it played the better I felt. I stopped at the bottom of the steps and scanned the courtyard and the buildings on either side for any sign of Auburt Hall. No luck. There were also buildings behind the library and realizing this I decided that I'd skip my class and go back to my spot. But before I made another move a very thin kid walking down the steps bumped into me on accident and printed on the back of his shirt was a wavy white arrow and slightly aslant and pointing past his left shoulder was the arrowhead. What was there to lose?

I walked across the courtyard in the direction of the arrowhead and the first building in my path had a big plaque above the front steps labeled Aubert Hall. I went inside and thought, *That's a sign for the books.* And then emerged another sign of sorts. For the entire class on the top of my head pricked a persistent itch and after this my world became increasingly uncanny.

The second week of classes the roughness began. The itch on my scalp had claimed its presence indefinitely. What this sign was or meant I did not know. But it grew from an itch to irritation and by the end of the week my head beneath my hair was also inflamed. If there was a good part to this situation, nothing was visible to the naked eye except for a tint of redness here and there and one day all around. That one day I was in calculus class and thank the gods it couldn't be noticed beneath my hair. I sat in a seat by the window and let the breeze ease the itch. The TA asked a question. I raised my hand.

"Yes, *Andy*," she said.

She was just about four years older than me, the TA, and she was very very comely. The guys from her past had shown her no curiosity. And I have to admit, I liked her. Sometimes she teased me and I readily played along, because after all we were only in class and class can easily get dull.

"You wanted the derivative."

"Yes."

"Four thirds," I said.

"That's correct."

The only cute girl in class turned her head and looked my way as if surprised that I had answered the question, and then the TA followed up with another question and the girl raised her hand to show that it was on. The TA called on her. "X approaches positive infinity," she said.

"Good job. That's right."

The girl squared herself in her chair and flipped her hair and glanced my way.

"Those are good thoughts," said the TA, also looking my way. "Good job. Good thoughts."

The girl looked back and it was clear that she had won. She was very cute, didn't smile and I liked her style. She was sensible, not overly outgoing. Maybe it was a friendly kind of urge, something that to hold back is very hard to do; I wanted to go up to her and give her a hug. But like most cute girls that are young, behind her pretty innocence butter inside her mouth wouldn't melt. I gazed outside at the courtyard and thought, contemplated, drifted. What the TA said had sounded vaguely provocative; I had a good idea of what she carefully insinuated. I was a mixed-up twenty-year-old, sorely distracted by an irritated itch on the top of my head. Times were strange and withal tough.

Over the weekend what previously seemed unable to get worse got worse. The time spent in class was an awful reverie. This might have been because what rest I didn't get at night I tried to get in class. I had always been a light and troubled sleeper, but the itch on my head made matters worse and over the course of just a few days insomnia set in. Helplessly at night amongst the essence of sleeplessness I tossed and turned and judged whether or not what Gil's mother had said on the first day had a layer of truth. One time I thought, *This is not sane—you need to sleep!* But I had only let her slanderous words get to me. Though I was right, I needed sleep!

Sleep in a way is a form of nourishment for your body. Without it your body will not function properly and this I immediately noticed. My stomach was all contorted, I swallowed excessive air, it was bloated, and I hardly had an appetite. There was no food on the table and when there was I refused to eat. In other words, I was malnourished and sleep deprived and this had an unruly effect with the rash on my head. Sometimes it stung like pinching the skin on the back of your triceps. Around the clock I was vexed.

Clearly this time at college things went astray unexpectedly fast. Exams lay just around the corner in every class. It didn't look very promising for me. How can you study and retain knowledge feeling utterly wretched? It's simple, you can't.

After finishing each of the three exams the pit in my stomach grew deeper. That empty feeling in my gut told me that I had failed all three. Later I found out that this was true for two exams, Materials and chemistry, but the calculus exam I had actually passed! The TA would have been so proud that I did if she had known about my great misery, and the cute girl would have gladly flipped her hair and given me a hug, but I never got to see their reaction because after that exam I fully withdrew from all of my classes. And there in my chest sat statically that bitter feeling that I might not see them again.

For the first time in my life I felt like a failure, and that night I had plenty of time to reel and think about this strange turn of events. There was no chance that I would have been able to go on like this for the rest of the semester, let alone for four years. The workload was overly demanding under these conditions. At

214

this rate, to keep up and pass each lab and class would have been too expensive and harmful in the long run. I told myself that I made the right decision, and now there's not a single doubt in my mind that it was. I lay in bed and thought, *Remember my boy, it's all in the attempt! At least I gave engineering a shot. And you know what that means… Now you can do what you really wanted to do. But first, get better. Start from the bottom and build from there.*

Chapter 33

As soon as I withdrew from classes I tried to land a job. For work, basically all that was available and easily accessible was across the street at a gas station. I needed a few days to recover from my latest failure, then the following Monday I went to the store and applied for a position as an assistant sandwich maker. Why I settled for this line of work, I didn't have the lucidness that you need to write, and I thought that I could heal and clear the fog through menial work, but I never had the chance to try. The manager seemed interested in hiring me during the interview, and I gave her my consent for a background check, but I never got a call back. She saw the arrest, the pending charges, the black and white smudge on my record. That's what happens when an employer purely uses a background check to determine which applicant is best for the position. Their ignorance is no better than an individual's. It was either that or she happened to find a highly qualified sandwich maker and then hired this prodige instead. I wasn't upset, I was glad, and the feeling was probably mutual.

Now that I had a lot of time on my hand I wasn't really sure what to do with all of it. I tried to get back into reading even though I didn't have the brain power or attention span to see a novel all the way through. But short stories were all right. I read a dozen stories a day and some days many more. My routine was simple. I'd get up in the morning after tossing and turning for most or all of the night, then wash and bathe, get dressed and eat, and then go to the library just to get out of the house. Not a lot had changed since I was actually a student; the library was still my spot! Libraries are quiet, peaceful, full of information, full of productive energy. I felt better and alive on the inside of this sedately tranquil space, doing something productive, surrounded by knowledge, even though what I was doing was on my own terms, for myself and nobody else. I gladly read Hemingway, O. Henry, Carver, King, Murakami, Bukowski, Miller, and more. I found anything autobiographical enjoyable and most relatable, and there's not a doubt now or then that realistic dialogue was my favorite component of each story. It adds heart and momentum to the page and this was practically new to me. When someone's own life is being written about in first person, that's genuine, that takes guts. And when someone else's thoughts and adages are close to your own, and it sounds almost as if they're written precisely for you, that's brilliant. Put yourself in their shoes, try not to judge solely from a reader's point of view. These selected writers were solid all the way through and each had his own claim to fame. Hemingway and Carver knew how to lay down a line. Their lines had flow and rolled easily across the page. Bukowski had the secret to the line and said a profound truth in a simple way. Murakami added a dash of magic to the page. And King wore the crown for twelve thousand days. They were all on top of their game and each writer left behind iconic literature. Reading these authors and many others was the best way to spend my time wisely. The pattern seemed universal. As long as writing is profound you will learn and get something out of it, and good writing can be hard to find but once it is found and gently read it's started by one reader and finished by a different person. And if the writing reads fluidly out loud and lives in your mind it will stand the test of time. A mind with knowledge has real power, and the more I read the more I wanted to write, and what a great urge I had to speak my mind, to use its power and play with words on the page, to record the ordeal and a few stories and thoughts in a book. I just hoped that people would actually buy it—not just lend and borrow it. It costs about as much a breakfast with coffee, and the difference between the two is more or less one thousand calories and caffeine versus rare amusement and awareness. It's unlikely that a coffee would ever be shared, so why pass around the chapters? Maybe it's just a universal principle: slight the writer at his own expense. Take his thoughts and ideas, style and soul, scorn his work, and let him starve. Despite this, I still eagerly hoped to soon sit down and commence this project good and proper, and then at last after finishing, after having to write through the night because of long hours at work and school, tasting the peculiar satisfaction that comes from creation. That is, creating raw and well-thought-out art from the evocation of experience and memory and forming on-the-spot associations! My mother asked if I'd be excited once I finally get my degree and I said no. Anyone can get a degree if you conform to the excessively protracted, trying and trivial studies, but to write an authentically complex and ornately powerful book at the same time, that's remarkable, and I'll only be excited once and if I actually get it right, but it's not easy! Especially after writing, editing, and proofing the entire project meticulously, intentionally bending the rules, at times leaving out certain punctuation and basically creating an alternative meaning for selected words when it's suitable, and using intuition to know when to do this and when to hold off. Try and think of a book as a work of art—a painting of words and marks and flows on a page—you can find meaning from it if you want, and if you don't want to, you won't. But of course there's much more to the page than what meets the eye—that's a technique called the iceberg theory. Looking back at it, all along this exhaustive journey I knew that to write a book you have to constantly sit down and write the book, unapologetically spill your guts like it's confession and leave everything that you have up to that point on the page save for what feels good, for your own sake. But at this time the problem might have been that I didn't have the slightest clue where to begin, let alone the actual zeal, fire, patience or assiduity for a presumably straightforward task that's necessary to write a book. And in that case, long time not now, reading any book and building a solid foundation of knowledge at the library was a good way to spend my time when I had nothing else to do. Each day dipping into different worlds, separate minds and lenses, ideas and perspectives, thoughts and memories, almost like telepathy. I spent endless time there in that firm leather chair at the library.

But as it were, turmoil all but erased this memory. I can hardly recall anything about the actual library, but perhaps knowledge that is once retained is always retained no matter what. That's why it's important to expose your mind to the self that you would like to be.

Back at the apartment everything was worse, and it was worst at night on the verge of sleep. I had no hope that while I was here things would get any better; the whole situation had been rapidly exacerbating. That's why it was utterly urgent to go home. To figure out my unnoticeably flushed head and trouble with sleep meant that I absolutely had to leave Orono. Google suggested that I see a dermatologist and I knew that there were a few in Portland. After that, I'd find a quick job through Bonney Staffing, just a temporary position until spring semester started, and this would leave more than enough time to complete my community service. So without question I went home.

I rode home with Mack Daniel. I thought, *the great one.*

Later that month I planned to drive back and get the rest of my belongings. The landlord had been very understanding and luckily I got out of the lease. It was medical—my traumatic brain injury. And in a way it truly was.

On the drive home Mack asked, "Wait, what were you studying again?"

"Civil engineering," I said.

"*Oh!* When I first transferred to Orono I was thinking about switching to engineering, but it's too hard."

"Well. Now I know…"

At first the idea had sounded great, especially during and after the time in the hospitals. Lying there in various hospital beds I was lost and didn't know where to go or what to do and I thought that engineering was the answer to those questions. It made perfect sense to give it a try—having been a childhood aspiration for some time in the past. And that's exactly why this ambition went amiss. When lost, the old self is gone and it might be that the only way to find a new self is through change, trial and error. It was the whole idea of being an engineer for a profession that actually made it appealing, not the grind to get there, it was mostly this idealized idea. Like most long-term determinants, an idea related to work will either sound a lot better or worse in your head than it actually is when you get there. Becoming an engineer is hard work and this work might be rewarded in the end or it might not.

Life as one is brief, and as one in this life we all have a purpose. But regardless of what it is this life is a gift, and it can pass too fast when it's ignored and too slow when it's observed. Take it as it comes, and do what you can with what actually does.

That last stream of perspective was formed after nine months of uncertainty and ache and then abandoning my newfound hope. Left in the world directionless. This might have been true during this time, but as time goes on the direction will shift; naturally the show proceeds. The problem here, and even the tragedy, might have been that I had a goal, an ambition, a serious want to be an engineer, and I sought to understand and learn about how to become an engineer rather than about the man who was trying to become one. For a short frame of time a few years earlier that was what I wanted to be, and for reasons that were out of my reach for better or worse it didn't work out. Somewhere along the passage of time perspective changed. It wasn't the engineer that changed; I did. Every person is the product of time and circumstance, but as time elapses, circumstances change, experiences grow, each person develops a distinct perspective, a fresh character, shift in position. There's meaning, but what does it mean?

I knew that I would try to find some sort of meaning through writing, but it would have to wait until the time was right. First I had a huge array of complications to fix and along with these the community service to complete. One hundred and three problems to resolve. With plans to enroll at the University of Southern Maine for the spring semester, I had a vague idea that I would have the time to start thinking and writing then. And maybe I would finally wake up.

Back in the car, a black blob on the side of the road caught my attention. We sped toward it. Drove by. Lying bare on the ground were the plump remains of an animal that was now a black blob in the breakdown lane. Mack swerved on the highway.

"Watch the road, Mack."

"Sorry…"

"Thanks, Mack."

"So Terr," he said. "Are you done with school?"

"No, I'm not brave enough."

"Brave enough," Mack laughed.

"I've made it this far and pushed through hell just to get here. Might as well finish what I started and get a degree."

"That's smart. Are you coming back to UMaine?"

"No. Actually I'm transferring to USM."

"I can't tell if that's sarcasm."

"It wasn't."

"Terr at USM." Mack laughed. "What will you study?"

"Going back to business."

"Nice. I study marketing."

"I've heard that's like a daydream."

"Yeah, it's something. What area are you thinking of?"

"Something straightforward. Probably death on credit."

"What?"

"Management."

"Terr, you're in a bad mood today."

"That was sarcasm. And you would be too, Mack. You would be too."

"I understand, but I don't really know."

"Well, I guess not. But you could always try."

"So you're thinking about management?"

"¡Ay caramba!"

"What Terr?"

"Just—what you said."

"Management."

"Mm-hm."

"Now I think I get it," said Mack. "But are you sure that's what you want to do with your life?"

"No, I'm not really sure."

"Yeah, I feel that."

"There's always tomorrow to figure it out," I suggested.

"True. Well what do you want out of life?"

"I'll have to think about that."

And then we drove on and at my request pulled off to the side of the road and behind a tree I took a leak and there in the woods it appeared at last.

Peace, freedom, and memories, I thought.

Chapter 34

Home suddenly felt faintly dark and detached. The short autumn days cast a somber shadow over all forms of life. Trees had entered dormancy and in a way so had I. This lasted for only a few days and then a few days later I went about solving my problems. First I went to see a doctor, Karen Davis the dermatologist, and she had a one-star review but improper biases aside she was very friendly and benign. What weighed her down was actually the receptionist, that surly hag. Good reviews mean a lot and they're more or less a reflection of your hard work. One day what might be the case is that not just created work or provided service will be subjected to a rated review, but people too. Everyone—the average Joe and the basic Betty. Think about how ugly that would be! For now, I'll try to be proper, and try to realize that one will be much obliged to a good rating or review. Either will go a long way.

At the appointment, as it turned out, Karen informed me that I had an acute case of dermatitis, and it didn't take her very long to figure this out. She quickly examined my scalp by parting the hair atop my head and the skin underneath flared and puckered like a highly ticklish allergic reaction.

"It's all red!" she said.

"That's not good."

"I've seen *much* worse. We'll get you cleared up."

"Okay."

"Have you noticed inflammation on any other part or parts of your body?"

"No, it's just on my head."

"What about under your eyebrows?" she said. "You have really nice eyebrows."

"No."

"Excellent. We'll treat this customarily."

Karen explained that this kind of acute dermatitis can break out unexpectedly after stressful or physically traumatic events, and in my case, I had been brushed with both one after the other over the course of just a few months. But it seemed as though the stress was not quite over. Of course I wanted the treatment to work but apparently there was a very tragic catch. She said that inflammation from the dermatitis can cause a disturbance to the hair follicles, and along with excess stress hormones and lack of sleep this type can gradually cause hair to thin. She said temporarily, and I thought *Who cares?* It's yet another strange scar from bad luck but never worse luck, and I remembered good old Mike from the meeting at Spaulding and sanguinely shrugged my shoulders at the memory of his character, that kind of dominance, and thought, *By God, knowing me—maybe someday!*

But today there was an urgent matter in need of attention and improvement. It affects the mind, body, and above all, the soul. I had never been the type of person who needs all that much sleep to function, but since the third week at Orono, going on five weeks now, soundly sleeping at night had been a seldom occurrence and some nights it didn't happen at all. It's hard to get up tomorrow when you don't sleep at all today. Your conscience tells you to get up, your body says stay in bed, and it's a constant battle until you give in one way or another. Whatever it is, that's your choice.

Since cannabis seemed to fully exacerbate each problem and instantly flush my spirit with anxiety—this had been going on since before I withdrew from classes—I chose to try and get help with sleep from a different kind of drug. It was a legal, over-the-counter, inadequate attempt at any rest through a pharmaceutical. It was an antihistamine called *BowelBlocker*, brand name Unisom. Its intended purpose was hardly effective at all; I slept in a state of unrest and woke abruptly choking on a lemon. I was glum, sour, and lethargic for the entire day and these days were slow and colorless. But I stuck with the *BowelBocker* called Unisom because that's what you do when you're desperate.

It was not in my nature to stay in bed deep into morning—I'll feel guilty if I do—but this drug really enticed me to be indolent under the warmth of the covers. On the surface it was languorous, but underneath that layer of pleasure it drained what little energy I had gained from the disturbed rest that I had gotten, and there I was lying lifeless in bed at noon. This became the daily routine, a baneful routine at that, until one day when I withstood the narcosis and got out of bed and drove into town to look for employment.

That night I set an alarm for six the next morning and woke seven hours later absolutely exhausted. I chose to search for a job and I actually found one, and now I was obliged to get up and go to work and arrive on time. Honestly I was kind of excited to leave behind my repetition of nothingness. If only for a day, I told myself, if only for a day.

I showered with ridiculously cold water to shock my drugged mind back to normality. The half-life for Unisom the *Bowel blocker* was a full twelve hours, but with the dose that I chose to take, its soporific effects were still noticeable when I was ready to take the next dose the next night. I was drowsy twenty-four seven; I just couldn't sleep. But it was nothing that a fresh cup of coffee couldn't fix, and after I had three cups in the kitchen my bowels actually moved! There was still time for breakfast and I ate apples and eggs and thought nothing of it, and then I sat and waited at the bar until I left for my new job at a warehouse in Portland.

Behind the warehouse was a broad dirt lot nestled beside a pair of railroad tracks and hidden from the world by a line of oaks on either side and to its rear. I parked my car facing the warehouse and the entrance around the corner. Sometimes I wonder what I'm doing, where I've been, where I'm going, and this was one of those occasions. I got this gig through an agency called Bonney Staffing and they completed a background check and paid no mind to the pending charges. Very considerate people.

I had arrived at work early and sat in my car side by side with another employee who sat in his car. We waited until the workday began and to pass the time he talked. Ten times out of ten I'll say no to a cigarette, but this time when he offered me one of his, being the new worker here I felt almost obligated to accept it.

He flung a No. 27 through the window. I cupped it in my hands. "I need a lighter."

He smiled and threw a lighter through the window. I caught it, sparked the lighter and lit the cigarette. I inhaled, exhaled, tossed the lighter back through the window. He seemed very happy this morning.

"Are you new?" he asked.

"Yeah."

"Bonney?"

"Yes…"

"Me too! My name's Ernie, but some people call me Ern."

"Andy," I told him over the subtly euphoric buzz. It had been a long while since I had a cigarette last.

"Nice to meet you, Andy. Let me tell you. Compared to the last place that they assigned me for work this place is like recess."

"Well I like recess much more than I like school."

"Are you still in school?"

"I'm going back to college in a couple months."

"Nice! What are you studying?"

I didn't want to say it, but I said it. "Business management."

"Management huh? Maybe someday you'll manage me."

"No."

"No?"

"Absolutely not."

"Good man," said Ernie. "Come on, let's go inside."

We walked through the dirt lot and went into the warehouse and found our boss in her office out front. She was writing herself a reminder on the whiteboard. She turned around. "Hi! You must be Andrew."

"Yes I am."

"I'm Mary."

I smiled and we shook hands.

"Do you go by Andy? You look like an Andy."

"Sometimes."

226

"You have better a better face."

"You can all me Andy," I said.

"Okay!"

Ern's face crimsoned slightly. "She must like you," he said. "But don't let her boyfriend know. He's got a very big gun collection."

Mary laughed. "How about you show Andy the ropes today. He can work with you, Ern."

"Sounds good to me!" said Ernie.

"You might want a jacket. It gets pretty cold in here. And if you have headphones you can listen to those too."

"All right," I said.

"And Andy, one more thing. I tell everyone from Bonney this. You don't have to show up again if you don't want to. There's no explanation needed."

"Well I'll see how it goes."

"Yes!" Mary turned around. "Now where was I..."

Ernie showed me to the break room and inside we each made a coffee and at the table Ernie told me, "People from Bonney are always coming and leaving. There's a new one every week. You seem like a good worker. You wouldn't believe the one that we had last week. Every other word out of his mouth was a swear. 'Fuck' this, 'shit asshat' that..." Ernie looked around to see if anyone had heard. "He called me an asshole. He said that if you're once an asshole you're always an asshole, and there's only one exception to this but he wouldn't tell me. What do you think of that? He might be right, but I don't think I'm an asshole. You're direct, you know what to say. Oh look, it's already that time."

We clocked in and walked across the assembly floor and went up the stairs to the second floor and in the far corner stood our workstation. A pile of white cardboard with foldable ridges and a crate of plastic hooks and hangers sat on the floor. Our job was to make display racks for this coming holiday season. One after the other we folded the cardboard and fastened the hooks and inserted the hangers through the front of the racks. We stood them off to the side like a cluster of Christmas trees, and pretty soon they filled our entire workspace, and after a while I began to feel as though I was actually one of them, folding their corners in, pinching my fingers, setting them aside, starting again. I stopped this humdrum method of work and took a sip of coffee. It was disgustingly tepid. I looked at the progress that we had already made. There was no way to tell how much would be sufficient. I went back to work—standing in one spot any longer would have likely put me to sleep.

A couple hours after we first began assembling the racks a woman walked back to our spot in the far corner. At this point I was near-asleep but just the sound of a womanly voice aroused my conscience ever so slightly. Ern jumped back, apparently surprised by our visitor. She was only here to help. Mary wanted her to hang a whole array of Christmas cards on the hooks of finished display racks. Each card featured a different breed of dog and all of which were dressed in holiday outfits.

"Aren't they cute?" said Sarah.

"Oh yes! I like that one," said Ernie.

"This one's my favorite—" she pointed to a poodle with a red ball on its nose and tangled in a cord of white Christmas lights: all class. "What about yours?"

"I can't decide," I said.

"You must be new here."

"Yes I am."

"It's his first day," said Ernie.

"*Oh*, first day. Well I'm glad you're here. I'm Sarah."

"I'm Andy."

"I'm not sure if Ernie already told you. I'm a seasoned worker so if you have any questions feel free to ask me."

"Okay."

Sarah flipped her hair and then we were back to work, folding the cardboard and assembling the hooks and placing the hangers into the racks. Sarah hung the cards in an orderly arrangement off to the side and even though her work was light she tired very fast. "Man," she said. "I could really use a smoke break."

"You can have one of my cigarettes," Ernie offered excitedly.

"No, not that kind of smoke."

"What do you mean?"

"Never mind."

"Wait a second," said Ernie. "I know what you're talking about. Why don't you meet me out back after work."

"*Okay.*"

Whatever this mysterious activity was, I was too tired to care. All of my energy and reserves were gone. My eyes had a hard time staying open. Ernie and Sarah talked ceaselessly and the imaginary clock ticked very slowly. I paid no attention to anything, and when you don't pay attention to the time much more will elapse than you might think. Pretty soon we all clocked out for lunch.

I ate in my car with the windows rolled up and wallowed in the perfect peace and quiet. I reclined the seat and took a ten-minute nap. I didn't fall asleep but resting my eyes was wonderful—even just for a minute, and I got ten times that! I went back inside much more energized than the first time. I clocked in and went upstairs and assembled the racks and hung the cards and by the end of the day had produced well over one hundred.

"Good job guys!" said Mary. "Thanks for your help!"

Everyone left our little huddle and walked toward the timecard machine. Mary pulled me aside.

"How was your first day?" she asked.

"Good," I said. "Look at all we did."

"I know, you did great!"

"Thanks."

"What do you think about working here?"

"It's fine." I shrugged. "Right now work is work."

"Work is work," laughed Mary. "Remember what I said. You don't have to come back on Monday if you don't want to."

"Are you sure? Or you don't want me to come back."

"No, I'd love it if you came back. I just think that you're better than this."

"Well." I thought for a moment but there was nothing in my mind to think about. "We'll find out on Monday."

"Yes! Have a good weekend! It looks like the timeclock crowd is gone."

I clocked out and went out back. I noticed Ernie drive off with Sarah in his car and thought, *Looks like they're going to smoke*, and at that I laughed. Even though I had been seemingly oblivious in the warehouse I knew what they were up to. They were going to waste their minds thoroughly with their kind of smoke, whereas my mind finally felt suitable for the good kind of smoke. I got in my car and drove home and there I went down in The Basement and retrieved The Goldstein and then my weed and ground it up and stuffed the bowl and ripped it. *Long time no taste*, I thought giddily, and then five minutes later the cloud of dread swept over. Playing on the tv was the Celtics, and in my mind it was a battle. "It's just the weed," I told myself as my ailing heart throbbed like fear itself. "And it's always better in the shower."

This turned out to be true, but five minutes of bliss turned into a very long night of unease. Cannabis can heavily exacerbate any negative emotion and I told myself that I would have no more until times were easy. Before I got in bed I had another dose of Unisom the *BowelBlocker* and then fell right back into the self-inflicted cycle.

Chapter 35

Monday came slowly but it surely came and along with it a powerful cyclone named Elsa, a big mess in her wake. She had cropped up to my surprise. I never watch the news, hardly watch tv, and I only faintly heard my mother mention the possibility of a windstorm over the phone. That night Elsa swept through and in my room I heard her wind rattle and shake the house like a lovely feminine breath. Under the synthetic stupor from my heavy dose of Unisom this rhythmic noise put me to sleep. Four hours later I woke to a lightless house and strident howls puffing through the walls like a splendid symphony. I rubbed my eyes and then walked downstairs apathetically.

My mother was sitting at the bar in the kitchen. I opened the refrigerator and looked around blankly but I wasn't exactly sure what I was even looking for. Orange juice. Milk. Focaccia bread. Butter. I grabbed the container of blackberries.

"Don't keep the refrigerator open long. You're letting the cold air out."

I turned around. "What."

"Close the refrigerator. Our food will spoil."

I shut the door and ate a blackberry.

My mother was on her laptop. Her eyes peeked my way above the screen. "Don't you just hate it when we lose power?"

"I certainly don't like it," I said.

"They said that there were gusts of wind over seventy miles an hour. Our street is completely flooded. Look outside, it's wild."

"I heard it all night."

"How did you sleep?"

"Not good." I walked over to the sliding door and looked out back through the window. The treetops bent violently to the right and branches shook to and fro. Lying across the yard in a rippling puddle was a fallen tree and its splintered stump at the edge of the wood. The air was opaque and a layer of fog covered the shed and the space behind except the trunks.

"Neither did I," said my mother.

I went into the kitchen and poured a cup of coffee and sipped and stirred it as is.

"The wind and rain are supposed to continue all day."

"I believe it."

"You should—"

I choked on the coffee and coughed it up.

"—call into work and make sure that they're still open before you drive there. A lot of businesses are closed today."

"I will in a minute," I said.

I topped my mug with coffee and went upstairs and called the warehouse. The phone rang several times incessantly. There was no one there nor even an answering machine. But I didn't have an answering machine either, or even a voicemailbox, until two years later when I finally gave in. I didn't believe that I needed it.

Next I called Bonney Staffing. A receptionist who introduced himself as Dan answered.

"Hello, Dan. Is *The Dog In Us* closed—the warehouse?"

"Andrew? No, as far as I know we have not received any word of cancelation."

"What was that?" I said. "I can barely hear you over the sound of the storm."

"It's not closed!" said Dan. "Get to work!"

"You smell like dirt?"

"Get to work or you're fired!"

At that point either Dan hung up or the call was disconnected. The noise of the rain was all there was. Pelting the windows and walls in torrents.

I set off for the warehouse amid the tail end of Elsa. You could tell by the way the trees shook in the wind. They weren't being forced; it was almost as if they were dancing. Had it been summer and the trees covered not bare their leaves would not have shown their silvery undersides. A sure sign that the storm is over. But she left behind a mess of debris and water everywhere.

And it came as no surprise that I was nearly the only one on the road. Everything along the way was closed, schools, stores, clinics, cafes, and inside all, it was very dark. In every dip in the road stood a deep pool of water. Perhaps if the weather was warmer within these very large puddles kids would have been playing, laughing, splashing. I know that I would've liked to. I was hardly affected by the dreariness of the day. It fit my mood perfectly.

When I arrived at the warehouse from the outside it looked almost the same as everything else. The doors were shut. Inside it was dark. There were no lights on or cars out front. I drove slowly along the dirt driveway and stopped just before the back lot. I could drive no further. The entire back lot was now a pond, completely flooded in greyish brown water. It looked murky and dirty and kind of like Elsa's excrement. Not repulsive; only natural.

There was not a single employee around. The warehouse was evidently closed. I stepped out of my car and into the drizzle and picked a flat-faced rock off the ground and flung it at the pond. It skimmed and bounced once off the water and flew into the brush at the edge of the lot. I got into my car and drove home. I listened to Mary and never went back.

The power stayed out for close to week. There was nothing to do. Keep on keeping on. From the womb to the tomb. This is what I told myself as each day passed and darkness endured. Not only did the house and the sky outside lack essential light, so did I. With constantly disturbed rest and hardly any sound sleep it was pretty hard to function and I didn't mind doing the bare minimum. Get out of bed in the morning, bathe, muddle and putter around the house, eat, resist the urge to get fresh air, and very lackadaisically, I read. Then after five days of living on the back burner the sun finally peeked out from behind the clouds!

Even though my mind and soul were both sad I drove to Back Cove and walked around the Boulevard. I was certainly not the only one to take advantage of this unusually nice weather. Many people walked along the path and birds flew the skies and chirped in tune. The sun was very strong for the middle of autumn and its rays felt warm and pleasant on my skin. I meditated for the entire walk and then went home to a powered house with working lights and warm water and managed to find work for community service at a food pantry. This wouldn't start for another week; apparently there were many other offenders working out their court orders and I sat the bottom of the list. It seemed like a great opportunity to catch up on sleep but sleep refused to cooperate.

After the perfect mid-autumn day I have to admit that I indeed slept solidly that night, but then once again my precious rest began to deteriorate. The Unisom was seventy percent to blame for this, and almost entirely because of the dreams that it produced when I actually fell asleep. It's true that these dreams were problematic, but at least they kept me on my toes unlike the other detrimental problems in my life, which mainly forced me to sit and do nothing. That's what killed me during this intermission between activities. But as wasted as I tend to feel when I sit and do nothing, this might be one of the best things to do. Ask a monk, he will probably agree. But as for my decline in sleep, the other thirty percent was mostly a mix between the dermatitis, the stress, the overall discontent.

Stress dreams after a brain injury are wondrous and wild and one night after falling asleep prone on my stomach I dreamt of an uncanny city street and all around a starless night and air so brisk it could not be felt and from my mind a lone black vehicle appeared at the corner on the curb and I ran toward it. At which point a loud pandemonium broke out and shattered the silence and splitting the darkness a storming sputter commenced unbroken. Three red dots appeared on the ground and one on the vehicle where a face inside sat dimly lit and perhaps ugly. He motioned urgently to move faster and hurry as each blasting crack from a stoop far back cut through the space like solid butter. And then sudden silence induced a still darkness and the back door opened and I mechanically hopped in. As if I had entered someone else's body and he was in control. His arms were weak, hands were damp, skin too pale, legs too long, to come close to me; I was in a strange frame in a hectic world with a clear

234

perspective. I saw the case and he opened it—*click click*—bit the fruit from the serpent, sparked the match, took the cash, and burned it. And at once a silent flash and the whole world stopped and lit up. And I woke up. Sweating, panting, centsless. It was over and that was that for that dream that night.

Chapter 36

The following week went by and during that time the environment completely changed. Winter was on its way and on its way fast. Outside it was often overcast and cold and when the skies cleared and the sun shone it was a bright sun but its rays were weak and they gave off very little warmth. I hardly went outside after that surprisingly nice day the week earlier; I fell right back into a case of seasonal doldrums. Each night was a battle for sleep and I seldom won. And then when the day came to start chipping away at my community service I was not well-rested for this kind of work. Yet here I was, standing inside of the garage of yet another warehouse, looking outside at the freezing rain of yet another autumn storm. The sky was immensely dark and the rain fell down and froze upon contact with the ground. I wondered if I'd actually do one hundred hours of work at this food pantry or try to find a different agency.

It was my second day at the pantry and by the way things looked and felt, it didn't appear as though it'd be much better than my first. The day before I had spent seven hours in the warehouse—that's where they told me that I would work—loading banana bins with canned foods and carrying them one by one across the floor to the display shelves. I packed them, carried them, unloaded them, and perpetually repeated this process while the manager and another volunteer watched me. The manager's name was Roger and the volunteer was a former heroin addict meandering his way through recovery. He openly talked about his daily struggles and it undeniably excited Roger whenever he mentioned an addict who had previously worked at the pantry.

"Maude," said Roger. "I love her! How is she?"

"She's dead."

"You hear that kid. Stay away from drugs!"

I told them frankly that cannabis and an occasional drink was good enough for me.

"Oh yeah, what do you drink?"

"Whisky in the winter, wine in the summer." *Unless, of course, activities permit otherwise.*

Other than that I paid them no mind. They talked and watched and gladly let me carry the load. The bins were heavy, each one well over fifty pounds, and this was not the sort of weight that a heroin addict wanted to bear, and neither did Roger! I bleakly went home a languid hunchback.

Overnight I recovered only slightly, and Roger told me that it was just him and I today. He called out from across the warehouse, "Hey, you've been in the garage for long enough! Get over here! I have something else for you to do!"

I walked across the warehouse floor and stood before Roger. He sat on a forklift looking at his phone. He laughed unnaturally, maybe intentionally ignoring my presence. "Take those," he said at last. "And separate them by category."

I reached down and picked the bin off the floor and anchored the weight to my hip. This bin was filled to the brim with canned green beans.

"See those green beans," said Roger. "They last forever! I read somewhere that divers found a sunken ship in the Mississippi. They found trunks filled with canned green beans. Forty fifty years past the expiration date. Opened one. Smelled it. The beans were still delicious! The expiration date means nothing. Canned green beans last forever!"

"That's incredible," I said.

"Have one!"

"A can of green beans, right now?"

"Yeah, just try it."

"I'm good."

I turned around and slowly walked toward the display shelves.

"Hold on," said Roger. "You remember how to do that?"

"Just separating them by category, yeah I do."

"Don't do it too fast! I need to figure out what you're going to do next."

I carried the bin across the floor and unloaded them in their particular shelf—a full rack actually, designated entirely to canned green beans. I did as Roger said and took my time. I looked at my phone—had only been at the warehouse for one hour. I had about ninety-two hours of this kind of labor left to complete. Or did I?

When I finished unloading the bin I walked over to Roger. He hadn't thought of something else for me to do, and after surveying the warehouse from his spot on the forklift he told me to empty the recycling bins filled with boxes into the dumpsters out back. Outside it was dark as night and along with freezing rain and sleet, very heavy snowflakes swiftly fell from the sky.

"You have a jacket?" asked Roger.

"Yeah."

"Go get it," he said. "And bring me a can of green beans!"

I walked over to the shelf by the door and slipped into my sweatshirt.

"You'll need this!" Roger yelled across the warehouse, holding a utility knife in the air. "You have to break down the boxes!"

I walked over to the forklift and grabbed the knife.

"Be careful with that. It's sharp and rusty. It's been my lucky knife for the past seven years… Now wait a second! Where are my green beans?"

"There's a shelf full of them in the display area."

"Aargh… Go take care of those boxes!"

I wheeled the industrial recycling bins one at a time across the warehouse through the garage and across the lot to the dumpsters. Heavily bombarded by sleet and freezing rain and snow I lost my balance numerous times along the pavement, covered in a sheet of thin ice and water. The weather was cold; my heart and soul were both frozen.

After ten minutes of breaking down the boxes I had altogether made very little progress. Then a red car pulled up front and

Roger ran over and stayed within the reach of the overhang. "Hey Larry!"

An elderly man stepped out of the car and climbed the stairs and stood on the ledge of the loading dock with Roger. "Hello, Roger. How do you do?"

"Fine. Went hunting last weekend!"

"You get anything?"

"No... Hey," Roger shouted. "Get back to work!"

I picked a box out of the bin and cut the tape and broke it down and dropped it flat into the dumpster.

"Who's that?" Larry asked.

Roger leaned in and whispered a lousy joke in Larry's ear. They both broke out in laughter, and then Larry whispered a question in Roger's ear.

"I'll just make him do it!" he said. "I'll make him do anything!"

"That's right, Roger!"

They laughed and howled like pigs in a gate, and when I looked up the two trolls were standing side-by-side looking my way. With that, I went inside and signed the sheet and walked through the doors and out to my car and never looked back. There was a thrift store across town that I had called when I had called a handful of agencies during the power outage, and they also told me that they had plenty of volunteers at the moment but to check in with them in a week or two. That was it. I reversed my car and drove to the thrift store.

As soon as I got off the exit and onto Congress a line of cars filled the street. I was one of one hundred in a traffic jam. Now slightly closer to the ocean, Casco Bay and the Fore River, the precipitation was strictly rain and it poured on the street from thick and dark clouds. We slowly inched closer to the intersection of Congress and St. John and standing on the corner was a group of cops and blocking the right lane was a cruiser. *Of course*, I thought. *Have some consideration. The weather's terrible outside!* But what they were doing and what they were blocking I wondered about. And then it came into sight—lying on the side of the road was a corpse! Half of her body lay flat on the sidewalk and the other half was sprawled out onto the street. *Hey look, it's Maude!*

When I drove by I made no attempt to study the scene, but from the corner of my eye indeed it appeared to be an overdose. Her awkwardly laid body and closed eyes and soaked clothes were all that I noticed before turning into the plaza. I parked my car in a spot close to the store and thought, *This oughta be rich.*

On my way through the parking lot a pack of vagrants who for some reason were still in Maine despite the harshening weather nodded and said hello. I opened the door to the thrift store and a set of jingle bells strung together and dangling from the top of the frame slammed against the window and *ding-a-linged* as I stepped inside. Sitting behind the counter an eccentric lady lifted her head and smiled, and then she dropped her head toward the counter on which a black and white magazine sat crinkled and open. She had wildly curly hair, and the noise had apparently caught her attention but only so much as would a sneeze. I walked over.

"Excuse me," I said.

She listlessly lifted her head. "How can I help you?"

"I'd like to volunteer—for community service."

"Were you the one who called?"

"The other week, yeah."

"Hold on. Let me radio Melanie." She grabbed the two-way radio off the counter and brought it to her mouth. "Melanie."

"Yes."

"There's a boy out front who'd like to volunteer."

"Oh, okay. I'll be right out."

She set the radio on the counter. "Melanie's the manager."

I said thanks and she dropped her head toward the magazine. In just a few seconds Melanie came strutting around the corner, tall with black hair.

The lady behind the counter made an awkward gesture at me. "This is—"

"Andrew," I said.

"He called a little while ago about volunteering. Does that ring a bell?"

"Yes! I do remember speaking with you. I'm Melanie."

We greeted each other with a casual handshake.

"Pleased to meet you," I said.

"I'm Esther," said the lady behind the counter.

"Hello, Esther."

"I'm going to call you Andy," she said.

"If you'd like to."

"So you have some community service to do—is that right, Andrew?"

"Yeah."

"How many hours do you have left?"

"Ninety."

Esther and Melanie both looked at each other bewilderedly. As if the number was unexpected.

Melanie smiled. "Well that might take you some time. You'll be here for a while!"

"I can tell that here I'll be in it for the long haul," I said.

"When would you like to start—would you be able to start next week? Whenever it's best for you."

"Next week is perfect."

"Awesome!"

"I'll start on Monday."

"Perfect. Our hours are ten to six, seven days a week, and feel free to come by whenever you can."

"Thanks Melanie. See you next week."

"Yes, see you on Monday!"

Chapter 37

Work at the thrift store had started on the second Monday of November and there was no rush to finish. Melanie and Esther were glad to see me plugging away at my hours and they let me work at my own pace. On average I clocked in about four hours each day that I worked, and by doing this roughly four or five times a week, with some last-minute hustle I would easily finish before Christmas! But to set the record straight, finishing my community service before Christmas was not a priority. Actually I could not have cared less. But a wise person will set a deadline for any kind of work that they do. That's the easiest way to get anything done.

The actual work at the thrift store was slightly tedious but it certainly beat the back-breaking labor called work at a warehouse! I hung, sorted, and folded clothes, cleaned, vacuumed, and washed the windows, priced, tagged, and carried donations. All of this I either did alone or with another volunteer, three of whom were girls from the county jail. They worked at the thrift store to shave time off their sentence. Alexus was in the slammer for a driving incident about which she would not talk; and similarly, Lily was there for driving intoxicated with a suspended license; and I believe that for Dani it was drug related. Either jail had rehabilitated the three girls nicely or they had always been naturally sweet.

Everything was going smoothly, and for the most part it was uneventful, but ever since I started working here I had constantly been on the qui vive for anyone that I knew or who might know me. Small talk in a thrift store while doing mandated community service was something that I did not want to happen. And there I was, of all days on a Sunday, vacuuming dust and dirt underneath a rack of jackets, when the front door opened and the jingle bells jingled and then commenced a strange commotion. A man and a woman entered speaking in jitters. I was off to the side of the store and then walked toward the center to get a better view.

"Oh, I know her," Dani said to the other girls.

And what a small world in which we live. I did too!

"Her name's Sarah," said Dani. "She's a junkie."

Indeed it was Sarah from the warehouse, but she seemed to be much more strung out now than she was in memory. She walked listlessly and wrapped around her aura was a coat of doubt and desire and then she stopped. She turned around and to the man she was with she said, "That's not what it's for, Ern!"

"Shh!" said he, and he was the Ern who had also worked at the warehouse. A small world indeed.

They bumped into each other, and then Sarah knocked over the sidewalk sign advertising a ten percent sale storewide and she tried her best to pick it up. But she struggled to do this more than the average person, and while standing in the same spot Ernie vacantly looked at the art on the walls. He picked his nose and said, "What are you doing?"

Sarah shrieked. She gave up on standing the sign and instead she asked Esther who stood behind the counter for the key to the changing room.

"You don't have anything to try on," said Esther.

"Can I have it?" She held out her hand and nervously it shook.

"This is too much," said Dani, and she left the other girls in amusement and walked out back to the break room. Good idea, I followed right behind her.

Ever since my appointment with Karen the dermatologist my dermatitis dramatically worsened. I figured that this was because winter had come early this year and the dry air only aggravated this difficult condition. Maine winters offer you nothing in return for everything.

Dani and I sat at the table in the break room and soon Lily and Alexus joined us.

"You look tired," Lily said to me.

"It's been a while since I've slept."

"Why?"

I didn't say anything but patted the top of my head.

"You think and you dream too much? Your mind is always working."

"Sure, right now."

"Hey look," said Alexus. "A penny! You think we could go on a honeymoon with this Andy?"

"I think we'll need a lot more of those first."

The jail girls laughed at that. I poured a cup of coffee and sat in my seat. I fanned the brim, stirred the spoon. Outside in the hall I heard Melanie and Esther talking. I tried to block out the chitchat at the table.

"Those two out there," said Esther. "I'm telling you, they're high on something."

"Well what do you wanna do?"

"I thought you would know."

"I've been on the phone with Tobias for an hour—I don't know."

"Oh, not him!"

"But it was," sighed Melanie.

"That man out there—his name's Ern I guess, or maybe Ernie, and hers is Sarah—he's dressed in a camo outfit and he wanders around the store going up to customers one after the other. They look pretty upset."

"What is he doing?"

"I don't know. I saw him stuff his pockets with silverware. And just a minute ago he came up to me—he was all fidgety—he asked if I've seen his knife. I said 'no' and told him that we're going to check his pockets on his way out."

"His knife?" said Melanie. "Gosh. Some people around here."

"Mm-hmm," mumbled Esther.

"Maybe I should give Tobias another call."

"No, don't tell him. I'll keep an eye on those two."

"Yes, I'll go out on the floor with you. We need to make sure that nothing else happens. And that the store stays in order."

After that, Esther and Melanie walked away and I got up and did the same. Who had been watching the store just then, and what else had Ernie stuffed into his pockets?

I watched the man in camo move erratically between the racks, and then he noticed me and from across the store he rushed over hurriedly. I can still hear the sharp *ding* that the plastic tip of his shoelace made against the metal legs of the clothing racks. Like two wine glasses touching at the stem, mutual eye contact. Nothing else has come close to replicating that noise or the situation. You don't forget these things. It's been over two years—you wouldn't forget it after seven.

Ernie excitedly came up to me and the smell on his breath was putrid. Mostly I was confused, wondering how he didn't recognize me just two weeks after working together, but maybe during that time I had lost some shine too. Tiredness will do it.

"Listen," he said. "Do you have my knife?"

"No."

His eyes darted in all directions at once, unaware of where he was or that his former coworker stood before him. "Well have you seen it?" he asked.

"No," I said. "Step back a little."

Ernie moved in closer. "Where—where is my knife?"

"Would you give me some space."

He did not, and from the rear a clothing rack blocked me in and on either side it was too tight. There was nowhere to go.

"Ern, back up. You need to let me breathe."

"How did you… Where is my knife!"

"Please."

"Where is my knife! Where is my knife! Where is my—"

"Relax. There, relax. I don't know what to tell you."

His eyes had glazed over and there was a drastic change in the tone of his voice. "I've had that knife all my life," he said between snuffles. "It's mine, you hear."

"I believe you."

"It's this big." Ernie stuck his fingers in front of my face about five inches apart. "That's a big blade you know."

"That's nothing!"

"Would you help me find it?"

"No."

"But I can't—"

"If you're supposed to, you'll find it."

I pressed against the clothing rack and scooted aside and freed myself from the nonsense. I went to find Esther for my next task—testing electronics for proper functionality—and two hours later I finished. I had been in the back room for the entire time, plugging power cords into an outlet, powering each device, handling them with care, but rough enough to make sure that they're in working condition. I recorded my hours for the day and signed out on the sheet and walked into the store and there they were, still hanging around. Ern and Sarah were finally getting ready to leave. In Sarah's hand was one shirt that she had spent all of this time to find. Ernie moped around the checkout line while waiting for Sarah and based on his tone of despondence it was safe to assume that he had no luck finding his knife. They both appeared to be highly slothful, lost in the midst of a harsh comedown. Their kind of smoke was much different than my kind of smoke, but my kind of smoke was still out of the question, my cannabis. The difference between mine and theirs was like night and day. To each's own.

I realized in the middle of the store that I forgot my coat in the break room and went out back to get it. I thought, *Don't need to lose another one of these!* and by the time I came back the situation had completely changed. Sprawled out and wailing on the floor in a childlike tantrum was Ernie. Patrons in line at the registers were all very confused, and Ernie was unquestionably upset. To no one in particular he cried out, "What! No. No. No!"

"I saw you," said Esther, standing behind the front counter.

"I didn't take those!"

"They were in your pockets. Yes you did."

"Listen, no, I swear, no, No, NO, *NO!*" Now pitifully crying, Ernie dolefully repeated, "No way, no way, no way…"

"You need to get off the ground, sir."

"*Oh, oh, oh*—" the cries of a sad man "—where is my knife?"

"Uh—"

"*Oh, oh, oh*, my precious knife…"

"The man just wants his knife," said a patron nearby.

Melanie came out of her office and stood beside me. "What's going on?" she asked.

"Ernie lost his knife," I said.

"They've been here all day."

"I know."

"Oh hey, two pennies on the ground—both heads up."

Melanie reached down and grabbed them.

"I'll take those," I said. "They're for a special fund."

Smiling, she handed me the coins, and then over the pitiful cries of the man in camo Esther asked, "Melanie, what should we do about this—tell Tobias?"

"Yes, I'll call him right now!" Melanie walked away and went out back to her office.

Ern's missing knife had really sent him into a rough patch, and when I walked closer to the scene I saw on the counter two forks and a spoon that had been in his pocket only about a minute earlier. The spoon I thought could have been useful to him, but he went overboard with the forks. For utensils all that was missing was a knife, and Ernie let the whole store hear about his heartbreak. "It's my knife," he cried. "*Oh, oh, oh*. My knife…"

Melanie walked past me and went behind the counter. I walked toward the door; it was time to leave.

"Wait till I tell the girls about this tomorrow," Esther said as I walked by.

And there in front of the door stood Sarah, bewildered in a state of deep abstraction. I scooted to the side and opened the door, and apparently the bells woke her from her trance. "Wait," she said. "I think I recognize you."

I turned around. "No, Sarah."

"How, wait, who?"

I nodded to the wall on which the one hung, and then I turned around and said no more.

"Humph. Oh…"

Chapter 38

About a month's time had passed and the days grew short and the nights came early and around the clock it was frigid. This was the time of year that will make you appreciate the warm weather in the summer but dealing with the cold drains all warmth and memory of warmer days out of you. Winter in Maine as a kid was great but as you grow in age the cold can penetrate your sternum and chill your heart. No wonder bears hibernate during the winter months; they know that outside it is very dreadful, and I certainly knew this too. Over time, every other day in the past month had even made me become seriously dreadful. This was not your average seasonal blues; this was low, lower, lowest.

The thrift store was nearly all the same. The only difference was that in the beginning of the month we had decorated the store with Christmas lights and secondhand ornaments. All of us helped and given our location in town on St. John street we actually made the store appear rather inviting. For much of that day I worked on a ladder and toward the end a highly hyper kid almost knocked me off. Had it not been for my deep despondency it's possible that I would have lost my temper. In those days, after nearly knocking me off of a ladder there was a good chance that I'd express my ill humor toward whoever it was, especially after lying on the wrong side of the bed at night and the next day simply going through the motions. Around the clock I was temperamental and touchy, and rightly so, but now that kind of mood is very uncharacteristic of me. Not to mention, I knew that it wasn't on purpose.

After that day I had about forty hours of community service left to complete, and I worked continuously through the middle of the month, straightening clothes, moving chairs, lifting shelves, and every once in a while, helping people find what they were looking for, if they even knew what it was. In other words, I did what I had to do, good and proper.

Then at night, after getting home and wandering idly around the house and finally settling in The Basement only to wallow in my own solitude, I was far too morose to actually fall asleep. But luckily this happened only four or five times each week. Excessive sleeplessness will not end well and knowing this I always tried to make the most out of those wakeful nights. At the time, the only way to do this was by listening to music, and at four in the morning music had a profoundly positive effect on my previously anguished mind. The music was therapeutic and almost always instrumental, and for that brief period of time, listening to track after track was a way to feel superbly fearless. It was the same kind of fearlessness that Ern and Sarah had felt after hitting their dope pipe. A different method, the same result, both of which caused a significant release of endorphins. And surprisingly, just as they had experienced their own kind of ghastly comedown, when the new day dawned and my glumness recurred I even felt rather ghastly myself. My once warm heart now harmful in time beat rapidly.

Days blended together. Nights the same. Time was slow. And I have to admit, over the past few months I had plunged into deep misery and grief. Lack of sleep and prejudicial rumors led me into a state of near-despair, a conceivably fleeting kind of hopelessness, and ironically the thrift store's name was Interwoven Hope, and it was especially ironic that my work there would come to an end in a very short time. For now, I was utterly alive and at the same time searching for peace, meaning, some kind of outcome, something that I wasn't even sure existed. And if it existed and it *was* in fact real, was it a feeling or belief, a meaning or reason? Did it have a name, and if it did, how is it spelled? Perhaps whatever it was it was something preordained. And there in my room, lying under the sullen morning sky, I'd often think, *Oh, hell. Why get out of bed today, and what's a survivor still drudging for?*

It was my last day of work at Interwoven Hope and the air felt promising—that's why. I had to do four more hours of community service and that would be that. One hundred hours of work would finally be completed, and I ask, for what reason exactly?

Nonetheless it was a good day; I was glad to get that monkey off my back. Despite the time of year and the fact that Christmas lay just around the corner the store was remarkably uncrowded. A few lone patrons roaming the floor brought forth dismal feelings. In the later years, those short holidays, those sad seasons.

I stood waiting outside of the donation room. Inside I heard the jail girls talking and possibly bickering, and then as they walked out and I walked in we greeted each other in the doorway. Pricing items in the middle of the room stood Esther. A bag of Christmas toys and lights sat by her feet and donated clothes lay all around. "Hi Andy," she said.

"What's next on the list?"

"Did you ask that guy to leave?"

"Yeah."

"He was very rude."

"He's gone."

"The Christmas trees?"

"Done."

"You're ahead of your time."

And for a brief moment this lifted my spirits appreciably.

Esther looked around the room at the everlasting clutter of junky donations. Trash bags full of odds and ends that may have been there for decades and may remain for decades to come.

"Go take out the trash," she said.

"The trash," I repeated.

Esther smiled. "Yes. The trash."

With that, I sank even lower in my stance and did what I was told to do. The weather was dark and dismal and dreary. Thick mist floated, stagnating in the air. Behind the dumpster and on the other side of the train track was the county jail. Two prison guards stood smoking on the front steps. They had the right idea, and after I had dumped the last bin I also waited outside to pass the time. *Only three hours left*, I realized as the cool drizzle sprinkled upon my upturned face.

I sat on the back steps and blankly thought about something and mostly nothing. The night before I had sold some Bitcoin and the unexpected success of this pioneering cryptocurrency had very little effect on my snowballing unhappiness. A helplessly tragic tale if I must say so. If you don't know, you don't know.

Naturally under the refreshingly wet conditions of the placid atmosphere I began to meditate. Then just as a sense of oneness crept in the back door opened and a girl from jail sat down on the steps beside me. "Andy," said Alexus. "Do you have a cigarette?"

"No."

"Well thanks for being handy, Andy."

"I hardly smoke cigs," I said.

"I bet you smoke weed."

"Yeah, but I'm taking a break right now."

The girl sighed.

"Have you found anymore pennies?" I asked.

"Yes! I've saved thirty-two cents."

"Thirty-two, we're getting there."

"Have you saved anything? I bet you don't even care."

I reached into my pocket and gathered the pennies that I had brought to work every day since Ernie and Sarah showed up.

"Here," I said.

"Two pennies," said Alexus. "You're a tightwad!"

"It's better than nothing."

She gently took the coins from my hand and as still as a child's thought she sat on the steps and didn't say anything.

Inside I sat at the breakroom table and ate fettuccine alfredo for lunch. Don't think that it was a very good meal; it was the last of the food that Esther had gotten for everyone from Olive Garden. Now they were leftovers, and nearly inedible at that! After wolfing everything down I made a coffee and quickly drank it to wash away the rancid aftertaste. That's what you get for not packing your own lunch.

For the next ten minutes I sat at the table digesting the food, dawdling over a newspaper, and then I got up and left the room in search for my next task. And this turned out to be pricing the *new* china, cups, and glasses, as Esther called it, but to me they seemed to be slightly more antiquated. Some of them could have made for a thoughtful present, considering the crowd that normally shopped at Interwoven Hope, and cherished greatly by the giftee.

Esther said that I can take my time. She and Melanie knew that it was my last day and they wanted to make it easy for me. As they'd suggested, I leisurely plodded away at pricing the tableware and for a good half hour I mainly worked undisturbed. A full shelf had to be tagged. Then in the middle of this monotonous task my elbow swiped a teacup off the shelf and it shattered on the floor. I looked around to see if anyone had heard. Not a single patron was in the store. But then, just as I reached down to pick a piece of ceramic off the floor, the front door open. The jingle bells jingled. And not a jolly kind of jingle. A disturbingly flat and forceful jingle.

I slowly rose from behind the shelf and marching side by side past the shopping carts were three cops. My stomach sunk and growled as they approached. I made my face appear as ordinary as possible. It was anyone's guess what I looked like—three days in a row without sleep, three months without peace—probably like an antelope. But they paid no attention to me, standing there with shards of ceramic scattered about around my feet. They walked out back and talked to Melanie in her office.

Being basically the only person in the store, it seemed like the best thing to do would be to step away and hide. To the donation room, I told myself, and in there I thought that I heard something in the parking lot. Yelling, or maybe it was cheers of joy. I opened the door and there was Alexus. She instinctively spun around and saw me.

"What are you doing out there?" I asked.

"Nothing."

"You were up to something."

She made her way over. "Maybe I was but I can't remember."

"Three cops just walked out back," I said.

"Three cops—what are they doing here?"

"Talking with Melanie. I think they're here for you."

"Andy, are you serious?"

"That's what they said."

"Seriously?"

"Maybe, but I can't remember."

"Oh, Andy," sighed Alexus. "You wouldn't talk to the cops."

"I'll talk to anyone who's respectful."

"*Andy!* Should I be worried?"

"No."

"So I was right?"

"Yeah, you were right."

"See, I told you!"

"I know. I didn't talk to the cops."

Alexus smiled. "Good boy."

Then she went ahead and met up with Lily and Dani in the middle of the store. They were tagging clothes, and I returned to the shelf of tableware to clean my mess and finish my task. By the time I found an old broom and swept the bits and pieces of ceramic into a dustpan the cops had emerged from Melanie's office. They walked back and forth several times, apparently determined. The jail girls stood off to the side and watched.

"He has a high forehead and he's hot," said Lily.

"I—"

"He's mine!"

"Was just saying…"

Then all that I heard was ribald laughter, whispers, titters, and more laughter.

I walked to the donation room and then to the break room and sat at the table and waited for a short while. Again I picked up the newspaper and dully skimmed through the pages, stopping just briefly to read the police beat, and that was when I wondered how long it had been since I had even held a newspaper in my hands. I prefer books.

After this I went out front and Esther assigned me to my final task, moving around and organizing furniture, and two hours later

I finally finished—done with the undeserved community service at last! It was an incredible feeling walking out back for the last time, knocking on Melanie's door and saying goodbye.

"So this is it?"

"This is it."

"Well it was a pleasure to have you around, Andrew."

"I was glad to be here."

"Were you really?"

"Yes I was."

"*Oh*," she said. "Well please come back. You're welcome back anytime."

"See you Melanie."

"Bye Andrew. Have a merry Christmas!"

And then I grabbed my jacket and walked out front. I would've liked to say goodbye to the girls but while I was talking to Melanie Esther had walked them back to jail. So long Alexus, Dani, Lily. So long Interwoven Hope. It's been over two years since I had worked there and I haven't heard from the girls since. I wonder where they're at right now, which side of the law they're living on, and after all this time how many pennies has Alexus found and saved? We never went on a honeymoon.

Chapter 39

Christmas happened and as a joke all that I got was a lump of coal in my stocking. Not to mention a completely restless night without a trace of sleep and the unbearable itch on the top of my head. The day drearily passed and concurrently laid down a bridge to the past apace, a dim beginning, a dull present, a day that melted away like snow. I settled into a snug spot against the arm of the couch and casually sipped insipid coffee, dozily watching the light snow fall in the morning fog, and as the clock ticked and my mug of coffee perpetually filled the snow fell from the sky in intermittent squalls. I sat rigidly on the couch for the entire day. I drank cup after cup of coffee to stay awake. And despite ingesting excessive caffeine I actually slept soundly that night. This was maybe the greatest gift that I could have asked for. A good night's rest.

As for its longevity, that actually seemed quite promising. I slept uninterrupted each night through the new year, and why there was such a sudden change in the quality of rest that I got probably had to do with my new and improved sleep hygiene. No more Unisom, that's what it was. As soon as I stopped taking Unisom my dreams returned to normal and normally my mind was clear. There was no more fog and nothing opaque to shade my wits. Any other reason was simply a Christmas gift.

And there I sat in The Basement on the 31 of December, well-rested and ready to go, but sitting on the couch is where the night started and sitting on the couch is where the night ended. This New Year's Eve I did nothing and the year before it was next to nothing. There wasn't anything better to do at the moment than to recall the night that was one clockwise lap around the sun. Thinking back to it, to exactly one year earlier, I remembered that the squad went down to UNH and we had a fine time and made a few memories but the memories that were made were mostly weak. Memories are delicate. If they're not with the right person or people over time they start to rust like iron left outside in the rain. All memories are best rinsed.

Some of those people I had seen before the new year and some after. One person was Cole, and the time that I had spent with him in The Basement was typical. We gambled minor sums of money on an online casino. Nothing major, no safe bets. We both ended the night as winners so to say, and we both capped off the evening with two heavy tokes from The Goldstein. But ultimately, from my perspective the night did not end very well. The cannabis made my mind reel until morning, but this happened before Christmas and before I had made the vital change to my sleep hygiene. After that, everything improved entirely.

The next person that I saw was Ricky. After nearly a year-long disconnect what the friendship once was endured no longer. There was little mutual reference and very few questions. And now that it's been over two years since any sort of communication I only impassively wonder what he looks like these days. People can change drastically over a short period of time, both physically and mentally of course, but it mostly has to do with appearance. Every year I seem to change considerably, and throughout the year of 2017 my appearance and perspective not only changed markedly but also quite frequently, starting off in a coma with absolutely no perspective in the worst condition imaginable, then bearing a close resemblance to an alien with a fairly dismal outlook, then getting unhealthfully husky and adopting a mostly carefree attitude, then appearing actively unhealthy while regaining an abundance of intellectual acuity, then appearing fit with all but only a hefty ounce of fat on this convalescing body, then after this sudden evolution perceiving the world fully and clearly, then seeming down in the dumps and glum with that standstill kind of mood, then basically returning to the state that it was in before the whole ordeal began, but this time around with many distinctive scars and stories, pacific and pensive.

In any event, at Ricky's request we ate grass brownies, and although it had been about four months since the last time that I had consumed cannabis on a regular basis, and even though my tolerance was incredibly low, Ricky ended up higher than me! He fell asleep on the couch and toward the end of the night my father had to drive him home—he was not in the right condition to walk. As for me, I sat awake and warmly euphoric and as soon as he left I went to bed and effectively slept until noon the next day. No stress, no fret. That's what did it—how I brought cannabis back from the past and into the rekindling picture. If only for a short while, it's wise to end on a *high* note. *¡Perdonen el juego de palabras!*

Now that I had a decent sleep schedule and a proper state of mind to alter its sobriety, for old times' sake I went back to the gym and rowed on the rowing machine for hours on end. If it hadn't been so crowded I probably would have dumb crawled! But too many people were actually fulfilling their New Year's resolution. I was lucky enough as it was to find an open rowing machine and once I did I was on it for the rest of the night. I took my time when I rowed, I considered it my workout, a fine workout at that, and I didn't stop once until the monitor read thirty thousand meters. And there's a reason for that specific meterage—that's just about the distance of the width of the English Channel! A treacherous body of water, one whose murmurs sound like fire. I always went home very happy.

It was no surprise that this drastic improvement in mood had a plainly positive effect on the dermatitis, and on top of that, shortly after the weekend with Ricky I had discovered a natural remedy to help control this pesky sickness. The trick was apple cider vinegar and MCT oil. I applied both to the affected areas, and in this case, that was my entire scalp. First I slathered the oil onto my skin and then in the shower I rinsed it off with vinegar. After only a day it had cleared everything. No itch, no inflammation, my problems were gone. I was back on the right track and with that went down to Boston.

It was time to see a close friend. Her name was Mia, and we reserved a room at the Beantown Boston Beacon Hill. Ironically the hotel was located about one block over from Mass General and this I didn't find out until that night.

Online I bought a round trip train ticket and rode the Amtrak into Boston and along the way took a very light nap and sipped a hot tea and gazed out through the window first at the passing trees and as we approached our destination the triple-decker apartments of Somerville. By now you can probably tell that I enjoy looking out through a window, and while this scenery was seemingly bland I was lost in admiration. I am where I am not.

We arrived at the TD Garden and I stepped off the train and maneuvered through the crowd and went outside and the cold wind shook me awake. Down the sidewalk I walked, both hands tucked snug inside of my jacket pockets, the only one in sight on the streets. This time of year there's often a somber loneliness in the air that can sometimes feel especially good. The wind blew from behind and my mind skipped ahead to the future.

Outside in front of the Beantown Beacon Hill I chewed on a mint. The doorman nodded his head. I checked to see if he was rubbing his thumb over the tips of his index and middle fingers, silently asking for money. He was not, but I would have tipped him if he was.

The lobby was overly crowded. They were hosting some kind of writing convention for amateur writers, people who would like to call themselves a writer but have not actually been there *been there*. It had probably cost them hundreds of dollars just to buy an entrance ticket, and maybe these people paid this fee because they thought that money spent to attend a writing workshop will earn them the title of being a writer. Not so fast! A writer observes but rarely spends, authentically invents new ways of thinking, peers inside the minds of others, speaks the truths that are left unspoken. A writer either has it in them from the start or they are not.

I entered an elevator and pressed number five and rode up alone. The doors opened to an alabaster lobby. I stepped out and walked to room 564 and knocked on the door. Behind the walls a gentle shuffle, nearing footsteps. The door opened and there in the entry stood Mia, wearing her hair back and a short black dress. The stillness of breath and time, the warm draft stirred and down the hall a door opened and closed. We had opened and then we closed and after all this time I breathed marvelously at last.

We walked inside and after a glass of highly tannic red we sat on the bed and lay back against the pillows. I kicked my shoes off and so did she. They fell to the floor with a bang and rolled around on the carpet together.

"You don't mind talking about it," she asked. "Do you?"

"No. I've talked and thought about it plenty."

"You had a—what do they call it—near-death experience?"

"Yeah. I mean I was told that I did die for at least a moment."

Mia bit her fingernail. "I've always wondered what it might be like."

"You have a peculiar curiosity," I said.

"Well what was it *like?*"

"Which part of it?"

"Tell me all of it."

"When you're ready I will. It's kind of hard to explain."

"Oh, no. Don't beat around the bush. Tell me."

"No?" I smiled. "I don't know."

"Come on…"

I looked at the ceiling and then out the window. The Charles River sat still in the distance and behind that was Cambridge, bare trees and buildings.

"*Tell me,*" said Mia.

I turned my head back toward hers. "That's the third time that you've said, 'Tell me.'"

She cupped my knee with her hand and held it there. "Haven't you heard—third time's the charm."

"Third time's the one," I said.

And there we were, both calm and quiet and we seemed to be thinking. The room lay perfectly still and in the stillness so were we. I thought about all that had been thought about superficially. I thought about the dream, and beyond the stars the third degree.

259

All was there, the world itself and life in actuality. I thought about nothing and pretty soon nothing was something.

The universe in its crudest state that can possibly be perceived while still physically on Earth might have been witnessed in the coma. As the perfectly dark unconsciousness slowly closed in the world itself all but opened up. Galaxies and seas of refracted light and distant stars so close together so far away they dot the space like sand and stones and shine on end and past their realm another realm and altogether a multiverse a cosmic complex of immense energy but who really knows what it was that was actually witnessed in the midst of the coma running from death while heavy narcotics and trauma pumped through the veins of this lucky survivor who was strapped to a bed and respirated in the ICU of a prestigious hospital in Boston Massachusetts. The true answer will be unveiled one day and this one day is certain for all. For now we satiate.

I lay in bed with Mia to my right and her hair on my face. Fruit and flowers and an afterscent exotic. It smelled very nice! I brushed it off and then we talked. She was going to Europe in the summer. I thought, *¡Qué bueno!* and said that I was planning to start a book in the summer as soon as classes end and I move out of the house. The time was right to start writing—all of that audacious energy from the past had turned into something wonderfully thoughtful. She liked that, and she thought that writing would be a good way to channel my energy. Up until this point and beyond it seemed as though my entire life had been misunderstood by too many people who in a peculiar way I still care about and even though life waits for no one it would be truly wasteful to not sit down and correct this misapprehension through the creation of meaningful art. Even though at this time in 2018 all of their unmindful assumptions are an obvious sign that they hardly care at all about me. There are many times when you have to step into the shoes of a bigger person with pleasure and failing to do so is a fully missed opportunity.

"You should smoke," said Mia.

"I would if I had some weed," I said.

"You don't have any?"

"Not with me."

"Why?" she asked.

"It'd end one of two ways. Either way I'd come out dry."

"Ew don't be dry. I don't like that word."

"What's the opposite of dry?"

"A better word."

Once again she asked about cannabis, forgetting that I forgot to bring my own today, and I told her, "I actually just started growing a few plants at home—inside a little grow tent. It's finally legal now you know."

Mia laughed, "What?"

"It's true."

"So you have a little grow tent and what, weed plants?"

"Yeah."

"This is funny. How big are they?"

"They're getting bigger. They grow pretty fast under the right conditions."

"They're growing girls."

"Yes." I smiled. "This talk is pretty dry huh?"

"I think it's fascinating."

"After they're cultivated and harvested I'm taking a break."

"You'll be done?"

"No. It'll be with me forever but I'm parting ways from it for some time."

"Why?"

"You can't write well under that kind of influence."

"You can't?"

"No."

"You can't do much of anything on it," she laughed.

"I know, it doesn't mix well with a lot of things."

"Especially with that thing."

"Ey! You're right."

Mia arched her back and spread her arms and reached for the ceiling.

"But it might have saved my life," I said.

"Oh yeah, how?"

"I'll put it in the book. It does have serious meaning."

"Will it be a serious book?"

"Yes and no."

"I like that. It can't be all serious or all funny you have to keep me on my toes. But what will you call it?"

"I don't know. Fire on the Water."

"That's sick."

"Yeah? I just came up with that one on the spot."

"Yeah, oh you're smaht."

"Maybe you're right."

"I am! Oh yes, but wait. One sec. Hold on one second. I want to ask—you know it might be kind of hard to write a book with no closure—have you ever thought about that?"

"Yeah," I said. "And that's where you're wrong. The book will be my best attempt at getting closure."

Much later I went outside and breathed a breath of Boston air and walked along the empty street and turned a left around the corner. Massachusetts General Hospital stood erect straight ahead and in my head it was the way to go. I strolled along the road and there to the right was the main arcade and entrance and beyond those doors and up the stairs and down the halls this very story began. Where corridors were roamed and the voice of Rosa filled the air and reached my heart. Her silvery vocals, Alfonso steering the chair. On a patch of grass to the left a single pigeon waddled and cooed as I walked along the empty road and in my mind all was there. Before time, the past year. That was that.

Made in the USA
Middletown, DE
24 August 2020